Management for Professionals

More information about this series at http://www.springer.com/series/10101

Alessia Zorloni
Editor

Art Wealth Management

Managing Private Art Collections

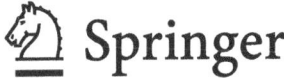 Springer

Editor
Alessia Zorloni
IULM University
Milan, Italy

ISSN 2192-8096 ISSN 2192-810X (electronic)
Management for Professionals
ISBN 978-3-319-79595-9 ISBN 978-3-319-24241-5 (eBook)
DOI 10.1007/978-3-319-24241-5

© Springer International Publishing Switzerland 2016
Softcover reprint of the hardcover 1st edition 2016
This work is subject to copyright. All rights are reserved by the Publisher, whether the whole or part of the material is concerned, specifically the rights of translation, reprinting, reuse of illustrations, recitation, broadcasting, reproduction on microfilms or in any other physical way, and transmission or information storage and retrieval, electronic adaptation, computer software, or by similar or dissimilar methodology now known or hereafter developed.
The use of general descriptive names, registered names, trademarks, service marks, etc. in this publication does not imply, even in the absence of a specific statement, that such names are exempt from the relevant protective laws and regulations and therefore free for general use.
The publisher, the authors and the editors are safe to assume that the advice and information in this book are believed to be true and accurate at the date of publication. Neither the publisher nor the authors or the editors give a warranty, express or implied, with respect to the material contained herein or for any errors or omissions that may have been made.

Printed on acid-free paper

This Springer imprint is published by Springer Nature
The registered company is Springer International Publishing AG Switzerland

Foreword[1]

Over the years, we have seen progress and setbacks, but there is no denying that art and wealth management industries today are closer than they have ever been before. The number and diversity of direct and indirect art and finance related activities that are now taking place shows that the market is starting to build momentum and critical mass. We continue to see new and interesting developments in the art and finance industry, with particular emphasis on the role of art and collectibles in the broader wealth management context. Moreover, economic uncertainty and financial volatility draw people toward art and the awareness and motivation for including art in traditional wealth management is becoming increasingly apparent, although not without its own set of complexities.

Art and wealth management is not a new concept. For many decades, private banks and wealth managers have helped address the needs of their clients regarding art and collectible wealth. However, with the increase in value and holdings of art and collectible assets among HNWIs and UHNWIs, a more strategic and holistic approach to art wealth management is required in order to fully meet collectors' demands and expectations. In this scenario, the increasing and fascinating phenomenon of private art museums is of great interest. Alessia Zorloni's *Art Wealth Management. Managing Private Art Collections*, the first book dedicated exclusively to the financial and managerial aspects of private collections, comes on a timely manner.

In fact, a new research report[2] found that there are 317 privately funded contemporary art museums around the world. A fifth of these were set up in the past five years and 70 % of the museums were founded after 2000. Europe is home to the largest number of private museums in the world, with 45 %. Asia takes second place with 33 % of global private museums, and North America is third, with 15 %. The growth in private museums has coincided with rapid growth in personal wealth worldwide, and the desire to build and leave a legacy for the local

---

[1] Barbara Tagliaferri is Brand & Communications leader at Deloitte.

[2] The Private Art Museum Report, an international research project initiated by the art collector database Larry's List and Art Market Monitor of Artron, is one of the first systematic efforts to understand the rapid rise of private museums over the past decade. The survey authors collaborated with 166 private museums from more than 40 countries.

community and future generations. According to the report, private museums seek not only to be a venue for exhibiting art collections, but also to demonstrate the philanthropic mission of supporting and enhancing a city or region's cultural landscape.

Moreover, key findings of the recent Deloitte and ArtTactic Art & Finance report 2016 identify priorities for collectors and wealth management which are perfectly aligned to the ones Zorloni examines in depth in this book. A large majority of collectors buy art for passion but also with an investment view. The emotional benefit of collecting, combined with the potential of a value increase and/or store of value, value protection and diversification of portfolio, is the driving motivation among most art collectors in the art market, still investment value is an increasingly important motivation among art collectors: after seeing an increase in motivations driven by "investment returns". This is an important point for private banks and wealth managers when designing and implementing art-related services. More and more wealth managers are now very aware that art and collectibles should be part of a wealth management offering. According to the report, this is the first time in five years of monitoring the art and finance industry that we see an alignment of the wealth management industry with collectors and art professionals, but still there's space for wealth managers to fully meet clients' expectations. On the other side art collectors appear to be increasingly focused on investment returns. Art professionals and collectors do agree on the portfolio diversification benefits that art could offer. Which are then the art related services collectors are asking the most to wealth managers and private bankers?

Collection management strategy: resale prices matter to collectors, as auction sellers are not inclined to sell if they are likely to make a loss. This supports the theory that there is much more to collecting art than following the simple conventional rhetoric of "just buying what you like and selling what you don't".

Diversification benefits of art: art and collectibles are increasingly playing a role in a well-balanced wealth portfolio, and both collectors and art professionals feel it offers a degree of safety and diversification in times of economic and political uncertainty. Variation in market prices, even for established artists, provides a means of efficiently diversifying art collections and reducing investment risk without having to hold a large number of artists in collections. Portfolio diversification and art as a "safe haven" was an important motivation when buying art.

Services aimed at preserving their clients' art and collectible wealth: services such as estate planning, philanthropy, and art-secured lending are increasingly becoming relevant, particularly as the financial component and motivation for buying art and collectibles are becoming important drivers. However, for the wealth management industry to be able to deliver these services effectively, more investment in ongoing professional development and education about the art market, the art itself, and other collectible assets will be essential.

Estate planning: among services above mentioned, it is evident from both art collectors and art professionals that issues related to estate planning are increasingly becoming a top priority. This is one of the most relevant wealth management services that wealth managers could offer with regard to art and collectibles. Wealth managers need to respond to their clients' growing estate planning needs in key areas related to art and collectibles, particularly with regard to valuation, taxation, inheritance, and succession planning.

Art-secured lending: the opportunity that collectibles can offer continues to increase, boosted by third-party lenders. Wealth managers said their institutions now offered services linked to art-secured lending, in particular the US art-secured lending market is expanding rapidly, aided by low interest rates, an expanding art market, and an attractive legal environment provided by the Uniform Commercial Code (UCC). With an increasing amount of capital tied up in art and collectible assets, art-secured lending can be seen as an effective way of enabling art collectors to access the equity value in their artworks without having to sell them.

Tax benefits: only 4 % of art collectors named tax benefits as an incentive for establishing a private art museum. The rules for a non-profit organization to qualify for tax benefits vary from country to country. Still, in many regions, these foundations can profit from tax advantages. This illustrates the close relationship between art and philanthropy, and an opportunity for wealth managers to address this growing trend among their wealthy clients.

Safeguarding collections: in recent decades, the art market has opened its arms to the world; it is global. New international collectors operate on a flashy art scene, with billionaires often going head-to-head for trophy pieces. Art collections represent a significant proportion of high-net-worth-individuals' non-financial assets (art accounts for approximately 17 % of their investments in passion assets). If you have been entrusted with the task of properly safeguarding a collection, protecting an asset in financial terms should be collectors' primary responsibility.

Wealth reports: art collectors want to include art and other collectible assets in their wealth reports in order to have a consolidated view of their wealth and of the financial aspects of their art collection. Integrating art and collectible assets into wealth reporting is the practical way of improving the links between art and finance through a common reporting mechanism. Better integration of art and collectible assets would give wealth managers a unique insight into clients' total collectible wealth and allow wealth managers to tailor a set of art wealth management services around these specific needs.

Finally art market research and information is also increasingly seen as a service that wealth managers could provide.

This book stimulates reflections and provides analyses on all the issues here briefly introduced with a specific focus on the challenges that private museum founders, one of the most important and interesting stakeholders of the art market, have to face today. Through a sophisticated and exhaustive research, Alessia Zorloni offers interesting insights and practical recommendations not only to wealthy collectors, but also to family offices, wealth managers and art advisors.

Milan, Italy Barbara Tagliaferri
September 2016

About the Book: Introduction

Throughout history art patronage has played an important part in the wealth of ultra-high-net-worth families. Although the Renaissance is regarded as the golden age of patronage, the patronage concept was actually born during the Roman Empire. Rulers, nobles, and the very wealthy used patronage of the arts to endorse their political ambitions, social positions, and prestige. Over the course of time, patronage led to private museums funded by philanthropist collectors in order to celebrate their own tastes and leave a lasting legacy. Especially in the past three decades, private museums have been set up with increasing frequency, and today, the private collections of ultra-high-net-worth families can rival those of major art institutions and have a significant impact on the global art market. In Miami, art collector Martin Margulies and philanthropist and entrepreneur Ella Fontanals-Cisneros have opened galleries in old buildings. Don and Mera Rubell have funded the Rubell Family Collection, one of the world's most renowned collections of contemporary art. In the USA, Eli Broad, a philanthropist and property billionaire, has recently opened The Broad museum in Los Angeles. Mexico City's Carlos Slim, one of the world's richest men according to Forbes magazine, has opened his second museum, the Museo Soumaya, to host a collection of more than 66,000 pieces of art. Across the Pacific, Australian mogul David Walsh has established his Museum of Old and New Art on a riverside site just outside Hobart, Tasmania—a groundbreaking venue. Indonesian tobacco industrialist Oei Hong Djien, one of the most established art collectors, in 1997 opened the OHD Museum of Modern and Contemporary Indonesian Art, which serves as a national gallery, in Magelang in Central Java. Singapore has at least three private museums of contemporary Asian art, including Art Retreat, which was opened by the Indonesian collector Kwee Swie Teng and includes a gallery dedicated to the late Chinese master Wu Guanzhong. While China's government is focusing on strengthening state-run citadels of culture, an increasing number of wealthy philanthropists are constructing new showcases for their collections. Collector couple Liu Yiqian and Wang Wei launched their Long Art Museum in Pudong, Shanghai, and the Long Museum West Bund; Indonesian collector Budi Tek has branches of his Yuz Museum in Jakarta and in Shanghai, with a third set to open in Bali in 2017. The private museum model is also behind the recent inauguration of the Aïshti Foundation, a mixed-use cultural center, opened in Beirut at the end of 2015. Dedicated to presenting contemporary artwork from the private collection of Tony Salamé, CEO of luxury brand Aïshti, the Aïshti Foundation exhibition space will move Salamé into the league of fashion-entrepreneur megacollectors (Prada, Pinault, Arnault) who have opened museums in which to show their holdings.

The growth of the art world from a niche lifestyle sector into a nearly $60 billion global market has been accompanied by a sharp increase in art philanthropy, and today, as a result of the growth of art investing by a new generation of wealthy collectors, not only artists but also wealthy families, sophisticated investors, and their close advisors now face a more complex set of financial and managerial needs. The relatively recent emergence of art wealth management has meant that, until now, there has been little available research on this important trend. *Art Wealth Management. Managing Private Art Collections* is the first book dedicated exclusively to the financial and managerial aspects of private collecting, providing essential insights into art wealth management, art investment, art governance, and succession planning for art assets. It offers practical recommendations on sound art collection governance but also examines the background of art markets and price building, including the influence of fashion and trends. As such, the contributions in this book will be of interest to collecting families, family offices, and professional advisors seeking to integrate art into their overall wealth management strategy and to scholars in the fields of cultural economics, art dealers, curators, and art lovers.

The volume is organized as follows. The first chapter "Turning Collections into Philanthropic Opportunities" analyzes the global rise of private museums, providing insight into the motivations of museum founders and discussing today's challenges. Planning how to transfer a family collection to the next generation can be one of the most critical aspects of building and maintaining a successful financial plan. Deciding where the collection may reside, be it with a foundation, a family member, or a museum, also is a key consideration. In light of the potential tax and other financial liabilities, deciding on the best strategy early on can be of critical importance. The second chapter "Financial and Estate Planning for Art Assets" examines the role of art in the overall wealth management strategy of sophisticated collectors and the issues they face in managing a private art collection. Its conclusion offers general recommendations on what constitutes sound art governance in order to preserve and protect art assets. The third chapter "Assessing and Improving the Effectiveness of Private Art Museums" addresses a practical managerial problem—how to design a performance framework for private art foundations—and aims to construct a model using balanced scorecard (BSC) architecture, which integrates quantitative and qualitative criteria and examines performance and accountability expectations from both an internal perspective and an external, public-oriented perspective. In this way, philanthropic funders can better define, assess, and improve their effectiveness—and, as a result, their intended impact. The application of the balanced scorecard approach to a private museum is discussed in detail, and conclusions regarding the use of the balanced scorecard in a not-for-profit organization are presented. The appendix gathers together interviews with renowned museum directors and sheds light on their attitudes toward performance assessment. The interviewees are Julia Peyton-Jones (Co-Director, Serpentine

Gallery), Lars Nittve (Director, M+), James Bradburne (Director, Pinacoteca di Brera), and Elizabeth Macgregor (Director, MCA Australia).

Chapter "Celebrity Effect in the Contemporary Art Market" shows the results of empirical research conducted on a sample of the 155 most famous contemporary artists in the world in order to analyze the competitive dynamics regulating the system of contemporary arts. Results show that the contemporary art market is a winner-take-all market subject to network effects where collectors influence the artist's notoriety, making the artist even more attractive to additional buyers and accelerating the process of mainstream adhesion. This celebrity effect tends to reinforce the same artists in the art market, whereby the works of the most famous artists are the most demanded and achieve the highest prices on the market, while emerging artists face high barriers to entry.

Collecting contemporary art and supporting art projects can be a powerful means to develop an organization and to increase its capacity to create value. As a consequence, several of the industry's leading brands, including Prada, Trussardi, Louis Vuitton, Hermes, and Cartier, have begun investing in and supporting the fine arts through the establishment of their own art foundations dedicated to the collecting and presentation of contemporary art. The chapter "Deepening Business Relationships Through Art" introduces a framework to show how successful brands take advantage of the unique characteristics of the arts and lay the foundations for a series of case study analyses exploring the links between fine arts and luxury brands.

The last chapter "The Art Collector between Private Passion and Philanthropy" gathers together interviews with renowned private collectors worldwide and offers privileged access to firsthand information on aspects related to creating and managing a private art collection. The interviewees are Enea Righi, Bruna and Matteo Viglietta, Harald Falckenberg, Tony Salamé, Donald and Mera Rubell, Ramin Salsali, Uli Sigg, Renate Wiehager, Marina Dacci, and Massimo Lapucci. Finally, the text concludes with an appendix that contains a list of the most important private museums worldwide and their founders.

This book owes a great debt to all authors who have contributed. I would like to express my appreciation to Patrizia Sandretto Re Rebaudengo, Magnus Resch, Randall Willette, Antonella Ardizzone, and Sonia Pancheri. My sincere thanks go to all collectors and museum directors who agreed to tell their stories: Enea Righi, Bruna and Matteo Viglietta, Harald Falckenberg, Tony Salamé, Donald and Mera Rubell, Ramin Salsali, Uli Sigg, Renate Wiehager, Marina Dacci, Massimo Lapucci, Julia Peyton-Jones, Lars Nittve, James Bradburne, and Elizabeth Macgregor. I am also grateful to the senior editor of Economics/Management Science of Springer, Katharina Wetzel-Vandai, for her help in publication process. My final thanks go to my parents who over the years have always supported me and taught me to pursue my ideas and projects with courage and determination.

Milan, Italy Alessia Zorloni
September 2016

Contents

Turning Collections into Philanthropic Opportunities 1
Alessia Zorloni and Magnus Resch

Financial and Estate Planning for Art Assets 19
Alessia Zorloni and Randall James Willette

Assessing and Improving the Effectiveness of Private Art Museums ... 37
Alessia Zorloni

Celebrity Effect in the Contemporary Art Market 67
Alessia Zorloni and Antonella Ardizzone

Deepening Business Relationships Through Art 81
Alessia Zorloni

The Art Collector Between Private Passion and Philanthropy 95
Patrizia Sandretto Re Rebaudengo

Appendix: Private Museums and Their Founders 131
Sonia Pancheri

List of Contributors 161

Turning Collections into Philanthropic Opportunities

Alessia Zorloni and Magnus Resch

1   Introduction

American history is rich in art patrons who proudly created museums to serve the needs of the public, as well as their own. Since the first U.S. museum, the Peale Museum, was created by Charles Peale in 1783, the tradition of private collection museums has continued through to the present day. During the Gilded Age, many cities benefited from the trend among art collectors to establish private museums showcasing their collections (Letowski 2010). While the Gilded Age was an important period for museum founding and support, patronage of the arts through museum foundation has continued vigorously ever since. Especially in the past three decades, a growing number of private museums have begun to emerge, funded by philanthropist collectors in order to celebrate their own tastes and to leave a lasting legacy. An analysis of data published by Larry's List[1] reveals that there are about 350 private museums of contemporary art founded by living collectors. South Korea, the United States, and Germany have the greatest number of private museums followed by China and Italy. The founding dates of these private museums indicate that only 29 % were founded before 2000, with 53 % founded between 2000 and 2010 and 18 % after 2010. These numbers reveal the relatively new trend of presenting private collections to the public. While there are a number of factors driving the growth of private museums globally, a lack of public exhibition space

---

[1] Larry's List is an art collector database, containing more than 3,000 art collector profiles from over 70 countries.

A. Zorloni
IULM University, Milan, Italy
e-mail: alessia.zorloni@iulm.it

M. Resch (✉)
Zagreb School of Economics and Management, Zagreb, Croatia
e-mail: magnus@magnusresch.com

© Springer International Publishing Switzerland 2016
A. Zorloni (ed.), *Art Wealth Management*, Management for Professionals,
DOI 10.1007/978-3-319-24241-5_1

has played a major part. It is currently estimated that only a small part of the collections of major museums is on view at any time: the Tate shows about 20 % of its permanent collection, the Louvre 8 %, the National Gallery 5 % of its holdings, the Guggenheim a lowly 3 % and the Berlinische Galerie 2 % (Bradley 2015). Moreover, artworks gifted to large public institutions are in many instances stored for long periods and displayed infrequently. Museum directors are also seeing a drop in donations and the number of art objects donated to top museums has been steadily falling even as the value of those donations has increased due to the rising art market. Some museum directors are working to combat these trends by launching aggressive acquisition programmes, appointing collectors to their boards, and expanding their space to display more works and appease donors who don't want their gifts sitting in storage (Willette 2010). Private museums established by collectors have become an important factor in art popularization and art education, and their influences are becoming increasingly notable. They have been recognized as powerful tools for a wide range of activities and goals, from education to entertainment, from the enhancement of local art systems to urban regeneration (Evans 2005) and are part of what has been termed the "voluntary sector" and "third sector" by sociologists and economists respectively. This is said to be the fastest growing economic sector in developed countries. It is also the sector that generates "social capital": the ability of people to work together to solve problems. However, the diffusion and the dimension of this phenomenon raises a whole set of questions related to the nature, diversity, mission, and prospective evolution of these institutions. Is it possible to consider them as a unique population? What are the motivations behind private collecting? What are the challenges of creating and managing a private museum? Despite the increasing role played by private museums in the display of contemporary art and in global art ecology over the last three decades, this topic has mostly been ignored by academics. The existing literature is mainly descriptive and concentrates on presentation of the most important cases (Larry's List & AMMA 2016; Letowski 2010; Doroshenko 2010). By contrast, this chapter aspires to offer a comparative examination of how the process of the privatization of culture changes the museum landscape, through a critical analysis of the rise of philanthropic collectors and their role in shaping the contemporary art culture. Section 2 presents data about the global art collector scene, providing insight into the motivations of museum founders. In Sect. 3, a global overview of private collector museums will be presented in order to illustrate where these art philanthropy projects are born and the various ways in which they operate. The last section offers some general conclusions.

2 The Global Art Collector Scene

Collectors are not only the founders of their own institutions, but also the source of donations for many already established museums. According to a 2007 statement issued by the Association of Art Museum Directors (AAMD), more than 90 % of the art collections held in the public trust by America's art museums were donated by private individuals. While institutions may be better equipped to create more comprehensive collections, often for the sake of objectivity, private collectors can take risks on the unknown and the controversial and be as partial as they choose (Letowski 2010). Consequently, understanding collectors and their motivations can offer an important perspective when considering their role in shaping the contemporary museum landscape.

2.1 Geographical Allocation and Demographics

It is estimated that there are about 8,000–10,000 serious collectors[2] worldwide. North America and Europe home the largest number of collectors. Europe has the greatest share of art collectors worldwide with 38 %, followed by North America with 28 %; 91 % of these collectors are based in the USA. 18 % of global collectors are based in Asia. Of the remainder, only 8 % are based in Latin America, the Middle East and Africa account for a combined 5 % and Australia for the remaining 3 %. New York leads the list followed by London, Sao Paulo and Los Angeles. It is interesting to note that New York and London combined are home to 15 % of all art collectors; New York alone has more art collectors than all of Germany. This underlines New York's position as a global art capital. The remaining 85 % of collectors are divided between 600 cities. This shows the diversity of the market. Paris, for example, is ranked fifth, following by another European city, Berlin. With Seoul and Beijing, two Asian cities enter the top positions, while Tel Aviv and Chicago mark the last seats in the top ten ranking. Art collectors are a very special, relatively homogeneous subgroup within the general population—usually male, middle-aged and well educated. According to the Larry's List Report (2014), the average age of a contemporary art collector is 59. An overwhelming 90 % are over 40 and 71 % of the collectors are men. The number of graduates and persons who are self-employed or entrepreneurs are also remarkably high—four out of five collectors have a college or university degree, and close to half are self-employed or entrepreneurs, whereas only 25 % are employees (AXA ART 2014). When it comes to the industries in which collectors operate, there is greater diversity. Most collectors work in the financial services sector (12 %). Media and entertainment accounts for 11 % and is followed by the consumer products sector and the non-profit segment, each with 7 %. Health care takes fifth place. These top five industries make up only 43 % while other business sectors, such as real estate or legal, provide 47 % (Larry's List 2014). According to the international collectors survey conducted by AXA ART, *Collecting in the Digital Age* (2014) art collectors often live in childless relationships and the vast majority (82 %) collect

---

[2] Not every individual owning artworks is also an art collector. Here this term refers to a number of criteria, which were defined in the *Larry's List Report 2014*. These are a focus on contemporary art and a collection of at least 100 unique artworks by relevant artists. To be considered, the collector must be still alive.

contemporary art. Modern and impressionist art ranks second, with 39 % of collectors. Only a small minority collects older art objects such as nineteenth century art, old masters or art antiquities. Paintings and works on paper are at the top of the list of most popular collectable items; sculptures rank third with 60 %, and nearly half the respondents collect photography. Only 14 % collect contemporary installation and video art. This is supported by data provided by Larry's List, according to which, globally, video and new media art works are presented in only 10 % of global art collections. Amongst the largest video collections in the world are those of San Francisco-based Pamela and Richard Kramlich, Julia Stoschek from Düsseldorf and Penny Clive in Australia. In Germany, the collector by far the most committed to video art is Ingvild Goetz, whose collection includes more than 500 video and film works. She exhibits them at Haus der Kunst, Munich and in her own museum, Sammlung Goetz. With regard to the categories of objects collected, the results of the survey conducted by AXA ART (2014) show that tastes strongly depend on age. Collectors over 60 more often buy works from earlier periods, whereas collectors under 40 have a marked preference for contemporary artworks. A number of these young collectors are bankers or entrepreneurs who were educated abroad and have developed a personal interest in art. They hold important positions or have taken over their family business, developing it in a modern way. A couple of emblematic examples are Hong Kong entrepreneur Adrian Cheng and Filipino Robbie Antonio. The former has the vision of merging commerce and art and has pioneering new strategies to support Chinese art. Consequently, he developed the first "Art Mall"—called K11—in Hong Kong in 2009. The latter only began collecting modern and contemporary art in 2005, but his collection is already well established and includes works by artists such as Francis Bacon, Willem de Kooning, Andy Warhol, and Takashi Murakami. Their collecting approach is very different, one focusing on young and emerging artistic positions and the other on blue-chip artists. What the two collectors have in common is that they developed a passion for the arts and about collecting at a very early stage in their lives and that when modernizing their family businesses they decided to place art at their core.

2.2 Understanding Motivations

Collecting is often an expression of personal identity and gives the collector a sense of pride and satisfaction. The motivations to collect are many, including the preservation of memory, realization of self-worth, and achievement of financial wealth (Letowski 2010). Other motives for collecting art are the possibility of gaining prestige, social advantages, and distinction (Bourdieu 1979). Indeed, art is amenable to what Veblen (1934) has called conspicuous consumption: by consuming art, people can distinguish themselves from others. Besides the leveraged social status, collecting art and opening museums brings tax relief. Particularly in Germany and the United States, collectors achieve tax privileges through presenting their collections to the public, as a non-profit foundation. Collectors differ depending on their motivation and can be divided into three distinct types (AXA ART 2014):

The Art Aficionados The first group of collectors is focused on one or very few sectors of the market and is driven purely by the desire to collect art for its own sake, with a high level of knowledge and connoisseurship. They collect for passion, to express their personality and to develop new contacts or friendships through art. They tend to buy and hold pieces and are averse to selling them. For these collectors, the reduced profitability of investing in art is more than offset by the aesthetic pleasure they derive from the possession of the artwork, the so-called "aesthetic dividend" (Zorloni 2013).

The Traditionalists The second group collects to continue a family tradition. Despite their preference for paintings and contemporary art for their collections, they show a higher than average interest in traditional types of collectables such as furniture, jewellery, clocks and watches, ceramics, porcelain and wine. Traditionalists are frequently experienced, and often discreet, collectors. According to the survey conducted by AXA ART (2014) members of this group have been collecting for more than 20 years, and almost as many refuse to disclose any information with regard to the value of their collection.

The Investors The third type includes those who buy art as a status symbol and/or as a commercial investment, with financial expectations. They work either in the financial services sector or in the private equity and venture capital industry, and have shown themselves to be as energetic in the art scene as they are in finance by actively engaging in the art circle, some even contributing greatly to public museums. In America, we might recall hedge fund managers like Daniel Loeb, Steve Cohen, Daniel Och, Daniel Sundheim and Kenneth Griffin. These collectors were driven by a combination of aesthetic and investment concerns and often made more diversified purchases across a range of categories. Often younger with considerable wealth and disposable income, these buyers are sometimes driven by a need to display status in the process of immortalizing their name. An excellent example of this kind of collection is Robbie Antonio's $15 million house in Manila, designed by renowned architect Rem Koolhaas, which features a series of portraits of Antonio commissioned from the world's top contemporary artists including Julian Schnabel, Takashi Murakami, David Salle, Julian Opie, David La Chapelle, and Damian Hirst. The collection, collectively entitled "Obsession", includes some of today's most iconic contemporary artists all depicting the patron, who reportedly paid $50,000 to $100,000 for each piece (Tiglao 2013). When considering these profiles, it should be remembered that all three share one central characteristic—they are art lovers who take pleasure in collecting. Of course, the groups overlap in many ways: art aficionados also consider financial matters, and a family tradition may develop into an intensely personal passion.

3 The Global Rise of Art Philanthropy

The growth of the art world from a niche lifestyle sector into a nearly $60 billion global market (McAndrew 2015) has been accompanied by a sharp increase in art philanthropy. Art philanthropy, which is broadly defined as private action for the public good, can take on various guises. One such form is the collectors' involvement in public art institutions. Indeed, 37 % of global art collectors are active in an advisory role, as a committee member or a trustee in an art expert board of a public art institution or a public museum.[3] An example would be a collector who sits in the board of trustees at the Museum of Modern Art or who is member of Tate's Asia-Pacific Acquisitions Committee. The UK leads the list with 55 % of collectors being involved in public art institutions. In the United States there are 53 % engaged collectors, in Germany 43 % and in France 37 %. In other countries, 27 % of the collectors are engaged to a public museum (Larry's List 2014). Asked about his level of participation, the British collector David Glasser answered: *"I'm a 'Friend' of lots of institutions, I sit on the Court of a London University, I am on the advisory board of a wonderful quarterly magazine, and am a member of the Art Scholars Livery"*.[4] As Glasser shows, it seems to be completely natural for a British collector to be involved in different boards and friend circles.

Another form of art philanthropy is the undertaking of lending programmes and frequent donation of single artworks, entire collections or financial resources to public institutions. This is particularly deeply rooted in American and British museums. In 2014 U.S. donors contributed $358.4 billion to charitable organizations or public institutions. Additionally, according to the report compiled by Indiana University's Lilly Family School of Philanthropy, the estimated giving to art, culture and humanities grew 9.2 % in 2014, totaling $17.2 billion.[5]

To reward this generosity, some museums have been renamed in honour of their benefactor. This is the case of the former Miami Art Museum, renamed in 2013 as the Perez Art Museum in recognition of a donation of cash and art valued at $40 million from Jeorge M. Pérez (Rodriguez 2014). Moreover, a new generation of philanthropists is emerging in the contemporary museum scene, for which art is increasingly becoming an important component of their alternative investment strategy. These philanthropic collectors are no longer sponsors or partners of existing museums but elaborate new and independent visions and concepts that might sometimes be seen as early, if not utopian, working hypotheses. The most ambitious achievement of these actions is the creation of museums where collections can be permanently displayed. In this way collectors fill a gap by building the first contemporary museum in their respective city or even country and by opening them to the public. Overall there are 350 private museums located

---

[3] Larry's List database.

[4] Interview with David Glasser published on Larry's List. http://www.larryslist.com/artmarket/the-talks/the-odd-story-of-how-i-came-to-be-a-collector/.

[5] Lilly Family School of Philanthropy, Giving US, 2014.

in 46 countries.[6] The U.S. leads with 48 museums, meaning that, in percentage terms, 14 % of private museums are based in the US. Compared to a share of 25 % of all collectors worldwide and a contemporary art market share of 46 % (McAndrew 2015) this number seems to be rather small. Completely contrary to this is the situation in Germany, ranked second in the world with 45 (13 %) private museums: a figure that surpasses the market share of 1 % (McAndrew 2015) and the quantity of collectors worldwide (8 %). Interestingly the UK, with only 2 % of global private museums, does not even appear in the top ten. Overall the top five countries make up 44 % of the private museum landscape with the remaining private museums scattered over 40 countries. There are many examples worldwide: José Berardo founded a museum in Lisbon that bears his name; Victor Pinchuk set up the PinchukArtCentre in Kiev; Bulent and Oya Eczcibasi have provided backing for the Istanbul Modern; Lee Kun-Hee has funded the Leeum Samsung Museum in Seoul; and Alan Faena is set to open the Faena Forum, a major arts space in Miami which will be a branch of the Faena Arts Center (FAC) in Buenos Aires. Philip Dodd, former director of the Institute of Contemporary Arts in London and founder of the Global Private Museum Summit,[7] has introduced three development models for private museums at the summit. The first one is based on the iconic presence of architectures, whose eloquence more often overwrites collections and related events and on commercial activities. This entrepreneur model is represented by the Museum of Old and New Art in Hobart, Australia, that relies on revenue-generating activities such as a winery, a brewery, a restaurant and a boutique hotel on the same site. The second model empowers the collections and related curatorial activities, emphasizing their educational value. The education model is represented by the Sandretto Re Rebaudengo Foundation in Italy, which is devoted to the education not only of artists and curators but also the wider public. The third model is more directly engaged with its surrounding communities, and exploits collections mainly by looking at their capability of generating positive social impact. This regeneration model is represented by the Rubell Family Collection's projects in Miami and Washington DC, which have rejuvenated decaying communities through art museums.

The term *"venture philanthropy"* has also emerged with the rise of new entrepreneurs who apply business acumen, passion, and technology to art in the fulfilment of their philanthropic goals. Their generosity is stimulated by a passion for art and quite often these motivations are far stronger than any tax incentive they may receive. This new venture art philanthropy features four main characteristics (European Venture Philanthropy Association 2010). It involves high levels of engagement, tailored financing, multi-year support and performance based management with a strong focus on measuring outcomes and impact. These philanthropic projects are quite a diverse cluster that may include:

---

[6] Larry's List database.

[7] The first international forum devoted to private museums. http://globalprivatemuseumnetwork.com/.

1. Museums owned and operated by private individuals, families or corporations;
2. Museums owned by private collectors but operated by non-profit organizations;
3. Museums owned and operated by charities or non-profit-making organizations (such as foundations or trusts) that receive some government funds.

Some charge admission while others are free; but, in addition to fulfilling the fundamental functions of collection, research, education and display, they have four characteristics in common. They have independent or semi-independent boards, multiple sources of funding (including visitors, private donors, foundations, sponsors and service fees), budgetary control and are community focused.

The following section presents a global overview of private collector museums, intended to illustrate the various ways in which these venture philanthropy projects operate.

3.1 United States

The U.S. has a long history of privately founded institutions and while wealthy collectors have been funding museums for years posthumously, a new generation of collectors now want to open a museum during their lifetime. In America there are 48 private museums founded by living collectors (Larry's List 2014). Others date back almost a century. The Frick Collection in New York and the Isabella Stewart Gardner Museum in Boston opened their doors in the early twentieth century. In 1959, the Guggenheim in New York welcomed the first visitors to its Frank Lloyd Wright building. Other prominent private museums, including the J. Paul Getty Museum, the Hammer Museum and the Norton Simon Museum, have followed within the past 40 years. In recent years, a growing number of private collectors in the U.S. have been opening exhibition sites ranging from casual warehouse spaces to fully-fledged museums in order to share their collections and assert their aesthetic views. Among the most visible is the Rubell Family Collection, started by Mera and Donald Rubell, prominent Miami collectors of post-1980s art. Frustrated by the inability to see their collection all in one place, in 1993 they opened their space together with a public research library containing over 40,000 volumes and a comprehensive contemporary art bookstore. The Contemporary Arts Foundation (CAF) was created in 1994 to expand the RFC's public mission within the paradigm of a contemporary art museum. The works themselves are owned by the Rubells, who have set an example which has transformed Miami's art scene. The Foundation has been recognized as a pioneer in what has been referred to as the "Miami model" (private collections being converted into public institutions), a trend followed by the Margulies Collection, the Ella Fontanals-Cisneros Collection, the de la Cruz Collection and the Craig Robins Collection.

In another blow to established museums, more collectors are forgoing donations and starting foundations that essentially serve as lending libraries, loaning out works to institutions around the world. In 2008, Los Angeles-based collector Eli Broad defied expectations when he said he would not donate his 2,000 piece collection of postwar and contemporary art to the Los Angeles County Museum of Art (LACMA). He had already donated $56 million to the museum to open a building named after him,[8] indicating that he would give the museum the bulk of his extensive collection. Instead, 1 month before the Broad Contemporary Art Museum opened, Broad decided to retain permanent control of his works. He continued the lending library model he had been using since he started his own foundation in 1984 and in 2015 opened The Broad Museum, a $140-million building, with an endowment of $200 million (it is expected to generate investment returns of $12 million a year, enough to cover its operating expenses), which houses his collection and serves as headquarters for the Broad Art Foundation's lending library of contemporary works (Finkel 2014).

The Fisher example is similar to that of Broad in several ways. Donald and Doris Fisher, co-founders of the Gap, have provided San Francisco Museum of Modern Art (SFMOMA) with funding for a new building to house their collections, operating under the assumption that the art will eventually be permanently donated to the museum. They have created a trust, administered in collaboration with SFMOMA, to oversee the care of their collection at the museum, renewable after 25 years. Similarly, Eli Broad provided funds to Los Angeles County Museum of Art for the Broad Contemporary Art Museum building, with LACMA assuming the building assured the donation of the Broad collections.

Alice Walton, like the Broads and the Fishers, has a long history with the city in which she practices her "venture philanthropy." Like the Broads and the Fishers, her decision to build a museum to house her art collection is motivated by her commitment to her city. Walton's fortune stems from her stake in mega-retailer Wal-Mart, which her father founded back in 1962. She was raised in Bentonville, Arkansas (the location of the first Wal-Mart and the current Wal-Mart corporate headquarters), where she decided to open Crystal Bridges, a new museum of American art, to house her art collection. The museum was funded by Walton's personal wealth and supported by major contributions from the Walton Family Foundation, including a record cash gift of $800 million in May 2011 (Crow 2011) and a $20 million grant from Wal-Mart to eliminate admission charges for the museum in perpetuity (Reynolds 2011). Public investment in Crystal Bridges came largely in the form of tax breaks, which were developed specifically to benefit the museum. The extent of Walton and Wal-Mart's influence in the founding of Crystal Bridges was evident when the State of Arkansas passed Act 1865.[9] The legislation provided tax exemption for a "qualified museum for construction, repair, expansion, or operation," where a "qualified museum" was defined as one with a "collection with a value greater than $100 million[10] in Arkansas prior to January 1, 2013 (Davis 2011). Walton denied this legislature was meant to benefit Crystal Bridges, but there are no other museums in Arkansas that meet the requirements of

---

[8] The Broad Contemporary Art Museum at LACMA.
[9] ftp://www.arkleg.state.ar.us/acts/2005/public/ACT1865.pdf.
[10] State of Arkansas 85th General Assembly, "Act 1865 of the Regular session," March 16th, 2005.

a "qualified museum." The legislation was clearly designed and passed solely for Walton and Crystal Bridges. Crystal Bridges has already triggered a positive economic effect on Bentonville with restaurants and hotels that support the cultural tourism drawn by the museum (Reynolds 2012).

3.2 Europe

The European art collector market is strongly connected with a vast tradition of collecting art. Since the fifteenth century, rulers in Central Europe have fostered artists and collected art. During the seventeenth century with the opening of the market in the Netherlands more people began to develop an interest in collecting art. As a result the first auction houses, including Sotheby's and Christie's in London and the Dorotheum in Vienna, were incorporated. Alongside these, the salons of Paris, which are the precursors of the modern art galleries, were responsible for the enlargement of the art market and an increasing interest in art collection. The supremacy of the European art market continued until the late twentieth century. Today the import market in Europe is still huge: with a share of 35 % (McAndrew 2015) of global imports, Europe is the largest global importer of art. Moreover Europe has a global post-war and contemporary art market share of 26 % (McAndrew 2015), which is approximately as much as Asia, but not as great as the U.S. share (46 %). In terms of total numbers of collectors, Europe leads with a big advantage. More than 38 % of global collectors are based in Europe, compared to 28 % in North America and 18 % in Asia.[11] While European museums were historically institutions established by the state and part of the public sector, the situation has changed considerably in recent years. Now private museums increasingly attract a vast audience and have become a major tourist attraction, undertaking more market oriented policies than public museums. Many of the latest museums are more expansive than their older counterparts, with bigger staffs and larger buildings. Two of the most famous examples of this kind are those of the dueling French luxury company owners Bernard Arnault and Francois Pinault. Arnault, owner of the luxury conglomerate Louis Vuitton Moët Hennessey (LVMH), opened the Fondation Louis Vuitton in the Bois de Boulogne in Paris. The cloud-inspired, Frank Gehry-designed museum was met with local resistance, which postponed the project several times; however, the French Senate approved the project in 2011 (Elliot 2011). Sponsored by the group LVMH but run as a non-profit legal entity, the $143 million museum opened in 2014 and shows works owned by LVMH and Bernard Arnault (Vogel 2015). Pinault, owner of rival luxury company Kering, also met with Parisian resistance when he attempted to build a museum on the Ile de Seguin. Pinault became so frustrated with Paris that he took his offer elsewhere, refurbishing a historic Venetian palace, the Palazzo Grassi, to house his collection instead. The Palazzo Grassi project was so successful that in

---

[11] Larry's List database.

2007 the City of Venice gave Pinault control of another historic property, the Punta della Dogana, so it too could be converted into an art exhibition space, which now displays his vast collection (Goldstein 2011). Another private museum recently opened in Italy is the Prada Foundation. Though Fondazione Prada was established in 1993, the new 19,000 square-meter venue—an old distillery dating from 1910 and located in southern Milan—gives the foundation a permanent exhibition space, after years of hosting activities in spaces in Milan and Venice, and a number of international outings. The project, designed by OMA, the studio of renowned architect Rem Koolhaas, involved the renovation of seven existing buildings at a complex in Largo Isarco, as well as the design of three new structures: a cinema, a gallery, and a tower. Just 1 month later, Rem Koolhaas also completed the Garage Museum of Contemporary Art, the first institution in Moscow related to the development of Russian contemporary art, founded by Dasha Zhukova. The project was initially located in a glass pavilion designed by Japanese architect Shigeru Ban, before moving in June 2015 to its first permanent home: a groundbreaking project that transformed the famous 1968 Vremena Goda Soviet Modernist restaurant in Gorky Park into a contemporary museum. In the United Kingdom, the Saatchi Gallery is one of the largest and most contemporary collections of art to be found. It contains artworks by the YBAs alongside the young cutting edge. London is also the home of the newly opened Newport Street Gallery, which presents exhibitions of work from Damien Hirst's Murderme art collection. The project, which cost around £25 million, has been entirely funded by Damien Hirst (Anstey 2015). A similar size space, the David Roberts Art Foundation (Draf), opened in 2007 near the Mornington Crescent end of Camden High Street. These joined the Zabludowicz Collection, which has been housed in a former Methodist chapel on Prince of Wales Road since 2007. All four are private museums that display the wares of high-powered British collectors: Charles Saatchi, Damien Hirst, David Roberts and Anita Zabludowicz respectively. Each is free from state control, with no role for DCMS directives or Arts Council handouts, and are accountable only to the collectors who founded them. While London has more art collectors than any other city in Europe and dominates with 15 % of European collectors, a large number of private museums have been created in Berlin over recent years. Erika Hoffmann opened the Sammlung Hoffmann in 1997; Alex Haubrok the Sammlung Haubrok in 2005; Christin Boros the Sammlung Boros in 2008; and Thomas Olbrich the Me Collectors Room in 2010. There are also a number of private museums located in smaller cities—such as the Museum Ritter in Waldenbuch, the Weishaupt Collection in Ulm, or the Walther Collection in Nersingen—and even in the countryside. The Sammlung Klein, which is located in the village of Eberdingen-Nussdorf, and the Grässlin Collection in the village of St. Georgen are examples of such rural enterprises.

Eastern European oligarchs also use their collections to influence cities and their business. Several years ago, business industrialist and philanthropist Victor Pinchuk realized he needed an innovative setting, rather than the usual office or restaurant, in which he could bring new business interests in the Ukraine. In collaboration with curator Peter Doroshenko, in 2006 he opened the Pinchuk Art

Center in a historic neighborhood of Kiev, where he could meet with and entertain new business prospects in an exciting setting. While the new art centre served Pinchuk's purpose brilliantly, putting him in a position of power among business people who knew very little about contemporary art, it had another outcome as well: by operating as a museum open to the public, with staff, lectures, and educational programs, the centre introduced the local and national populace to contemporary art (RBC Wealth Management 2012).

3.3 Asia

The Asian art market is not as comprehensive and homogenous as the European or U.S. markets. Within Asia there are many different countries with completely different stylistic and artistic creations and tastes, as well as financial situations, economic developments, and market structures. This makes it difficult to consider Asia as one market as a whole. In recent years, several art market centres have come into existence in China, Japan, India, Indonesia, and South Korea, each with their own regional characteristics. Art collectors in these regions started out collecting what they recognize as art specific to their country, and every country has its own local art stars favoured by the local collectors. Nevertheless, the Asian collector structure is undergoing a process of internationalization, which has been supported by the establishment of international art fairs in these countries and the introduction of internationally renowned artists to Asian markets through auction houses and galleries. One example of the internationalization of the Asian market is Art Basel in Hong Kong (formerly Art HK). With galleries from 35 different countries, this fair seeks to attract dealers and collectors from both Europe and Asia, encouraging them to converge. While more established markets tend to have a large proportion of collectors who own museums, in this respect the Chinese art market is just getting started. Overall there are 17 private museums or exhibition spaces in Greater China, with Beijing clearly holding the most museums. Nevertheless, due to the growing economy and the increasing number of HNWIs, the number of private museums has been increasing in recent years and many collectors have expansion plans for their own museum. Art collectors Wang Wei and Budi Tek are two examples of this kind. Chinese billionaire couple Wang Wei and her husband Liu Yiqian are world-renowned collectors whose collection includes traditional, modern and contemporary Chinese art, as well as contemporary art from Asia and Europe. The couple founded the Long Museum in Shanghai, which now has two locations. The first venue, the Long Museum Pudong, opened in December 2012 at a cost of almost $50 million and more than $1.5 million annually on overhead. The Long Museum West Bund was launched in March 2014 in the Xuhiu District and concentrates on the contemporary art that the couple have acquired over the past 2 years. Wang Wei and her husband are also planning to open a third branch in Chongqing in the spring of 2016 (Tsui 2015).

Just 1 km along further down the Xuhui riverfront, Indonesian-Chinese collector Budi Tek has his own Yuz Museum, where he houses his personal collection of contemporary international and Chinese art. Tek started to dedicate himself to the building of an art collection about 10 years ago and in 2007 set up the non-profit Yuz Foundation to promote a wider understanding of contemporary art and artists. Tek, whose Shanghai Yuz Museum is the second museum to carry this name (the first opened in Jakarta in 2008), plans to open an Art Park in Bali, called Budidesa. Conceived as a new home for his Yuz Foundation in his home country of Indonesia, the park will be made up of a series of art gardens, exhibition spaces and a residence that together will form a unique combination of contemporary art in a tropical environment. Marked by large-scale contemporary art from renowned international artists such as Zhang Huan, Ai Weiwei, Anslem Keifer, Maurizio Cattelan, Adel Abdessemed, and Mona Hatoum, the quality and scale of the art within this tropical setting will create a global art attraction and make a lasting contribution to Balinese culture. Budi Tek and Wang Wei have joined a roster of existing contemporary art museums in China, established in the last few years. These include the Beijing Today Art Museum, China's first private museum founded by Zhang Baoquan in 2002; the Museum of Contemporary Art (MOCA) Shanghai, founded in 2005 by Hong Kong jewelry designer Samuel Kung; the Shanghai 21st Century Minsheng Art Museum, established in 2014 by China Minsheng Banking Corporation, China's largest bank; M Woods Museum, founded in 2014 by Lin Han in Beijing; the Sifang Art Museum, founded in 2013 by Lu Xun in Nanjing; the Rockbund Art Museum, a Kunsthalle that opened in 2010 in Shanghai; and the Shanghai Himalayas Museum, designed by Japanese architect Arata Isozaki and completed in 2011. Both the Rockbund and the Himalayas Museum are typical of many museum projects in China, linked with real estate developments, with the museums' primary role being to boost the commercial value of a development. The Rockbund was founded by Thomas Ou, founder and chairman of Sinolink Worldwide Holdings—a real-estate company listed on the Hong Kong Stock Exchange—as the centrepiece of a luxury redevelopment plan for Shanghai's prestigious Bund district. The Himalayas Museum was created by real-estate developer Dai Zhikang in 2011 as part of a development which cost about $480 million (Young 2013). The Himalayas Centre includes conference facilities, restaurants, shopping spaces and a luxury hotel; located on the top floor of the development is the Zendai Himalayas Art Museum, in which Dai Zhikang exhibits his art collection. At Zendai artists interact with families who have not necessarily come for the art, a synthesis that has also been promoted by entrepreneur and arts patron Adrien Cheng with his K11 Art Malls and his not-for-profit K11 Art Foundation. An innovative museum retail concept and a hybrid model of art and commerce founded by Cheng in 2008, K11 not only displays a permanent collection of young, local artists' works, but also allows the public to appreciate different local artworks and exhibitions during shopping and leisure through the provision of various multi-dimensional spaces. Works by Yoshitomo Nara, Olafur Eliasson and Damien Hirst, which form part of the K11 collection,[12] are dotted around the store

---

[12] http://www.k11.com/corp/art/k11-kollection/.

aisles, though none is for sale. The flagship K11 sites in Hong Kong and Shanghai were launched in December 2009 and June 2013 respectively. By feeding profits from the retail business back into the art foundation, Cheng is able to produce 50 shows a year and attract over 1000 visitors a day (Pollack 2014). K11 Art Foundation, which uses K11 shopping malls to bring art to the public, collaborates with the Palais de Tokyo and operates a residency programme in Wuhan, China.

3.4 Korea

The private museums in Korea have a history of about 30 years, with two exceptional expansion periods. In the early 1990s, Lee O-Young, the Minister of Culture, made a law to support the foundation of museums and galleries, which, as a result, stimulated the development of Korea's exhibition culture and greatly increased the number of private museums. The second expansion is currently taking place: the government has started to extend tax favors and ease regulations associated with the foundation and administration of museums. This current change in governmental support has resulted in the substantial growth of private museums (Da-eun 2007). Today, Korea possesses the largest number of private art museums in Asia behind China (approximately 75 % of Korean museums are private museums, of which about 80 % focus primarily on contemporary art), demonstrating its willingness and responsibility to promote art to a wider audience (Bouchara and Woo 2015). Art collecting and museum building in Asia is not limited to China and Korea. In Japan, collector and philanthropist Shoichiro Fukutake supports arts and culture projects through the Fututake Foundation under the collective name of Benesse Art Site Naoshima. The Art Site is concentrated on the islands of Naoshima, Teshima, and Inujima in the Seto Inland Sea. In 1992, Fukutake opened the Benesse House Museum designed by Tadao Ando. In 2004, with his own personal funding, he established the Naoshima Fututake Art Museum Foundation and in 2010 the Lee Ufan Museum. Thanks to his philanthropic interventions and passion for collecting contemporary art, Naoshima has become a contemporary art mecca recognized worldwide (Ardia 2015). In India, mother and son collectors Lekha and Anupam Poddar opened the non-profit Devi Art Foundation in the suburbs of New Delhi to showcase their collections of over 7,000 works, while Indian collector Kiran Nadar opened the Kiran Nadar Museum of Art, in a mall in New Delhi, to display her modern and contemporary Indian art collections.

3.5 South Africa and Middle East

In the environment of the African continent, where the infrastructural requirements for state-funded museum initiatives are frequently beset by bureaucratic problems, and regulations are either not in place or not fully actionable, large private initiatives make sense and may spark improvements for state infrastructure. The private collection of Jochen Zeitz is one such initiative and will be at the core of the

Zeitz Museum of Contemporary African Art (Zeitz MOCAA), opening in Cape Town at the end of 2016. The Director of Kering began collecting in the early 2000s and his collection has expanded with a strong focus on African and Caribbean art. The largest private collection of contemporary African art in the world, Zeitz's holdings feature works by globally established artists such as Chris Ofili, Kehinde Wiley, Glenn Ligon, Wangechi Mutu, Julie Mehretu, and Rashid Johnson. The collection also boasts a significant number of works by South African artists such as Marlene Dumas, as well as emerging artists from the region such as Nicholas Hlobo (whose work is represented in the Tate collection) and Nandipha Mntambo. Although it is not the only African private museum project, existing or in planning, Zeitz MOCAA is likely to set a precedent for the museum landscape in Africa. Its development may well be followed by other private initiatives of major African collectors, such as Sindika Dokolo (Luanda, Angola) or the Lazaar family (Tunisia) who have sizable foundations of their own with residency programs, educational facilities, publications, and in some cases future museum plans. While the reported $50 million museum is being built, parts of the collection are housed in the temporary pavilion of the Zeitz MOCAA in the Waterfront development in Cape Town, while other works are on display at the Segera Retreat in Kenya, a vast eco-resort founded by Jochen Zeitz in 2005 (De Sousa 2015).

Zeitz is not alone in his philanthropic mission to open up access to art in emerging markets; other cities are close to matching the pace. Within the next five years, Beirut will have five new private art museums (Chan 2015). The first of these, the Aïshti Foundation, belongs to Lebanese retail mogul and major collector Tony Salamé and opened in 2015 on the city's seafront. The Aïshti Foundation is part of an ambitious expansion of Aïshti Seaside by British architect David Adjaye, a huge complex of about 350,000 square feet, costed at about $100 million, with 60 in-store boutiques, six restaurants, a spa, a gym, a pool, the art foundation's space and a rooftop nightclub offering views of the Beirut skyline. Salamé, who created his foundation in 2005 and whose 2,500 piece collection focuses on the first decade of the twenty-first century, sees the Aïshti Foundation both as a place where Lebanese art can be in dialogue with international contemporary art, and as a new concept for the city: a total experience encompassing art, retail, lifestyle, well-being, and food (Douglas 2015).

3.6 Australia

In Australia, a handful of art connoisseurs have shown considerable altruism and dedication to establish purpose-built museums or open their own houses and invite the public to view their collections. One of the first to open its doors, thanks in part to the Federal Government's initiative in 1999 to encourage arts philanthropy, is the now publicly owned but privately funded TarraWarra Museum of Art. After 50 years of collecting, focusing on Australian art from the 1950s to today, Marc and Eva Besen commissioned architect Allan Powell to design a gallery for their collection of John Brack, Jeffrey Smart, John Olsen and other iconic artists, opening the gallery in 2003.

A more recent addition to the private museum scene is White Rabbit in Sydney, one of the world's largest and most significant collections of contemporary Chinese art. Funded by the $30 million foundation established by Kerr Neilson and his wife Judith in 2009, White Rabbit has a collection of over 1,000 works by more than 350 artists, capturing the explosion of creativity that has driven Chinese art in the past decade (Ardia 2015). Continuing a tradition of private settings being opened to the public to display personal collections, as well as the matching of distinctive architecture and art collections, is the Lyon Housemuseum in Melbourne's Kew. Designed by one of Melbourne's leading architects, Corbett Lyon, this building merges the public and the private setting of a family residence. A coherent contemporary collection of paintings, sculpture, video work and large-scale installations is juxtaposed with family living spaces, creating a unique environment for viewing the work. The owners, Corbett and Yueji Lyon, have been collecting Australian contemporary art since 1990 and their collection encompasses pieces by high-profile names such Tim Maguire, Callum Morton, Anne Zahalka and Patricia Piccinini as well as lesser-known artists.

Finally, one of Australia's most high-profile private collectors, David Walsh, has invested $75 million in the Museum of Old and New Art (MONA), to house his collections of antiquities and contemporary art (Barca 2010). MONA is the largest privately funded museum in Australia with an $8 million annual operating budget. The funding comes from Walsh (who made his fortune by applying his mathematical skills to a successful gambling system), and from other businesses Walsh developed on the Moorilla estate where the museum is located. The winery, brewery, restaurant and boutique hotel all benefit from a micro Bilbao effect, which in turn financially supports the museum (Hume 2011).

4 Conclusion

A new generation of philanthropists is emerging in the contemporary museum scene, no longer limited to sponsors or partners of existing museums. They elaborate new and independent visions and concepts, and are ready to concretely carry out projects that might sometimes be seen as early, if not utopian, working hypotheses. They are permanent, vital additions to the cultural fabric of the city, with a full range of curatorial, conservational, public and scholarly programmes. They do not compete with public museums, but complement their cultural and educational activities. In developing countries these museums will assume the responsibility of public museums, as examples in South Africa or China have already shown. At first glance, some brief reflections can be expressed. First of all, it must be said that all these projects have a physical aspect that requires a significant and continuous commitment, both in financial and organizational terms. It follows that all these projects have shown a remarkable ability to attract professional and intellectual resources. Due to their size and aims, these projects were developed in the medium-long term, thus revealing themselves to be independent from the financial situation. Another characteristic of this kind of museum initiative is the complete independence of management bodies from external political or administrative conditions, even if they cooperate with various local entities. Lastly, there is a consideration that is already implicit in the previous remarks, but still important to understand the reasons that lie behind all these projects: the will to propose something new, not merely for the sake of novelty, but for the real need of filling a gap, moving museum research and practice forward. These projects have been supported by the local government not for traditional reasons like the preservation of collections and scientific research, but in order to meet new goals such as encouraging tourism (one of the world's biggest industries), urban regeneration (with former industrial sites being transformed into museums), and city branding (to attract new industries and investment, which brings added value to the economy). With the price of homes near major creative centres increasing, even residential property developers have been naturally keen to be involved in this global art phenomenon. This has led to the emergence of art-led residential developments such as Dallas's Arts District in Texas, the West Kowloon Cultural District in Hong Kong or the Saadiyat Cultural District in Abu Dhabi. Without the restrictions of government boards and public accountability, or the pressing need to make a profit, private museums can provide an insight into private aesthetics, additional outlets for artists and an extra dimension for the art-going public. These intimate museums will continue to play a formative role in the public's understanding of art, its interpretation, function, and patrons, while challenging their directors to seek out new opportunities to engage wider audiences. And as museum standards impact collectors more directly, we will see more collectors seeking the advice of professionals in the field, resulting in collections better prepared to long outlast their creators.

References

Anstey, T. (2015, October 14). Hat-Trick: Caruso St John Architects Unveil Liverpool Philharmonic, Plus galleries for Damien Hirst and Larry Gagosian. *CLADglobal*.

Ardia, X. (2015, December 11). 10 Most influential Asian art collectors. *The Culture Trip*.

Association of American Art Directors. (2007). *Art museums, private collectors, and the public benefit*. New York: AAMD.

AXA ART. (2014). *Collecting in the digital age. International collectors survey*. Cologne: AXA ART.

Barca, M. (2010). Private passions become public. Australian Decorative and Fine Arts Societies Bulletin, *19*(1), 6–9.

Bouchara, C., & Woo, K. (2015, September 16). To be part of the big leagues: Savina Lee on private art museums in Korea. *Larry's List*.

Bourdieu, P. (1979). *Distinction: A social critique of the judgement of taste*. Paris: Les Editions de Minuit.

Bradley, K. (2015, January 23). Why museums hide masterpieces away. *BBC*.

Chan, M. (2015, July 17). Beirut at a turning point: 5 New museums and art centres on the horizon. *Art Radar*.

Crow, K. (2011, May 6). Record gift: $800 million. *Wall Street Journal*.
Da-eun, K. (2007, March 26). Private yet public. *The Yonsei Annals*.
Davis, B. (2011, June 23). Seeing through crystal bridges. *Artinfo*.
De Sousa, B. (2015, July 14). From private collection to mega-museum: The Zeitz MOCAA, Cape Town. *ArtSlant*.
Doroshenko, P. (2010). *Private spaces for contemporary art*. Brussels: Rispoli Books.
Douglas, S. (2015, June 29). Making waves: Tony Salamé's Aïshti goes big in Beirut. *ARTNews*.
Elliot, H. (2011, March 31). LVMH moves forward with Gehry Art Museum. *Forbes*.
European Venture Philanthropy Association. (2010). *Establishing a venture philanthropy organization in Europe*. Brussels: EVPA.
Evans, G. (2005). Measure for measure: Evaluating the evidence of culture's contribution to regeneration. *Urban Studies, 42*(5/6), 959–984.
Finkel, J. (2014, June 4). Eli Broad says patience is not his strong point. *The Art Newspaper*.
Goldstein, A. (2011, March 14). Francois Pinault Hone his grip on Venice by reorganizing art sites. *Artinfo*.
Hume, M. (2011, January 2011). Wild at art. *W Magazine*.
Larry's List. (2014). *Art collector report 2014*. Vienna: Modern Arts Publishing.
Larry's List & AMMA. (2016). *The private art museum report*. Vienna: Modern Arts Publishing.
Letowski, J. (2010). *Museum-making: Transitioning from private collection to public museum*, Unpublished Manuscript. Washington, DC: The George Washington University.
McAndrew, C. (2015). *TEFAF art market report 2015*. Helvoirt: TEFAF.
Pollack, B. (2014, July 16). Adrian Cheng: Building up a New Chinese Culture. *ARTnews*.
RBC Wealth Management. (2012). *Global shift: Transforming the art world*. Breakfast panel at The Raleigh, Miami, on December 9.
Reynolds, C. (2011, November 11). Backed by Wal-Mart millions, a museum is Born in Arkansas. *Los Angeles Times*.
Reynolds, C. (2012, October 14). Crystal Bridges Art Museum is reshaping Wal-Mart's hometown. *Los Angeles Times*.
Rodriguez, C. (2014, February 8). Meet the billionaire behind Miami's artistic rebirth. *CNN*.
Tiglao, R. (2013, June 23). A P1-Billion 'Museum of Me'. *Manila Times*.
Tsui, E. (2015, October 6). Billionaire Shanghai art collectors Wang Wei and Liu Yiqian have big plans for their museums. *South China Morning Post*.
Veblen, T. (1934). *The theory of the leisure class*. New York: The Modern Library.
Vogel, C. (2015, February 2). Bold addition to Paris Skyline gets art to match. *The New York Times*.
Willette, R. (2010). *Global trends in private museums*. London: Fine Art Wealth Management.
Young, M. (2013, May 21). Shanghai's private museums. *Asian Newspaper*.
Zorloni, A. (2013). *The economics of contemporary art. Markets, strategies and stardom*. Heidelberg: Springer.

Financial and Estate Planning for Art Assets

Alessia Zorloni and Randall James Willette

1 Introduction

Having created or inherited an art collection, many families will wish to ensure it is preserved both during their lifetime and for future generations. Planning how to transfer a family collection to the next generation can be one of the most critical aspects of building and maintaining a successful financial plan for art assets. Deciding where the collection may reside after it passes from a family's control, be it with an institution such as a museum, a family member or a fiduciary structure, is also a key consideration. In light of potential tax and other financial liabilities, deciding on the best strategy early on can be of critical importance in valuing and transferring a family collection. Often, the family's overall financial needs may help to determine the specific vehicle chosen to transfer all or part of a collection from one generation to another. Questions concerning whether children will have the organizational and financial resources to care for a collection and whether there will be sufficient wealth to bequeath an inheritance outside of the collection itself may have to be resolved. Regardless of whether the children have an interest in a family collection, decisions about its disposal can be quite emotional. One key to making sure a collection does not damage family harmony is to work towards open communication and look for creative ways to include family members in the decision-making process. Creating the right financial plan for an art collection requires a personal touch, taking into account unique financial needs, interest in providing for heirs and other beneficiaries and the nature of the assets involved in order to chart a creative and sound financial course that serves the family effectively

A. Zorloni
IULM University, Milan, Italy
e-mail: alessia.zorloni@iulm.it

R.J. Willette (✉)
Fine Art Wealth Management Limited, London, United Kingdom
e-mail: rjwillette@fineartwealthmgt.com

over time. This chapter examines the issues faced by sophisticated collectors in managing their private collections. Section 2 examines in detail the motivations for investing in art; Sect. 3 analyzes why it can be useful to create a fiduciary structure that preserves and protects the family collection; Sect. 4 considers the use of art financing to unlock equity in art; Sect. 5 provides a comprehensive analysis of the essential elements of art governance; Sect. 6 provides advice in defining an effective art succession planning; and the final section offers general conclusions regarding art wealth management.

2 Exploring the Motivations Behind Investing in Art

To understand what drives the art market, it is important to recognize that the overriding motivation is not simply to buy art. Artworks are bought and used not only for their intrinsic value or ability to fulfil a material need, but also for the many connotations they take on in a cultural environment. The need to collect works of art, which has emerged ever more clearly as Western standards of living have improved, stems from the desire to affirm one's own personality through a process in which artistic values take material form (Molfino and Mottola Molfino 1997). As a luxury good, art serves to express mature capitalism and post-industrial society (Vettese 1991). Several studies have examined the demand for the visual arts. Most of these focus on auction sales on the secondary market (Anderson 1974; Stein 1977; Baumol 1986; Candela and Scorcu 2001) and assume, explicitly or implicitly, that art is bought for purely speculative reasons (Goetzmann 1993; Locatelli-Bley and Zanola 1999; Mei and Moses 2002; Pesando 1993; Frey and Pommerehne 1989; Buelens and Ginsburgh 1993). In reality, as Moulin (1967) noted, motives for buying art are complex and ambiguous; they are simultaneously conscious and unconscious, altruistic and selfish, philanthropic and mercenary. The psychoanalyst Anthony Storr (1983) noted that collecting leads to classifying, and the ability to classify accurately correlates with the urge to make order, to comprehend in order to predict, and finally to master what had previously seemed beyond control. Knowledge, mastery, and control are therefore three recurrent motives for collecting. Other motives for collecting art are the desire to affirm one's identity, and to gain prestige, social advantages, and distinction (Bourdieu 1979). In fact, art is amenable to what Veblen (1934) has called *conspicuous consumption*: by consuming art, people can distinguish themselves from others. In principle, collector demand comes from four socio-economic groups: private collectors, businesses, public institutions, and cultural institutions. Looking at some distinguishing marks of the demand for works of art makes it possible to define four models of consumption that are linked to the needs and demands of each of the categories (Zorloni 2013).

1. The first model is linked to cultural interest motivation: it stems from a completely inner, aesthetic need, in which the consumer's emotive side predominates.

2. The second model comes from a decorative need to establish a pleasant working environment; the functional aspect is foremost here.
3. The third model is financially motivated, bringing together passion for artwork and the need to invest savings beyond the reach of currency fluctuations and fiscal risks. Here, economic criteria are the most important.
4. Lastly, societal motivations frame the collector's activity not as an end in itself, but as a source of social prestige with symbolic value.

Art can therefore be seen as having the capacity to satisfy a cultural and aesthetic need, but also the increasing desire of businesses and institutions to preserve contemporary creativity for future generations, to convey an image of prestige to their interlocutors, and to invest a portion of their savings in alternative markets. This trend is supported by a recent report by Deloitte and ArtTactic (2016) according to which 72 % of art collectors said they bought art for passion with an investment view. Despite the growing pattern of high-net-worth individuals (HNWIs) viewing art as part of a portfolio diversification strategy, the emotional and social value of art remain the primary reasons for its purchase. Other reasons include the desire to derive pleasure, preserve control, achieve social impact, and secure wealth across generations. Closer examination of each of these factors offers insights into the art-as-investment mindsets of HNWIs and family offices.

Derivation of Pleasure. Enjoyment is by far the most important motivation for direct investment in art. This fact supports a view that art should be regarded as part of an individual's personal holdings rather than as a separate asset class within an investment portfolio. An individual's personal holdings comprise all those assets that play a role in their lifestyle, such as personal property and treasure, and for which financial characteristics are less important than the use or pleasure they provide (Barclays 2012).

Preservation of Control. Direct investment in art is a good fit for family offices whose strategy is to be active and maintain a high level of control over the underlying investment; in essence, for those who want to physically own the art. Family offices must use the expertise of internal and external teams to assess economic conditions, financial and art market dynamics, and other variables that may influence the prices, activity, supply availability, and future appeal of opportunities identified for investment. These opportunities are generated by the underlying dynamic of the art market, which is inefficient and illiquid, lacks price transparency, and has highly differentiated products (Zorloni 2013). Similar to private equity, a family office must not only engage in the right transaction at the right time and the right price, but also must enhance the value of each artwork through a variety of curatorial and marketing activities commonly practiced by successful collectors and dealers.

Social Impact. Investing directly in art also provides a greater opportunity for collecting families to maximize social impact. Wealthy collectors who nurture living artists, protect the works of deceased artists, and share their collection in museums and exhibitions play an important role in enriching cultural life.

Although there may be some cultural value associated with loaning works of art to museums and exhibitions, the motivations for lending items are not always altruistic. Sarah Thornton (2010) notes there is genuine philanthropic desire to enrich the lives of others, but it is often mixed with other motives. Collections are more likely to increase in value if they are seen by the general public, because art accrues value through exposure. The willingness to share possessions with society varies widely from one country to another. According to a study conducted by Barclays (2012), investors from the Middle East and India are most likely to agree that there is a duty to share valuable possessions for the good of society, while investors from the U.S., Japan, Hong Kong, and the U.K. are least likely to hold this view. This suggests that countries with large quantities of newly created wealth may have a propensity to demonstrate status through valuable collectibles.

Securing Wealth Across Generations. Finally, direct investments in art and art-related businesses offer scope for financial return. This economic motivation is clearly rooted in the desire to achieve family wealth sustainability. For example, a family office may pursue investments across a broad range of regional, decorative, and niche opportunities in both the primary and secondary art markets. Works may be purchased for long-term appreciation or short-term arbitrage. Family offices can provide art dealers, auction houses, and other market entities with the resources necessary to make timely investments where traditional banks, unfamiliar with art world practices and dynamics, impose prohibitive terms. The attraction of co-investment opportunities includes the fact that the family office typically has a demonstrated expertise and ability to add value beyond capital (e.g., via business skills, art expertise, proprietary deal flow, or art-market intelligence). A family office may seek to identify two broad categories of co-investment opportunities: buying art works in partnership with art dealers and co-investment with auction houses.

- *Buying art works in partnership with art dealers.* While a single family office will generally acquire direct ownership of an art work, in certain circumstances it may own an art work in partnership with an art dealer or another family office. A family office may also enter into an arrangement with selected dealers to share in the potential upside of a painting by receiving remuneration when the painting is sold.
- *Co-investment with auction houses.* A single family office may also seek higher returns by selectively deploying capital to auction houses and by participating in guaranteed pre-agreed terms and conditions extended by the auction houses to a select number of important sellers. In return, family offices enjoy a share of the financial upside or downside of these transactions.

When considering the potential investment benefits of adding art to a portfolio, investors should consider the possible long-term advantages of inflation protection, volatility reduction for the overall portfolio via low correlation, and higher risk-adjusted returns. One must balance the potential benefits of art investment with other client-specific requirements and consider liquidity needs and time horizon.

Most importantly, investors should be aware of asset class specific risks and liquidity related risks associated with art investment, each with its own potential consequences.

3 Preserving and Protecting a Family Art Collection

According to a study by Accenture (2012), over $12 trillion worth of financial and non-financial assets are changing hands, moving from the "Greatest Generation," those born in the 1920s and 1930s, to the Baby Boomers, born between 1943 and 1964. With significant sums involved in this intergenerational transfer of wealth, wealth managers will increasingly have to offer advice regarding art legacies and the most effective way of preserving their emotional, financial, and cultural value. Planning how to preserve and protect a family collection can be one of the most critical aspects of building and maintaining a successful financial plan for art assets. Deciding where the collection may reside after it passes from a family's control, whether with an institution such as a museum, a family member, or a fiduciary structure, is also a key consideration. Ownership through a trust structure can offer significant advantages over direct ownership in terms of preservation of wealth both generally and in relation to art collections in particular. The very wide range of fiduciary structures available and the huge flexibility that careful drafting can incorporate into trust instruments allow structures to be tailored to the needs of the particular client and collection. According to Willette and Litten (2014), the types of structure most appropriate for dedicated art collections now include:

(1) Reserved Powers Trusts
    This is where the trustee retains legal ownership of the artwork in the trust, but the donor is given power to select and manage the artwork (e.g. deciding when certain works should be sold). Care must be taken to ensure that the extent of the powers retained by the donor will not cause legal and taxation issues in their own country of residence (e.g. risk of "sham" or co-trusteeship).
(2) Private Trust Company (PTC)
    The donor can form his/her own, exclusive, trust company to administer the family trusts, supported by a professional trust company. The PTC will be incorporated into and administered by an international finance centre. Typically, the donor along with certain family members and professional advisors will constitute the Board of Directors of a PTC, along with a professional fiduciary company which will add its expertise, and undertake day-to-day administration, accounting and corporate secretarial matters.
(3) Private Trust Foundation (PTF)
    This is very similar to a PTC, except that the Foundation itself (rather than a company) will act as trustee to the various family trusts. This structure is simpler, as the 'orphan' nature of the Foundation means no shares are issued (in contrast to a PTC). Some jurisdictions will require a professional fiduciary to be one of the Councillors. As the foundation will have no beneficiaries—and

its purpose will only be to act as trustee, an independent "Guardian" will need to be appointed (similar to the 'Enforcer' role, to ensure the PTF fulfils its purpose).

(4) Foundations

A Foundation is quasi-corporate in nature, and may appeal particularly to clients from civil law jurisdiction where the trust concept is not as well known or understood. As with a PTC, the client, the family members, advisors and a professional fiduciary can be appointed as Councillors to manage all the affairs of the Foundation. Foundations can own higher-risk assets: like a company, the foundation enjoys separate legal personality and will own assets itself. As such, the beneficiaries will therefore have no rights over the assets; this contrasts with the beneficiaries' property rights over a trust and the trustee's overarching duty to act prudently in their interests.

(5) Purpose Trusts/Hybrid Trusts

A Purpose Trust has no beneficiaries, but instead one or more "purposes"—such as holding designated works of art, or for a philanthropic mission. These trusts can be established to last in perpetuity and are particularly useful for keeping collections together for enjoyment by future generations. As the purpose of the trust is to hold the artwork and nothing else, the trustee cannot be held liable for non-diversification of assets. These purposes can also be combined with a physical class of beneficiaries to create a "hybrid" trust, where family members can benefit from the trust (e.g. to enjoy the artwork).

The study conducted by Willette and Litten (2014) highlights that when establishing a fiduciary structure, it is essential to consider how ongoing costs will be met—including art insurance, restoration and professional fees such as for trustees and advisors. The worst scenario to avoid is a forced sale of certain works to fund the ongoing costs of the rest of the collection. Ideally, liquid assets will also be placed into the fiduciary structure to provide long-term cover for fees and expenses. Should these funds ever become seriously depleted, the fiduciary will need to consider the following ways to raise funds, in discussion with the family:

1. Loans of artwork to galleries, museums and individuals/corporations;
2. Potentially borrowing against the artwork (as a temporary measure);
3. If no liquidity can be generated, then as a last resort considering the sale of certain pieces of artwork. The specific pieces that might be sold in such circumstances should be identified in advance with the donor.

4   Use of Art Financing to Unlock Equity in Art

Individuals seeking loans secured by private art collections typically fall into two categories: those who are asset rich and cash poor and need to raise capital for a particular purpose and those looking to monetize their art holdings, historically an illiquid asset, and to use the resulting liquidity for other investments (Gyorgy 2010).

Typical art rich, cash poor borrowers would be people who have inherited an art collection, which they plan to sell, but on which they need to raise money quickly to pay the estate or other inheritance taxes that are due within a short period of time. In other cases art lending makes it possible to redeploy their capital into other art acquisitions or investment opportunities. Beyond these basic priorities, collectors may utilize their art and collectibles as collateral to gain liquidity for the following goals:

- To manage short-term cash needs
- To free up equity to redeploy capital into other investments
- To provide orderly liquidation to achieve long term estate planning goals
- As a bridge loan to auction or private treaty sale
- To manage tax and capital gains

As Ultra HNWIs are investing an increasingly larger portion of their wealth in artworks, art loans can be seen as an effective way of enabling collectors to access the equity value in their artwork without selling their collection. Loans secured by art come from private banks, niche art financiers or auction houses. Historically, banks that lend against art have done so primarily for relationship reasons and have been reluctant to use art financing as a means of differentiating themselves in the market. While the majority of art financing by value at present remains with banks, the number of specialty lenders that carry out art financing activities is growing. This trend is coinciding with the rapid growth of the global art market, and as more capital flows into the art market, the need for financial services, such as financing, is rising. Lenders can currently be identified as recourse lenders and non-recourse lenders depending on their assessment of the borrower's credit worthiness. A recourse loan is secured by the art assets but also guaranteed by the borrower, which implies the borrower's full credit is essentially backing the loan. A non-recourse loan, on the other hand, is secured solely by the art asset underlying it. Because this is a higher risk loan it will typically incur a higher interest rate, as the art acts as the only source of collateral for the loan (Gyorgy 2010). Recently, new specialist art lenders have entered the markets in the U.S. and Europe to tap into the increasing demand for financing by sophisticated collectors. These lenders are often referred to as asset-based lenders and offer "non-recourse" lending, meaning they will accept the art as the only collateral with no right to claim on any of the client's other assets. Another type of non-recourse lender is the auction house, which offers clients a loan against an artwork or collection that they will sell at a later date. This is a tool often used by auction houses to win the right to consignments. Art-based lending can currently be divided into three main categories: term loans, bridge loans and lines of credit.

4.1 Term Loans

Rarely longer than 3 years, term loans can range in structure from interest only, partially amortizing or fully amortizing. A typical example of a term loan would be where a private collector uses their existing collection to unlock equity in their art and uses the proceeds to diversify their portfolio and gain a higher level of return. For this group the prevailing mindset is that every asset should be an available source of liquidity for investment.

4.2 Bridge Loans

Some of the major auction houses offer art-based finance to assist prospective consignors in need of liquidity by lending prior to the sale of the art in the short or longer term. These loans constitute an advance that is paid off with the proceeds of the eventual sale, making them essentially bridge loans. Amount is determined by the value of the art and not the credit-worthiness of the borrower as in the case of bank loans. Loans from major auction houses are generally extended at 40–50 % of average low presale auction estimate.

4.3 Lines of Credit

Some collectors may also wish to isolate their art collecting from their other business activities by establishing a revolving line of credit secured by their existing collections to acquire additional works. Few banks lend up to 50 % of the art's estimated low auction value and loans are typically priced at traditional bank rates (Gyorgy 2010). However, rates vary substantially depending on the credit worthiness of the client, the underlying art, and other collateral which may be pledged.

Terms on art loans vary widely, based on the quality of the art, the lender's policies, and the borrower's financial condition. While some bank lenders may require a borrower to have a collection with an overall value of $10 million or more (Arena 2013), there are specialist boutique lenders that will consider smaller values. Furthermore, collections must usually have diversified holdings among artists and time periods, although art loans based on one particularly strong piece of art are possible. The loan, once approved, will be documented and closed with all the requisite information such as bill of sale, insurance certificates and appraisal. In the US, collectors can maintain ownership of the collateralized artworks and usually will still be able to display the pieces as they normally would or, with appropriate insurance, guarantees and other agreements in place, the works may be lent for display in a gallery or museum (Arena 2013; Gyorgy 2010). However, most bank lenders in Europe will require the art to be held in a secure storage facility if it is to be taken as collateral for a loan.

5 Creating an Art Governance System for a Family Collection

Many ultra-high-net-worth families are art lovers, own collections, and require a holistic approach to art management that is tailor-made to the family collection. A family art collection requires the same strategic planning as other financial investments. Once a collection has passed a certain threshold, according to Willette (2013), a wide range of financial planning considerations come into play, making it important to create an art governance system to preserve and protect the family collection (Willette 2013). It is difficult to define family governance because the term is interpreted in different ways. Sometimes the term is used interchangeably with family office—a central administrative function that manages certain aspects of the family's affairs, such as its investments—but the two are not synonymous. Family governance is commonly defined as a process to help make better, more informed decisions. A sound family governance system for a collection often comprises both structures and documents. Because each family's needs are different, there is no real standard or template to follow. To be most effective, however, the system should facilitate three essential functions: creation of a framework for decision-making; identification of the governance model; and agreement on shared values.

5.1 Creation of a Framework for Decision-Making

While agreeing upon shared values is a necessary step in establishing a robust family collection governance system, it does not create a framework within which a family can actually make decisions. According to Willette (2013) this requires the formation of a family art council, a structure bolstered by a well-thought-out collection policy and set of bylaws, that is typically the chief decision-making body for managing the collection. A family art council is the single most important structure a family can put in place to help address and resolve issues regarding the family collection. These may include:

- Ensuring the strategic and tactical plans of the collection conform to the family's core values.
- Determining the kind of legacy for which the family should strive.
- Preserving and protecting the family's art assets.
- Planning for the transfer of the collection to the next generation.
- Identifying charities to which the family might make gifts from the collection and any restrictions it wishes to place on these gifts.
- If the decision is made to sell the collection, developing an orderly disposal strategy.

Once these questions have been thoroughly discussed and a consensus has been reached, many families create a document that officially establishes and empowers the family art council and delineates its role and functions. Depending on the nature of the family's concerns, the family art council also can address curatorial management issues relating to setting standards of best practice for art due diligence, valuation, and collection management. The family art council can be an extremely powerful part of a family's strategic plan for the preservation of the collection's legacy and culture, and for managing potential family conflict. It may also provide useful guidance to trustees as well as serving as a reassuring check on their powers.

5.2 Identification of the Governance Model

In order to evaluate potential governance options for a family art collection, it is important to understand the fundamental issues related to museum governance. Governance refers to the authority under which museums are organized, and identifies the governing body, and legal and fiduciary responsibility, for the museum. Museum organization can be seen as a continuum with 100 % publicly (or government) owned institutions on one side and 100 % privately owned institutions on the other. In the center of this continuum is a range of museum types. The institutional form is closely connected with the structure of financing the museum, which influences the incentives and behaviour of the museum directorate (Frey and Pommerehne 1989). Directors of public museums rely exclusively on public grants. In practice, they not only receive sufficient funds to cover the expenses allotted to them in the budget but also have a deficit guarantee, at least to a certain extent. This institutional setting provides little incentive to generate additional income or to minimize costs. The directorate will not allocate energy and resources to generating additional income because, if the museum makes a surplus, its future subsidies will be reduced, if not completely cut. Directors of public museums are less interested in the number of visitors because they are not dependent on income from entrance fees or shops. Therefore, exhibitions are designed to please an insider group of art lovers and visitors' amenities are usually poorly developed. Little attention is paid to the profitability of museum shops, restaurants, and cafeterias, which most often are contracted out (Frey and Meier 2002). On the other hand, directors of private museums have a strong incentive to increase their income because their survival depends on such sources of money as entrance fees, restaurants, shop surpluses, and additional money from sponsors and donors. If private museums generate a surplus, they are able to use it for future undertakings. Therefore private museums seek to maximize revenue by differentiating entrance fees according to presumed or estimated price elasticity of demand, as well as to engage visitors in certain activities that public museums do not provide. As a consequence, private museums undertake more market-oriented policies than public museums. This is shown, in particular, in the amenities provided for visitors, such as more flexible opening hours and excellent restaurants and bookshops (Frey and Meier 2002). Lord and Lord (2009) point out that most museums fall somewhere in the middle of the continuum between totally private and totally public. These public-private partnership models have three characteristics in common:

Financial and Estate Planning for Art Assets

- *They have independent or semi-independent boards* (governance that is separate from government).
- *They have budgetary control*, with multiple sources of funding including government, visitors, private donors, foundations, sponsors, and service fees.
- *They are outward-looking*. Since they must look outside for financial support, they forge more links to the community.

5.3   Agreement on Shared Values

To foster agreement on shared values for a family collection, creating governance-related documents, such as a collection policy, can be truly valuable. If a family can come together and engage in the collaborative process necessary to produce such a document, there is a good chance it will emerge with a set of principles that reflect what is important to the family, what kind of legacy it would like to achieve for the collection, and how to accomplish it. A collection policy should address the following issues.

The Range and Limits of the Collection.   Usually the collection policy establishes a qualitative statement of the objective of the collection, with beginning and end dates (if it is a historical collection), the geographical range, and the material (for example, ceramics or glass) to be collected. An art collection may aspire to be comprehensive or systematic; some art collections aim at a representative sample of a particular period. The criteria for inclusion in the collection should be specified, including size, demonstrated authenticity, established provenance, clear title, and condition.

Development Strategy. A collection policy includes the development strategy, which should usually begin with a qualitative analysis of the collection that identifies its scope and range; its international, national, or regional significance; its outstanding pieces; and its uniqueness. The qualitative analysis establishes the collecting priorities and projects the trajectory of the collection's intended growth.

Acquisition Procedures. The collection policy should establish acquisition procedures for donations (gift agreement) and purchases. Usually the collection policy disallows gifts "with strings attached" and requires donations to be transferred wholly and entirely without qualification of the museum's use of the acquisition. In view of the importance of collection development, many collecting families appoint an acquisition committee from among their members. Such a committee should develop specified and approved acquisition methods, which may include purchases, gifts, bequests, and deposits from other private collections or museums (Lord and Lord 2009).

Deaccessioning Policy. The deaccessioning section of the collection policy should make it clear that, in general, deaccessioning is to be regarded as an exceptional activity. Both the International Council of Museums and many countries' museum associations have published deaccession principles and rules. Deaccession principles outlined by the International Committee for Museums and Collections of Modern Art emphasize that deaccessioning is only justified in order to improve the quality or composition of the collection, and requires the same deliberation and rigour applied to acquisition. Criteria for consideration for deaccessioning should be listed. These should address objects that do not fit the collection's mandate, objects acquired illegally or unethically, duplicates that are inferior to more recently acquired examples, and objects in a condition that is not cost-effective to restore.

Lending Policy. The collection policy should include the policy on loans. It should distinguish between long-term loans or deposits to other museums or collections and short-term loans (both incoming and outgoing) for temporary exhibitions. The clause for short-term outgoing loans should identify the approvals required (such as the curator or even the family art council for some objects, with still others never to be loaned), and require that the borrowing institution complete a satisfactory facility assessment form and provide condition reports at each packing and unpacking point. The policy may also require that couriers accompany certain loans to supervise their installation and demounting (Lord and Lord 2009).

6   Art Succession Planning

After investing time, effort and financial resources to establish an art collection, many collectors find it difficult to consider its future and final disposition. Unlike other financial assets or real estate, art is intensely personal. As a result, many collectors find it extremely difficult to make planning decisions about the ultimate disposition of their art. However, the very personal connection to art, and the fact that art cannot be sold as quickly as other financial assets, makes it essential to diligently plan ahead (Drossman and Slugg 2015). Defining an effective art succession plan requires taking into account the unique financial needs of heirs and other beneficiaries and the nature of the assets involved. The potential problems and pitfalls facing collectors and owners of art are numerous and need careful consideration in order to ensure the best results for the collection, the collector and potential beneficiaries of the art. A number of practical issues will need to be considered, including the potential rights of heirs and, where claims can be made, the jurisdiction in which the trustee is to be located, the jurisdiction in which the assets themselves are located, and the proper law of the trust. Creating the right succession plan for an art collection requires a personal touch, taking into account unique financial needs, interest in providing for heirs and other beneficiaries, and the nature of the assets involved to chart a creative and sound financial course that serves the family effectively over time. Here are a few suggestions for developing a well-designed plan.

1. *Maintain a complete inventory of the collection.* When creating and updating a wealth transfer plan, proper documentation of the art assets is vital. An up-to-date inventory, as well as authentication documents and provenances (origins or source of the art and collectibles, and histories of subsequent owners), should be included. Where this is not possible, written opinions from one or more recognized experts in the field regarding the work's authenticity and dating should be obtained. Complex collections may benefit from specifically designed software.
2. *Know the collection's value.* For art and collectibles of any significant worth, an appraisal or valuation of each item in the collection should be acquired from a qualified professional. Value is not just important for insurance and tax purposes, but enables the trustees to monitor the performance of the asset class in relation to the remainder of their investments.
3. *Plan in advance.* With some forethought and expert art advice, careful planning today can yield significant benefits in the future, including financial security for the family, minimizing potential tax liability on the art, and the chance for the owner to leave a lasting legacy through proper preservation.
4. *Consider charitable gifts.* When philanthropy is a goal, consider beginning discussions early and establishing formal agreements with the recipient charities. Identify early on which charities the owners would like to benefit from gifts from the collection and any restrictions on these gifts. Keep in mind, however, that significant changes in the art world have made it more difficult to give a collection to charity, and many museums have become more selective in accepting art works.

How these collections will be managed in estate planning will have tremendous implications for collectors and their families as well as wealth management professionals. This is supported by the Art & Finance Report 2016 published by Deloitte and ArtTactic, according to which 82% of wealth managers surveyed stated that estate and succession planning around art and collectibles are increasingly becoming a strategic focus in the coming years. In light of potential tax and other financial liabilities, deciding on the best strategy early on can be critical in valuing and transferring a family collection. Questions concerning whether children will have the organizational and financial resources to care for a collection and whether there will be sufficient wealth to bequeath an inheritance outside of the collection itself may have to be resolved. In order to plan for the ultimate disposition of their collections, collectors and their heirs should be aware that they have five basic options: (1) sell the collection; (2) donate it to a charitable beneficiary, such as a museum; (3) create a lending library; (4) establish a private museum; (5) donate it to a non-charitable beneficiary.

6.1 Selling the Collection

Many great collectors see their collection as a self-portrait, so selling a collection is likely a last resort as this would mean dismantling a lifetime of work and ripping up that portrait. However, if a collector decides to sell part or all of a collection to create cash for living expenses, he/she should be aware that it is more expensive to sell art than many other assets (Drossman and Slugg 2015). This is because the overall return on investment in art depends only on the market price at the time of sale: this is the technical cause of the greater volatility (riskiness) of investment in art compared to that in capital assets, which yield regular earnings. Moreover as Zorloni (2013) noted, it is necessary to take into account that calculated return is usually net of tax burdens, but involves high costs that may end up crowding out the possible returns.

- *Transaction costs*: intermediation is paid both by the seller and by the buyer. With reference to commissions, for the purchase of a work of art from auction it is necessary to calculate an average 20 % buyer's premium (25 % for a value up to $50,000, 20 % for values between $50,001 and $1,000,000 and 12 % for higher prices). Imports from countries outside the European Union involve import tax equal to 19 % that must be added to the final price of the work of art. VAT is then added to the auction house commission, as well as 2–3 % cost for transport expenses.
- *Resale rights*: alongside the commission for brokerage, the right to resale (droit de suite) is paid to the artist or his heir if the painter died less than 70 years ago. This allows the artist or his descendants to receive certain tax benefits calculated in various percentages on capital gains earned by public sales (i.e. the difference between the selling and purchasing prices). The resale right only applies to sales where the price exceeds €3,000, and the maximum amount that an artist can receive as resale right for a single sale is €12,500. The percentages that authors receive according to the sale price of works of art are as follows: up to €50,000, 4 %; from €50,000 to €200,000, 3 %; from €200,000 to €350,000, 1 %; from €350,000 to €500,000, 0.5 %; from €500,000, 0.25 %.
- *Insurance premiums*: premiums against theft and/or destruction can be up to 0.5 % of the artwork's estimated price.
- *Time of resale*: art can be a good deal in the medium-long term; this means that. at a commercial level, the initial results are seen at a distance of 5–10 years from the time of purchase. However, it is important to remember that art, by its nature, does not allow an immediate disinvestment as for most bonds and shares on the stock market, and selling a painting can take several years, a period during which the return may completely decline because of the artist's exit from fashionable circuits.

6.2 Donations to Charitable Organizations

Whether during the collector's lifetime or after death, giving art to a museum can offer meaningful tangible and intangible benefits, and can be accomplished in a number of ways. Donating art to a museum is a personally satisfying gesture that bestows art that was once in private hands to the public for their enjoyment (Drossman and Slugg 2015). In some countries there are also tax advantages, especially if the work is donated while the collector is alive. In any scenario involving donations to institutions, it is important to specifically describe the conditions under which the art should be displayed—in a special wing, for example, with the collector's name on it—and any special rules pertaining to the exhibition, care and upkeep of the artwork. It is preferable that this be agreed to before delivery of the artwork (Beck 2014). Conditions that are too onerous may actually reduce the value of the collection and jeopardize the charitable deduction for estate, gift and income tax purposes.

6.3 Creating a Lending Library

Collectors acquire objects for many reasons, but the core of the process is often their passion for the art. Along with passion comes a strong desire to maintain control of the manner in which that art is displayed when a substantial collection is amassed. However, a donation to a museum may not result in the collector's wishes being carried out. According to Mendelsohn (2007) 95 % of a typical museum's collection is in storage at any given time and museums have sold pieces to fund other museum purchases (Bowley 2013). One approach to maintaining control, as well as maximizing tax benefits, is the "museum without walls" concept (Mendelsohn 2007). This concept utilizes a private operating foundation to hold and manage the collection by making them available to exhibitions travelling to various venues. This model was used by Eli and Edythe Broad, who in 1984 established The Broad Art Foundation as a way to keep their collection in the public domain through an enterprising loan program that makes the art available for exhibition at accredited institutions throughout the world. The result is a lending library of contemporary art and an expansive collection that is regularly cited as one of the best in the world.[1]

6.4 Establishing a Private Museum

There is a long and storied American philanthropic tradition behind creating individual and family museums, dating back to the Frick Collection in New York and the Barnes Foundation in Philadelphia, alongside other famous museums that originated with individual bequests from wealthy individuals. For instance, the City

---

[1] http://www.broadartfoundation.org/mission.html.

of Miami has seen a number of private museums take shape—as venues to exhibit their art, to maintain the integrity of a collection and to gain some tax advantages. For collectors who wish to maintain their collections intact and leave a lasting legacy, there are several factors to consider before establishing a private museum, including the size and value of the collection. As pointed out by Beck (2014), a person with a $100 million collection is a better candidate for a private museum than someone with a $5 million collection, due to the relatively high fixed costs involved in the creation and upkeep of such an institution. Moreover as pointed out by Drossman and Slugg (2015), collectors should be aware of the need to provide substantial financial backing to cover the museum's operating expenses, from curation to conservation, and ongoing maintenance of the facility. If a collector can afford to establish a museum, he should also consider the sustainability of the endeavor in the chosen community. Even though each private collection is different, a collector must consider the community and other leisure activities that could compete with a new museum. New museums should fulfill a specific need or at least complement existing institutions, rather than reproducing already extant collections or experiences.

6.5 Gifts to Non-Charitable Beneficiaries

Another option to pass on artwork to the heirs is through stipulations in the collector's will. A collector could arrange to have a particular painting go to someone who has always liked it, or might divide the collection according to the heirs' preferences. An alternative to both lifetime gifting and testamentary transfers that may be less complicated is to establish fiduciary structures, such as trusts or foundations, for the long-term protection and management of family art collections. Often, the family's overall financial needs help to determine the specific vehicle chosen to transfer all or part of a collection from one generation to another. The main areas in which trust structures can offer advantages over direct ownership are in succession, asset protection, tax planning, and efficient management of the collection. Ownership through a trust simplifies the situation on the death of the collector. There is no change in legal ownership, which remains with the trustees, so the need to comply with probate formalities is removed.

7 Conclusion

Economic uncertainty and the volatile return of other traditional assets in recent years are forcing HNWIs to consider a wider spectrum of alternative assets, including art and collectibles. According to a number of research reports, art and collectibles represent a significant proportion of the total assets of many HNWIs. This trend is supported by the rise in the past three decades of private museums funded by cultural philanthropists. Growing numbers of contemporary art collectors are building private museums to display their collections so that today, the private collections of ultra-high-net-worth families can rival those of major art institutions. An art collection requires the same strategic planning as other investments, and with the help of skilled advice can become an effective working asset. This suggests that wealth managers must take a more holistic approach to their clients' wealth, and develop management and reporting tools that combine both financial and non-financial assets. This chapter has examined the role of art in overall wealth management strategy and why it may be useful to integrate art into the family office platform. Significant sums are involved in the intergenerational transfer of wealth that is taking place, and this chapter has offered general recommendations on what constitutes sound governance in order to preserve and protect a family art collection.

References

Accenture. (2012). *The greater wealth transfer*. Accenture Wealth and Asset Management Services.
Anderson, R. C. (1974). Paintings as an investment. *Economic Inquiry, 12*(1), 13–26.
Arena, J. (2013). *Your art collection as loan collateral*. New York: U.S. Trust.
Barclays. (2012). Profit or pleasure? Exploring the motivations behind treasure trends. *Wealth Insights, 15*.
Baumol, W. (1986). Unnatural value: Or art investment as floating crap game. *American Economic Review, 76*(2), 10–14.
Beck, E. (2014). The real value of art. *Capital Acumen*, Issue 21.
Bourdieu, P. (1979). *Distinction: A social critique of the judgement of taste*. Paris: Les Editions de Minuit.
Bowley, G. (2013, August 27). Pennsylvania Museum selling a Hopper to raise endowment for contemporary Art. *New York Times*.
Buelens, N., & Ginsburgh, V. (1993). Revisiting Baumol's 'Art as floating crap game.'. *European Economic Review, 37*(7), 1351–1371.
Candela, G., & Scorcu, A. (2001). In search of stylized facts on art market prices: Evidence from the secondary market for prints and drawings in Italy. *Journal of Cultural Economics, 25*(3), 219–231.
Deloitte and ArtTactic. (2016). *Art & finance report 2016*. Deloitte.
Drossman, M., & Slugg, R. (2015). *Your art collection and legacy planning*. New York: U.S. Trust.
Frey, B., & Meier, S. (2002). *Museums between private and public. The case of the Beyeler Museum in Basle*. Working Papers 116. Zurich: University of Zurich.
Frey, B., & Pommerehne, W. (1989). *Museums and market: Explorations in the economics of the arts*. Oxford: Basil Blackwell.
Goetzmann, W. N. (1993). Accounting for taste: Art and the financial markets over three centuries. *American Economic Review, 83*(5), 1370–1376.
Gyorgy, S. (2010). The origins of art finance. In C. McAndrew (Ed.), *Fine art and high finance*. New York: Bloomberg Press.
Locatelli-Bley, M., & Zanola, R. (1999). Investment in painting: A short-run price index. *Journal of Cultural Economics, 23*(3), 211–222.
Lord, B., & Lord, G. (2009). *The manual of museum management* (2nd ed.). Lanham, MD: AltaMira Press.
Mei, J., & Moses, M. (2002). Art as an investment and the underperformance of masterpieces. *American Economic Review, 92*(5), 1656–1668.
Mendelsohn, M. (2007). *Life is short, art is long: Maximizing estate planning strategies for collectors of art, antiques, and collectibles*. New York: Wealth Management Press.
Molfino, F., & Mottola Molfino, A. (1997). *Il Possesso della bellezza*. Torino: Allemandi.

Moulin, R. (1967). *Le Marché de la Peinture en France*. Paris: Minuit.
Pesando, J. E. (1993). Art as an investment: The market for modern prints. *American Economic Review, 83*(5), 1075–1089.
Stein, J. P. (1977). The monetary appreciation of paintings. *Journal of Political Economy, 2*(1), 21–40.
Storr, A. (1983). The psychology of collecting. *Connoisseur, 213*, 35–38.
Thornton, S. (2010). *Seven days in the art world*. New York: W.W Norton & Company.
Veblen, T. (1934). *The theory of the leisure class*. New York: The Modern Library.
Vettese, A. (1991). *Investire in Arte. Produzione, Promozione e Mercato dell'Arte Contemporanea*. Milano: Edizioni Il Sole 24 Ore.
Willette, R. (2013). *Establishing sound governance for a family art collection*. London: Fine Art Wealth Management.
Willette, R. & Litten, M. (2014). *Ultimate trust: Fiduciary structures for family art collections*. London: Fine Art Wealth Management.
Zorloni, A. (2013). *The economics of contemporary art: Markets, strategies and stardom*. Heidelberg: Springer.

Assessing and Improving the Effectiveness of Private Art Museums

Alessia Zorloni

1 Introduction

Performance measurement systems have received much attention in recent years. Since the 1980s, a fundamental change in managerial culture has occurred in the nonprofit and public arts sector, with arts organizations showing a growing interest in managerial practices and ideologies stemming from for-profit business. The increased pressure on arts organizations to be more accountable for their behavior, to become less dependent on public funding, to stimulate audience participation, and to compete with the entertainment industry has, more specifically, resulted in the widespread adoption of performance measures. Organizations such as GuideStar have grown, dramatically expanding the types of data available about nonprofit organizations' operations. Academic journals such as the *International Journal of Arts Management* and *Nonprofit Management and Leadership* have begun publishing. Even federal policy has been directed toward increasing the effectiveness of nonprofit. The Obama administration has created the *Social Innovation Fund*, which includes among its objectives influencing philanthropy to work in a more data-driven way.

Although the overall incidence of the application of metrics by nonprofits and cultural organizations has been investigated (Carnegie and Wolnizer 1996; Gilhespy 1999; de Bruijn 2002; Paulus 2003; Finocchiaro Castro and Rizzo 2009; Weinstein and Bukovinsky 2009; Turbide and Laurin 2009), for most stakeholders in the museums sector, measuring museum performance remains an elusive goal. In a study of 14 art museums in France and the United States, Paulus (2003) describes the difficulties and challenges associated with an assessment based on measures of economy, efficiency, effectiveness and equity. She notes that only two museums in her sample used a written evaluation procedure and that in some museums the

A. Zorloni (✉)
IULM University, Milan, Italy
e-mail: alessia.zorloni@iulm.it

evaluation had no impact. Turbide and Laurin (2009) in their study on performing arts organisations in Canada found that the majority of organisations use multiple performance indicators to assess their own performance. The authors also found that even though performing arts organisations acknowledge that their most important success factor is artistic excellence, their performance measurement system places as much emphasis on financial as on non-financial indicators.

Overall, the results of these studies suggest there is value in contributing to the development of a performance framework that will enable museums to assess their institutional value and improve their effectiveness—and, as a result, their intended impact.

This chapter addresses a practical managerial problem—how to design a performance framework for museum activities—and aims to construct a normative model, using balanced scorecard architecture that integrates quantitative and qualitative criteria and examines performance and accountability expectations from both an internal area focus and an external, public-oriented focus. The balanced scorecard provides a framework for considering museum performance in a holistic way and seems to be a potentially useful managerial tool for achieving strategic alignment.

The chapter is organized as follows. In the first section, the chapter presents a theoretical framework that defines how to assess value creation in the museum sector, along with evidence regarding a lack of method for evaluating the performance of art museums. In the second section, it presents the balanced scorecard and discusses its use as a means for framing and focusing the strategic goals and activities of museums. In the third section it describes the research process and the methodological and research issues that guided the data-gathering activities. A short outline of the main findings from interviews with museum executives will be presented. In the fourth section, the application of the balanced scorecard approach to a private museum is discussed in detail. Finally, conclusions regarding the use of the balanced scorecard in a not-for-profit organization are presented. The appendix gathers together interviews with renowned museum directors and sheds light on the their attitudes toward performance assessment.

2 Performance Measurement in the Museum Sector

Leaders and employees of museums are constantly being pulled in different directions to serve multiple constituencies. In the business world, market forces serve as feedback mechanisms. Performance is relatively easy to quantify through earnings and return on investment (ROI),[1] and such metrics can be compared thereby ensuring that the companies producing the best results will attract new capital. However, assessing and comparing performance is a more subjective and value-driven exercise for museums than it is for companies. Given the diversity of

---

[1] Return on Investment (ROI) measures how effectively the firm uses its capital to generate profit.

the goals museums pursue, there is no single quantitative or qualitative metric against which performance can be evaluated and ranked. Even when several museums are aiming for the same goal—for example, to present outstanding contemporary art in all media—the absence of standard outcome measures makes it impossible to compare their performance. So what system should be used to assess quality and success in the museums sector?

In the awareness that the community does not possess the means or the culture necessary to judge the work being performed by museums, in some countries organs specialised in museum accreditation have been set up.[2] The purpose of these bodies is to certify the quality of the museum processes and the extent to which they conform to correct procedures: the codification of precise quality standards and the definition of systems of accreditation are specifically aimed at legitimising the work of the museum for its stakeholders (Sibilio Parri and Dainelli 2009) and at verifying the existence of the conditions considered to be minimum requisites for the effective performance of museum activities (Dainelli 2006). Weil (2005) makes a valiant effort to define the characteristics of a good museum, describing a success/failure matrix capable of determining the museum's overall performance. He identifies four key dimensions that must be present in a successful museum. First of these is the ability to articulate a clear and significant purpose; second, the ability to assemble the resources necessary to achieve that purpose; third, the possession of the skills necessary to expend resources to create and present public programs that achieve the articulated purpose (effectiveness); and fourth, the managerial skills necessary to create and present those public programs in an efficient manner (efficiency). Effectiveness is an indicator of the degree to which the museum is able to achieve its purpose. Similarly, efficiency is a measure of the level of resources that the museum has expended in seeking to be effective. Effectiveness and efficiency refer to distinctly different kinds of results. One is an evaluation of its program outcomes, the other is a measure of how much those programs cost (Fig. 1).

Weil (2002a, b) suggests that a successful museum is one that can produce positive outcomes for the communities it seeks to serve. A positive outcome means the preservation of collections for future generations and the introduction of beneficial changes for the communities it seeks to serve with the programs offered. This idea is not new: over 30 years ago, Orr (1973) first expressed the view that it was possible to consider performance measures as a continuum reflecting the

---

[2] The first accreditation models elaborated by sector associations emerged for American museums in the middle of the last century. From 1988, museum standards were introduced in the UK via a public governmental body (the Museums and Galleries Commission) and subsequently in other European countries such as Ireland, Holland and Denmark. In Italy in 2001 the "Guideline on technical-scientific criteria and standards for the functioning and development of museums" was issued (Sibilio Parri and Dainelli 2009). These standards represent a methodology for the definition of the minimum requirements for the existence of a museum and the criteria necessary to ensure its effective functioning (Jalla 2001).

Purpose	Resources
Effectiveness	Efficiency

Fig. 1 Success/failure matrix. *Source*: Weil (2005)

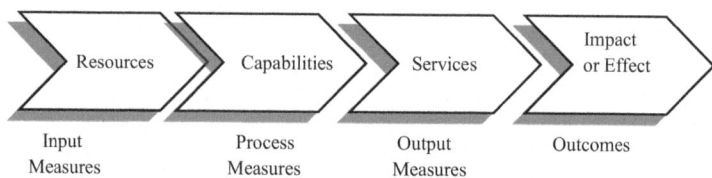

Fig. 2 General evaluation model. *Source*: Adapted from Orr (1973)

transformation of resources into goods or services and ultimately having an impact on society, as shown in Fig. 2.

Based on this perspective, the museum's resources are transformed and organized so that it has the capability to provide a set of services. Museum visitors then experience these services, which should have a direct beneficial impact or effect on the individual and directly or indirectly upon the local community. Orr's position is connected to that of Porter (2006), who suggests that each museum creates value through a chain of activities and the composition of the value chain determines the competitive advantage. Porter's value chain focuses on value-creating activities and mark-up, which, for museums, is the difference between social benefits and resources expended. Each activity is interdependent and can generate value directly or indirectly. In addition to single activities, connections, both between primary activities (the four lower dimensions) and between primary and support activities (the horizontal dimensions), are crucial to creating value (Fig. 3).

The views of Porter (2006) and Weil (2002a, b) underscore the point made by Koster and Falk (2007) that impact needs to be defined in a multi-dimensional way. According to Koster and Falk (2007), success needs to be defined as measurable value generated through socially, politically and economically sustainable practices and a museum's multi-dimensional value should include:

1. the good that the organization provides to visitors;
2. the assets of the organization, including particularly its collection, intellectual capital and brand;
3. the benefit provided by the organization to the community, including the fact that museums preserve collections for future generations;
4. the quality of the organization's workplace, meaning that each employee experiences continued growth and development;
5. the financial health of the organization.

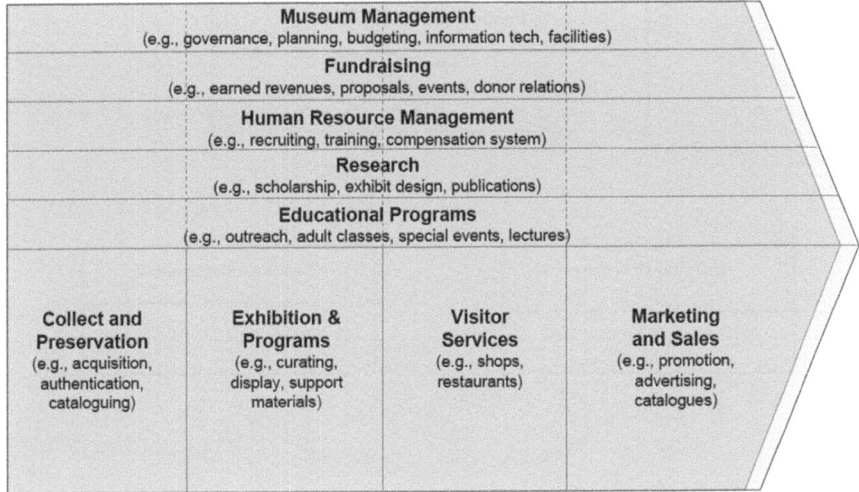

Fig. 3 The museum value chain. *Source*: Adapted from Porter (2006)

The implementation of the above concept integrates into the "THRIVE Assessment" proposed by Falk and Sheppard (2006), where THRIVE is an acronym standing for "Tools for Helping maximize Resources, Internal learning and growth, public Value and External relationships". Within this approach, the authors indicated four areas in which museums should invest and focus in order to measure the success of the organization: public value, internal learning and growth, external relationships and resources and finances.

2.1 The Use of the Balanced Scorecard in Nonprofit Organizations

The balanced scorecard (BSC) is a strategic planning and management system that is used extensively in business, industry, governmental and nonprofit organizations worldwide to align business activities with the vision and strategy of the organization, improve internal and external communications, and monitor organizational performance against strategic goals. It was popularised by Kaplan and Norton (1992) as a performance measurement framework that added strategic non-financial performance measures to traditional financial metrics to give managers a more balanced view of organizational performance. The BSC suggests that we view the organization from four perspectives, developing metrics and collecting and analyzing data relative to each. These are the customer perspective, the financial perspective, the internal processes perspective and the employee learning and growth perspective. A slight modification of the BSC developed by Kaplan (2001) for nonprofit organizations adds a "public value and benefit perspective" as shown in Fig. 4.

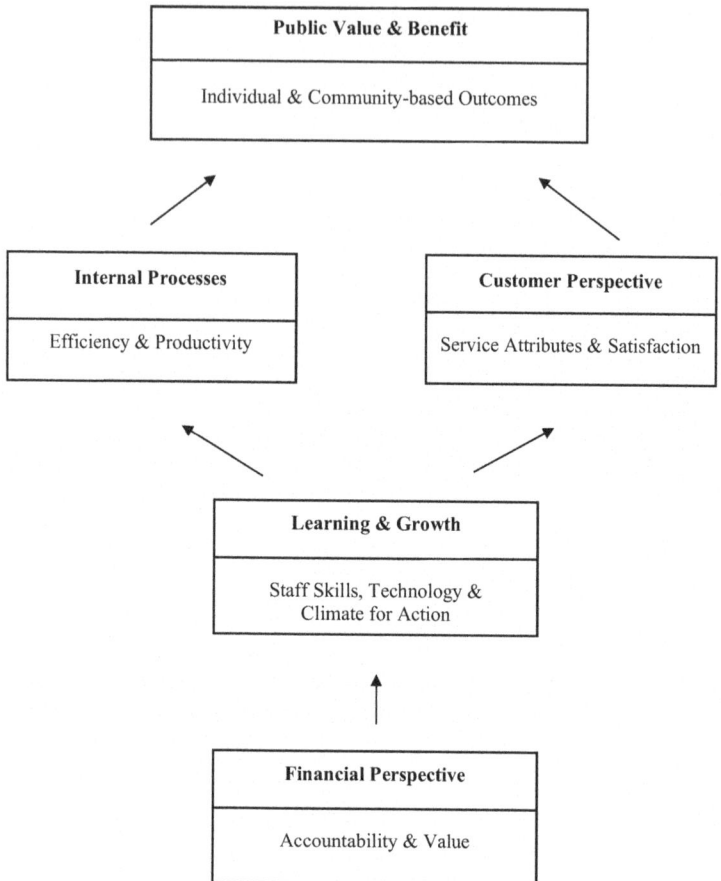

Fig. 4 Public value & benefit scorecard. *Source*: Kaplan (2001)

The BSC has been in use for over a decade and has been applied successfully in organizations around the world in almost every industry and public sector niche. Among some of the nonprofits that have adopted the use of the BSC are University of California Administrative Services, Fulton County (GA) Schools, the Texas State Auditor's Office, the City of Charlotte, the City of Brisbane, Australia, Singapore Public Libraries, and the University of Virginia Library (Matthews 2008). A review of the literature reveals that, despite the fact that the BSC has been applied successfully in different nonprofit organizations (Weinstein and Bukovinsky 2009), to date the only attempts to build a model to assess the performance of art museums based on BSC methodology have been accomplished by Fox (2006) and Falk and Sheppard (2006). The BSC has the potential to transform a museum by clearly communicating strategies, performance measures, targets and initiatives to museum staff members so that they can more closely align their day-to-day activities in order to achieve the museum's vision. A museum might be interested in implementing a BSC for different reasons:

1. *Better identification of performance measures.* A BSC will assist the management team in selecting the most important performance measures as well as understanding the relationships between each measure.
2. *Demonstrating accountability and communicating the value of the museum.* The BSC can assist the museum in better communicating to its funders and other stakeholders by presenting a more balanced view of the museum and its impact on its community.
3. *Focusing museum staff on the importance of achieving the museum's goals.* The BSC could serve as a management tool for museum staff members to measure their own performance relative to how effectively the museum is pursuing its mission and strategic priorities.

According to Kaplan and Norton (2000), the designing of a BSC should begin with the definition of a company's objectives and then proceed to the identification of critical success factors (CSFs). As every perspective of the scorecard should consist of a suitable combination of CSFs, the following section will introduce the methodology used for developing a working set of CSFs for visual art museums.

3 Empirical Examination

In order to identify the relevant factors for the success of visual art museums, a qualitative research approach has been adopted. The qualitative approach, based on in-depth interviews, document analysis and observation, was chosen as the most appropriate, given the exploratory nature of the research (Goodyear 1990). These methods had a dual role. Primarily, they were used to identify the CSFs of the museum industry. In addition, they produced insight on issues related to the process of designing a strategic framework and thus affected the model presented as a result of the study. The data was collected in 2009 over 7 months through face-to-face interviews. The sample comprises 41 museum executives of 16 institutions from Washington DC, New York and London. Organizations were selected on the basis of advice provided by a panel of experts, consisting of art managers, museum directors, and art academics. Each of the interviews took approximately an hour. Collected data were analyzed utilizing an open coding approach (Cresswell 2007) to develop meaning themes (Kvale 1995). The data were then organized according to the several themes that arose from the interviews. Finally, Kaplan and Norton's balanced scorecard model was adapted to design a museum balanced scorecard and to classify the themes within four perspectives.

3.1 Research Results

Among the meaning themes identified by museum executives, a clear distinction was drawn between internal and external factors. It was found that the balance of internal and external factors was dependent upon three key influences: political and economic environment; institutional setting; and organizational culture. Executives were able to identify different CSFs and cited critical external factors such as reputation and audience satisfaction. Internal factors such as artistic quality, employee satisfaction, museum governance, and organizational climate were cited as important in servicing their organizational goals. Furthermore, innovation, risk-taking, and internationalism were perceived as elements that best support the success of museums. In terms of information needs, it was clear that competitor intelligence, visitors' needs, and cultural policy trends were perceived as important in servicing their organizational goals, and that museum executives were all largely dependent upon their informal network of contacts for information. However, there was considerable agreement among all the museum executives interviewed concerning the importance of improving the sharing of information among institutions. Throughout the interviews, museum executives expressed a desire for better-defined and comparable measures of success, i.e. measures that were simple to collect, timely, relevant, and comprehensive. In the following sections, the themes that emerged from the interviews are presented and discussed.

Artistic Quality

The first category, artistic quality, is acknowledged as the most important and the most difficult to measure. One executive of a national museum cited the importance of artistic quality using these words: *"There is a powerful consensus across the organization that [name] should be driven by intellectual and artistic concerns. The role of the market as well as the need to generate both revenue and capital funds are both recognized as important factors for [name]; however it is keenly felt that these should not become the principal drivers"*.

When asked about the criteria used to assess the artistic quality a respondent commented that *"artistic quality can be supported in a variety of ways: for example, by working with international curators and institutions, involving diverse artists and audiences locally, nationally and internationally"*. Other respondents stated that international partnerships, the number of visitors, loan requests (reflecting the quality of the collection and how well recognized it is), repeat visits and participation in educational programs all help to assess artistic quality. The quality of both the collection and exhibitions is the primary goal of a museum but, as the interviews made clear, the evaluation of artistic quality is difficult and never truly objective. Anderson (2004) stated that judging exhibitions by the number of visitors is misleading. Instead, exhibitions should be judged by the degree to which they contributed to something. He proposed that museum managers consider the number of exhibitions in which one third of the works on the checklist have never been shown together before, the percentage of total exhibitions presented that were organized by the museum, or the number of exhibitions organized by the museum that travel nationally and internationally to other museums.

Reputation

A key success measure in the eyes of six executives is the museum's ability to build a good reputation. Two museums stated that they periodically engage in formal surveying in order to assess the visitor's impression of the museum's programs. Other respondents, working in marketing departments, cited the ability to gain respect among their peers and in media coverage of the museum and its programs as indirect indicators of their influence within the field. These indicators of awareness among other museums or the general public are closely linked to the reputation of the museum and are important factors of success. Three museums stated that they are engaging in formal brand audits to assess the museum's reputation. For many others, measurement of reputation is more concerned with informal information, largely driven by word of mouth within the museum community or press coverage of the museum and its programs. Another theme that emerged from the interviews was the idea that reputation was considered by museum executives as a highly important means to achieve the museum's mission. As one respondent noted, the museum's reputation is a very important factor in raising funds or influencing thinking within the field. These responses seem to suggest the hypothesis that, in the absence of widely accepted measures of performance, reputation can easily become a signal of quality and therefore a surrogate for museum effectiveness.

International Engagement

In Britain, national institutions such as the British Museum, the Tate and the Victoria and Albert Museum are promoting their international agendas assertively, using them to enhance their support from public and private funders, to develop new audiences, to forge new partnerships, and to gain access to artifacts and collections abroad. In other parts of the world, cultural institutions such as the Guggenheim Museum, the Centre Georges Pompidou and the Louvre are pursuing an active foreign policy. The Guggenheim Museum is opening a new outpost in Abu Dhabi to add to its franchises in New York, Bilbao, Venice, and Berlin. The Centre Georges Pompidou has developed new projects in Metz, France and in Malaga,[3] Spain, while in 2015 the Louvre opened an outpost of the museum in Abu Dhabi, lending not only its name but loans from its collection and exhibitions.

The context in which museums operate has changed radically as the art world has become increasingly global. This was a recurrent theme that emerged from the interviewees:

---

[3] In 2015, around 100 works from the Pompidou's twentieth- and twenty-first century collection have been installed in a temporary glass-and-steel structure called The Cube (El Cubo) in Málaga. The 2,000 square metre space will host the collection for 2 years, while a smaller area will be used for temporary exhibitions.

> [name] currently undertakes an impressive amount of international activities across all areas of the organization from exhibitions to interpretation and education, from collections to media ... [there] exists a rich matrix of relationships, projects, initiatives, professional contacts and networks (throughout the museum) ... the breadth and range of these partnerships contribute a distinctive quality to [name]'s work in the international arena... for many of its stakeholders, [name] represents a strong and trusted brand ... in order to build on this relationship of trust, we need to have a clear and credible international strategy.

These comments suggest that museums, in order to maintain their relevance and competitive edge, need to engage internationally. To be world-class they need to be seen on the international stage. Such analysis underscores the point made by McMaster (2008) that international comparisons are an important yardstick against which an organization can assess itself, and that working internationally is essential for artists and organizations to understand their work in a global context and to achieve and maintain world-class status.

Sharing Knowledge

The ability both to manage existing knowledge and to create new knowledge is widely accepted as one of the hallmarks of a successful twenty-first-century organization. Given their fast-moving internal and external environments, it is vital for museums to develop new systems and processes for managing and sharing knowledge. As one respondent in New York pointed out:

> I am part of a discussion group which connects people working in human resources in museums and in other cultural institutions in New York. We meet three times a year ... we have an online group on Google, where you have to be invited ... we use this to share documents, statistics, reports ... if I want to know what the average salary is for a marketing manager, I ask there ... [This group] started informally a couple of years ago thanks to a few museums.

The importance of competitor intelligence was a recurrent theme for the success of museums. In talking about the role of statistics, a director of visitor services in New York commented: *"Some museums never want to share their statistics ... I don't understand why ... when the 990 form is public"*. Another individual talking about the Association of Art Museum Directors Statistical Survey stated: *"The results of this survey are to be kept confidential at the request of the members and not disseminated beyond the museums surveyed even if these data are now public (with the 990 form)"*. When asked to indicate why there is a reluctance to disclose information (that with the introduction of the IRS 990[4] form is now in the public domain), a respondent working in the marketing department for a leading museum in New York commented: *"saying that data are confidential is just routine, it's a matter of tradition ... we never used to"*.

---

[4] In the USA, IRS Form 990 is the most commonly used data source about nonprofit organizations and is used by the Internal Revenue Service as an indicator that nonprofit organizations are meeting the minimum requirements for tax-exempt status.

Externally, a number of executives also saw the need to be informed about current visitor needs. They had, to a varying extent, implemented monitoring and evaluation procedures such as visitor questionnaires, statistics from programs, and program evaluations implemented by external consultants. When asked to indicate the information most critical for the future success of their institutions, directors working in both private and public institutions suggested: comparative figures across international organizations; comparative levels of public, charitable, and private income across different organizations; resources and published information detailing best practice in the sector; and partner-finding opportunities for funding from the European Union and elsewhere. A respondent in London in charge of international strategies stated that there could be career benefits from staff secondments and exchanges to share working practices across the sector. A director of development expressed a desire for initiatives that enable institutions to: (1) benchmark their practices and potentially improve them; (2) make the most efficient use of their resources; and (3) empower institutions with data that can enhance what they do and assist them in securing support from both public and private sectors.

The views of these respondents suggest that competitor intelligence is a strategic factor because it keeps executives up to date with developments in the field and allows them to access research funding opportunities. A variety of means were employed to gain such external information—the most important being the informal contacts they had built up. This network was maintained through meeting people at conferences, sitting on various local, regional, and national bodies, and joining various museum associations, professional societies, or informal discussion groups. However, the interviews suggested that there is value in contributing to the development of a common framework that will enable museums to share knowledge and learn from each other's experiences.

Effective Management

A recurrent theme that emerged from the interviews was the importance of the quality of management to the success of museums. Two respondents stated: *"the ability to create a good organizational climate is a sign of success"* and *"the quality of management could be seen as a direct influence of the museum's overall effectiveness"*. In an unstable environment—such as in a museum where employees often accept modest paychecks to do work they care passionately about—being able to create a good organizational climate and employee satisfaction are certainly signs of leadership success. This suggests that low employee turnover could be considered to be one signal of a successful organizational climate.

Related to the quality of museum management is the use of staff performance reviews. Clear staff performance goals, with written annual reviews, are essential for individual effectiveness and therefore affect the museum's overall performance. The existence of a rigorous and widely implemented process outlining the job descriptions, including written annual reviews of all staff within the museum is, in itself, a measure of effectiveness. Some museums, particularly the larger institutions, require written annual reviews of all staff. The Solomon R. Guggenheim

Foundation, for instance, uses an annual 360-degree performance appraisal process. This method allows every employee to receive written and verbal feedback from his or her manager, from his or her peers, and from his or her direct reports (if he or she is a manager) regarding the achievement, or lack of achievement, of their work goals. Every employee is evaluated according to 19 questions grouped into three work performance categories (general work abilities, management abilities, and interpersonal skills), based on those competencies that the Guggenheim considers most important.

Another factor crucial to the success of museums is governance structure, in particular a stable and autonomous board. As one respondent in New York noted, "*the relationship with the board is very important—when a director leaves the museum it could suggest a conflict with board.*"

Another respondent suggested that the board's autonomy, and its trust in its professional staff, is indispensable to implementing a coherent cultural strategy over the medium-to-long term. These findings underscore a point made by Anderson (2007) that transparency in museum operation and accountability is critical for the efficient functioning of a modern museum. According to Anderson (2007), the board of a museum should encourage a transparent and effective leadership. A transparent leadership requires the disclosure of information that has traditionally been seen as sensitive, such as details on what museums acquire and from whom, how museums attract support and spend it, whom they have succeeded in serving, and how they measure success. Transparency reveals not only the mechanics of museum operations, but also the philosophy of management. Full transparency helps prevent potential abuses arising from information asymmetry and permits museum stakeholders to make informed judgments. In this sense, transparency serves to achieve accountability and to improve museum performance.

4 Defining a Performance Framework for Museums Based on the Balanced Scorecard

As the interviews made clear, many museum executives are dealing with the challenges of measuring museum performance, but each is doing so alone or, at most, with informal support from colleagues. Some museums have implemented discrete measures, but none has yet put these together to form a comprehensive framework. With the exception of the simplest quantitative measures, such as the number of visitors, it is arguable that there is not a shared framework among museums or a coordinated attempt to collect museum statistics efficiently. Throughout the interviews, museum executives expressed a desire for better defined and comparable measures of success that were simple to collect, timely, relevant, and comprehensive. In particular, some expressed a desire for initiatives that enable institutions to benchmark their practices.

The interviews suggested that there is value in contributing to the development of a common framework that will enable museums to share and learn from

Assessing and Improving the Effectiveness of Private Art Museums　　49

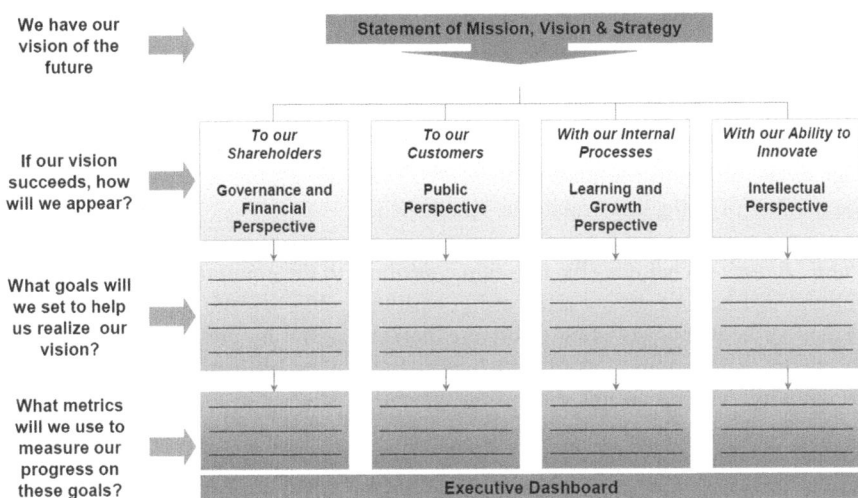

Fig. 5 Museum balanced scorecard. *Source*: own elaboration

each other's experiences. The approach I advocate in meeting those objectives is to build a common museum performance framework, using the balanced scorecard architecture.

The balanced scorecard proposed for art museums and shown in Fig. 5 is an adaptation of Kaplan and Norton's nonprofit balanced scorecard. It is designed across four dimensions based on the list of meaning themes identified from the interviews. The scorecard provides a "balanced" view of performance because it includes subjective measures and the input of external stakeholders, not just financial metrics. For instance, the BSC measures satisfaction and retention of both customers and employees. Moreover, the scorecard is balanced because it brings attention to possibly conflicting dimensions, such as productivity and employee satisfaction; high revenues and high perceived value, as measured by customer satisfaction; and low maintenance costs and minimal equipment downtime. This balanced perspective is critical for cultural institutions, which must consider the needs of a broad range of stakeholders—donors, employees, artists, local businesses, researchers, the public, and local authorities—and their often competing objectives. The public may seek education or entertainment, for instance, but local authorities are more likely to care about the impact that the institution has on the local economy, while donors want to be assured of financial sustainability before committing their support. With these challenges in mind, the BSC has been adapted to the specific needs of museums, creating four dimensions of value against which to measure performance:

Artistic Contribution How have the assets of the museum been developed and shared? A museum's assets include its collections, intellectual capital, and brand. Performance measurements in this dimension would typically include metrics such as the percentage of works on display, the number of pieces on loan to other art museums, the number and quality of institutions to which the museum has lent art and artifacts, the number of pieces purchased in the last year, and the percentage of permanent collections acquired and catalogued. Since research and knowledge development are also important, this dimension could also include metrics such as the number of articles published by museum staff in scholarly journals or the number of collections catalogues published.

Public Benefit What does the museum contribute to the community? A successful cultural institution forges a relationship with the public by offering programs and visitor services, by providing positive experiences, and by preserving collections for future generations—all of which lead to a favorable perception within the community. Metrics in this dimension typically include the range and variety of programs offered, the percentage of the museum's budget devoted to marketing, the percentage of return visitors, the increase in first-time visitors, and the number of schoolchildren who visit per year. More qualitative measures—such as increases in the community's cultural knowledge and awareness or greater public appreciation for a particular author or art movement—are also valuable.

Learning and Growth Is the museum a place where employees can flourish? An organization is only as good as its people, and providing an environment that promotes development and offers opportunities for professional and personal growth will pay major dividends in the long run. This dimension ensures that the culture supports the museum's mission, organizational learning is ongoing, and equal opportunity is provided to all. Typical metrics include the percentage of the museum's budget dedicated to training and career development, the percentage of satisfied employees, the use of "360-degree feedback" (that is, from subordinates and peers as well as superiors) to evaluate staff performance, and the degree to which employees are involved in the museum's governance.

Finance and Governance How well run and financially sustainable is the museum? A cultural institution must use its resources efficiently and effectively to achieve the trust of the public. Moreover, its finances must be transparent and the governance organization must be accountable. Typical metrics include the ability to meet fundraising targets, balance the operating budget, and meet revenue targets through diversified sources such as admission, shop and restaurant sales, and special events.

To deliver value in all four dimensions, museums must create the right metrics, set performance targets, define specific initiatives for achieving those targets, and then closely monitor results.

4.1 How the Model Could Be Implemented

The framework presented can be implemented relatively easily and inexpensively. Any museum can begin to monitor and improve its performance by collecting data, choosing the metrics that are most important to its strategy and within its budget. The development of a museum's BSC starts with a planning process that re-examines the museum's mission statement and its strategic objectives. Prior to embarking on the process of developing the museum's BSC, it is key to arrange meetings with a number of the museum's funding decision makers and other interested stakeholders in order to better understand their perspective on and experience of the concept of evaluating programs and services, and in general of assessing the value of a museum. The second step in developing a balanced scorecard is to create a list of the critical success factors that museum management deem important for their museum's departments. It may be beneficial to break down the CSFs into specific measurable activities and develop a preliminary list of possible performance measures for each strategic objective. A BSC contains a maximum of three to five performance measures for each perspective. Thus, the selection of each measure must be carefully considered from a list of other potential measures that might be used. This limitation forces the museum to identify few critical variables that represent the museum's strategy for value creation. The draft of the BSC is refined by exposing it to wider group of people. During short meetings with key interest groups measure's definitions are refined, targets set and measure's sources identified. After the museum has designed its scorecard, the museum should begin to ask their branch and/or selected departments within the museum to develop their own scorecards. This process is called cascading the scorecard. The scorecard concept is particularly useful in communicating with the museum's stakeholders. Typically an organization will present its BSC as a part of its annual report or through dashboards, which will allow stakeholders to view key performance indicators in graphs and charts (Fig. 6).

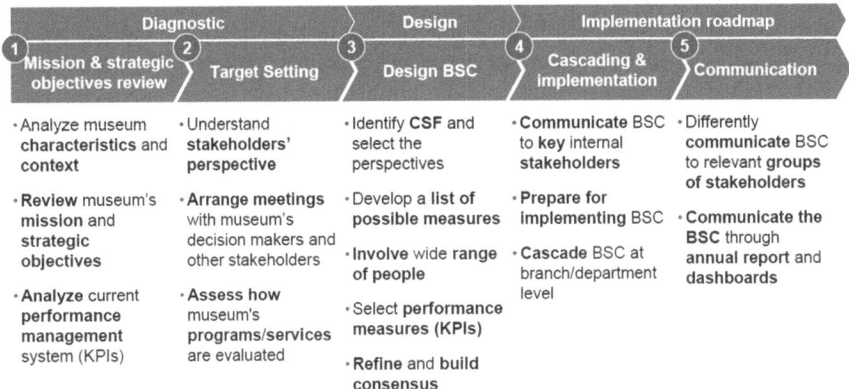

Fig. 6 Implementation roadmap. *Source*: own elaboration

4.2 Application of the Balanced Scorecard to a Private Museum

Founded in 1930, the Benaki[5] museum is Greece's oldest private cultural institution. It holds an important permanent collection of over 40,000 items focused on Greek history from antiquity to the early twentieth century, and operates several annexes in Athens, including one dedicated to Islamic art.

Over the years, it has expanded to fill six buildings with a wide range of unique collections, including prehistorical artifacts, art from the Byzantine era to the present, paintings, toys, and artifacts of Islamic culture. But shrinking private and public donations in the context of Greece's challenging economic situation have taken a toll on the Benaki. With rising costs and stalled revenues, the museum saw its financial future become precarious. A close analysis revealed a number of challenges. First, the museum needed to define and promote a more focused vision and mission. With such diverse collections—all very high quality—the Benaki needed to define a common thread so that it could communicate a compelling value proposition to visitors and donors while also articulating a focused program of exhibitions, events, publications, and educational programs. The museum also had to find new ways to generate revenue. Despite the museum's central location, the Benaki did not tap the full potential of the tourist market. Instead, visitors tended to be locals. Moreover, the Benaki's publications, events, educational programs, restaurant, and store earned less than might be expected, given the museum's quality offerings and strong brand. Finally, the Benaki's fundraising efforts were not optimally developed. Ultimately, the Benaki had to manage its costs more closely and strengthen its approach to governance, while empowering more of its employees.

Over the years, consultants have been utilized by the Benaki to assist in the strategic planning process. In 2012, based upon the input of the consultants, the management decided to utilize the concept of the balanced scorecard as a tool to cascade strategic planning throughout the entire organization. The ultimate goal was to have each area within the museum align itself with the overall strategic plan. Each area would then develop outcome measures that were aligned with the overall strategic objectives of the museum. To effectively implement the balanced scorecard approach within the Benaki, the participation and acceptance of the system by all personnel was essential. After a period of time the director was able to convince the top-level managers that the balanced scorecard approach would lead to more effective strategic planning for the museum. The BSC offered the Benaki a workable approach because it provides clear targets to drive greater transparency and accountability; it also encourages greater entrepreneurship, creativity, and initiative among employees.

The Benaki's balanced scorecard addressed the museum's challenges in the context of the four dimensions of museum value: artistic contribution; public

---

[5] An earlier version of this paragraph was published by Zorloni A., Egloff C., (2012) "Art & Business: Measuring a Museum's Performance", Making a Difference, 2012 Edition: BCG's Partnerships and Projects for Social Impact, Boston Consulting Group, Boston.

benefit; learning and growth; and finance and governance. The BSC included specific metrics and targets in each dimension and reinforced them with a set of clear improvement initiatives. For instance, to ensure a strong artistic contribution, the Benaki set an objective of lending its collections to top institutions around the world. One metric measured the number of institutional borrowers, with a target of lending to the world's top ten peer institutions. The museum also set up an annual exhibit plan and a calendar of events. In the dimension of public benefit, a key objective was to present first-class exhibitions. Metrics included both the number of positive reviews by critics per year and visitor satisfaction ratings; annual targets were set to achieve at least 80% positive reviews and 70% satisfaction rates, respectively.

To advance learning and growth, the Benaki aimed to increase employee satisfaction and retention, as measured by job satisfaction ratings and staff turnover rates. The museum's target was achieving employee satisfaction ratings at or above 80% and experiencing employee turnover below 15% per year. To improve communications and employee engagement, the Benaki displayed a scoreboard in each building to share information on current and upcoming exhibitions and programs, messages from the curator, employee suggestions, best practices, and fundraising progress. The museum has also focused on making sure that employees understand the museum's mission, what is expected from them, and how they can contribute to the museum on both an individual and collective basis. To improve finance and governance, the Benaki hired a fundraising manager to increase external donations and a finance manager to instil more discipline. One critical early success was an ambitious new fundraising program, which offers customized packages to companies and individuals. The new financial manager established a budgeting and control process aimed at managing costs more closely and increasing transparency. With greater financial controls in place and higher revenues being generated through fundraising, ticket sales, restaurant operations, and store and online sales, the museum is paving the way for a strong, sustainable future.

4.3 Implications in Using the Balanced Scorecard

The Benaki has experienced a number of benefits with the implementation of the scorecard. Perhaps the greatest benefit is the realization by personnel within the museum that strategic planning is a significantly more encompassing process than merely looking at long-range planning. With the utilization of the balanced scorecard paradigm, individuals throughout the museum have become involved in focusing on the linkages between each segment of the museum and the strategic plan. Another significant benefit concerns the focus on measurements or metrics within the museum. It is extremely difficult and time consuming to develop metrics in not-for-profit organizations. However, with considerable effort, the Benaki has begun to develop metrics that do provide linkages to the overall strategic plan. Museums that use the BSC to measure performance can fundamentally change the way they think about the value they deliver—and how they communicate that value to stakeholders. Moreover, the scorecard can help align the staff's efforts in support of the museum's mission and goals, and can increase employee satisfaction overall. For the Benaki, these cultural changes are as important as the renewed focus on the bottom line and enhanced financial sustainability.

5 Conclusion

Questions about governance, accountability and transparency have been at the forefront of current discussions concerning the management of museums and other nonprofit organizations. These are important questions because strong governance practices, rigorous accounting policies and regular public reporting are bedrocks upon which all well-managed organizations rest. Museum leaders have an imperative to operate as effectively as possible in the pursuit of social impact. Four core elements are essential to museum effectiveness: optimizing governance, setting clear goals, implementing coherent strategies and collecting relevant performance indicators. These are the required elements for achieving social impact. The aim of this chapter was to put forth a performance framework for visual art museums, using the balanced scorecard architecture that aligns well with Koster and Falk's (2007) thesis of multi-dimensional value and the holistic approach promoted by Porter (2006). Designed by Harvard's Kaplan and Norton to address the issue of performance evaluation, and adaptable enough to incorporate the unique characteristics of nonprofits in general and art museums in particular, the balanced scorecard is capable of meeting the demand for public transparency and accountability.

The contribution this chapter makes is as follows. First, the chapter presents the theoretical frame that defines how to assess value creation in the museum sector and discusses the balanced scorecard framework and its use as a means for framing and focusing the strategic goals and activities of museums. The second contribution of this chapter is the implementation of the balanced scorecard in a museum. In implementing the balanced scorecard approach, the Benaki has placed equal emphasis on the consumer perspective and the financial perspective. This equal focus is based upon the museum's need to carry out its primary mission for its consumers, as well as the necessity of maintaining financial stability within the museum. The emphasis on both of these perspectives has become a necessity in order for the museum to efficiently and effectively serve its customers.

While the use of the balanced scorecard in the long range planning process for the Benaki is relatively new, the process has been accepted by the management of the organization. The challenge ahead for the Benaki is to continue to develop outcome measures for the individual departments within the museum and to tie these outcome measures to the strategic objectives of the Benaki. It is recognized that this is an extremely difficult process as real outcomes are not easily measurable. The formulation of outcome measures is thus a continuous development process.

Appendix

Lars Nittve

Lars Nittve has been Executive Director of M+, a museum of visual culture in the West Kowloon Cultural District of Hong Kong, since 2011. He was Chief Curator of the Moderna Museet in Stockholm (1986–1990); the founding Director of Rooseum—Center for Contemporary Art—in Malmö, Sweden (1990–1995); Director of the Louisiana Museum of Modern Art in Humlebaek, Denmark (1995–1998); Founding Director of Tate Modern in London (1998–2001) and Director of the Moderna Museet in Stockholm (2001–2010). Lars Nittve studied at the Stockholm School of Economics, Stockholm University and New York University.

Alessia Zorloni As a leader of a non-profit arts and culture institution, what are some of the unique challenges you face?

Lars Nittve The single and unique difference compared to any type of business is of course that you in a non-profit arts and culture organization do not have a single, well defined goal to work against. In any business, you have to create a return on investment. It may be long term or short term, but there is always someone expecting a return on investment, and this is the ultimate success criteria. In a cultural organization there are always many and often conflicting goals and success criteria involved: a large audience; critical recognition; international recognition; local public trust; reaching new audiences. They may be defined by the government or funder, the history of the institution or the present management. The only way to lead in such a maze of conflicting success criteria (and they are often many more than the above) is to move away from leading by goals and targets and towards a leadership by vision. The vision has to be a "story" or set of stories that can be used in all types of decision-making, from program and acquisitions to basically what kind of coffee that should be served in the museum café. And the story should be "owned" by the entire staff and be reflected in every part of the institution. To get this right is the main challenge—everything else comes after.

AZ When can a museum be defined as successful?

LN As a consequence of the above, a museum is successful when it reflects the vision. Of course, when writing the annual report, a statement like that may not be sufficient, so the success in realizing the vision must be broken down in a number of criteria. It may be visitor numbers; it may be the percentage of first time visitors; degree of digital access and use of the museum's digital platforms; it may be local and international critical recognition; professional reputation; it may be financial targets which may mean that you can be uncompromising in what you show and how you do it, but also, if you are a museum of modern and contemporary art, your ability to, for example, attract a large and broad audience of "art lovers", while at the same time being seen as a relevant and exciting place for the young artists in the city and their entourage. Most likely it will actually be a mix of all the above. The interesting thing is that we all—all of us who work in the field—actually know when a museum is successful. It is about a whole, reflected in many details. Consequently, the details can also expose a museum on the decline, before it for example has started to lose its audience.

AZ *How do you assess the potential success of a particular exhibition, given the need to balance artistic direction and business development?*

LN The moment you choose to make an exhibition for business reasons, say to save a budget, you have put the carriage in front of the horse and will find yourself on a sloping floor. The trick is to balance the program over at least a 2-year period, so you can get the cost/income ratio right. There are always exhibitions that can be both net-income generating and artistically meaningful and "necessary" from an artistic point of view. Usually these exhibitions cannot be imported exhibitions, produced elsewhere, but have to be tailor-made for the specific situation your museum is in. This requires long term planning and that the team is good at generating ideas. You can never predict the numeric success of an exhibition, and the thinking has to be similar to a good magazine editor: the successful magazine is the one where the reader, when opening the magazine says "this is exactly what I wanted to read—but I had no idea I had that wish". It is ultimately about timing. And just as important to hit it "right' from the broad public's point of view with a certain frequency, it is important to be seen as taking "risks", to be out there early, to be a trailblazer. The museum that just produces blockbusters will lose public trust over time.

AZ *In terms of measuring success, and not just in terms of counting visitors, what other indicators or metrics do you use to gauge how well you are performing?*

LN The available metrics are limited. They may be visitor numbers; visitor mix; use of the digital platform; press, both international and local and categorized and measured along a positive-negative scale; it can be number of invitations for collaborations by other leading museums; loan requests (reflecting the quality of the collection and how well recognized it is); participation in educational programs etc.

AZ *According to your experience as a museum director, what are the most important factors affecting a museum's excellence?*

LN Getting a good vision in place, seeing it integrated in the museum's entire culture is critical. Everything else, as a matter of fact comes out of that, including your financial strength, which of course has consequences for programme, education, acquisitions, communication etc. The building in itself is over-valued. It should be seen, not as the same as the museum, but as a tool, albeit an important one.

Great museums can operate and have success in relatively modest and or mediocre buildings, and mediocre museums can be housed in great buildings.

AZ What led you to choose this profession?

LN My trajectory goes from academia to writing to curating to being a director. The ultimate choice had to do with the fact that I myself had a couple of, actually, life changing experiences through art, and I simply wanted to work in that field and try to create opportunities for others to have similar experiences (never believing that everyone, but perhaps just the occasional individual, would get such an experience). Moving from academia and writing to curating was just logical—I just loved the whole experience of curating, which involves the two other roles as well. Why then becoming a director? The simple answer may be that I was not so good at having a boss, so I preferred to be one myself. But I guess it also simply turned out that I actually had many of the extremely diverse skills and talents that need to be embodied in a single person in this strange and difficult role. You should, among many other things, be a respected professional in your field, you should be good with money, be social, a good communicator and writer, a leader and a manager (not the same) etc. As always, when you make a choice, you win something and you lose something. I have not curated so much in the last 17 years, after I took over my first big museum, but I have been closely involved in many curatorial processes.

AZ What inspires you and motivates you to work in this field, a leading arts institution?

LN My main driver is still the same—to try to create an optimized platform for the moment when art actually happens—when the art meets its beholder. To create the best possible conditions for the art and the artist, so they can realize their visions— and to do the same for the visitor, regardless of his or her background. Excellence and Access are my professional key words. We are here for the art and the artist— and for the public! My main inspiration is to see when this equation actually works out—it is fabulous!

Elizabeth Ann Macgregor OBE

Elizabeth Macgregor has been Director of the Museum of Contemporary Art since 1999. She was previously Director of Ikon Gallery Birmingham (1989–1999). Her first job was as curator and driver of the Scottish Arts Council's travelling gallery. For 3 years she organised and transported exhibitions on board a converted bus to Highland villages, inner city estates, schools, factories, hospitals and prisons. This experience informed what has become the driving force of her career—making contemporary art accessible to a wider audience. Macgregor's innovation and contribution to supporting artists and increasing access to contemporary art has been recognised with an Australian Federal Government Centenary Medal in 2003, the Veuve Clicquot Business Woman Award and the Australia Business Arts Foundation *Dame Elisabeth Murdoch Arts Business Leadership Award* in 2008. In 2011 she received the Australia Council Visual Arts Medal and was made an OBE in the Queen's birthday honour list.

Alessia Zorloni *As a leader of a non-profit arts and culture institution, what are some of the challenges you face?*

Elizabeth Ann Macgregor When I first took over the role of Director of the MCA Australia in 1999, my biggest challenge was overcoming the stereotype that contemporary art is elitist. Since then attendances at the MCA have increased substantially to just under 1 million in 2014. Balancing the business and fundraising aspects with the artistic and addressing the indifference of opinion formers in the political and business world to the importance of supporting living artists have been key facets of the job. Cultural institutions need to be entrepreneurial to supplement public funding. Costs rise and public funding stays static so the need to be constantly fundraising is a challenge. The business model needs to ensure a sufficient backbone of stable funding through commercial operations such as venue hire and store sales which can then be enhanced through fundraising and targeted philanthropic strategies. The activities of the MCA extend beyond the building to foster unique and innovative relationships between artists, the corporate sector and the community that show how productive an investment in the arts can be. One of the biggest challenges now is the changing relationship with the audience as a result of the astonishing changes we have seen in technology. Even more money is needed for the digital initiatives that are so essential. We need to work harder to counteract the demand for instant gratification and to encourage people to look at work rather than (or as well as!) take a selfie. However, social media offers unprecedented opportunities for the museum to reach young people especially. Finding a balance between funding the core business of collecting and exhibiting and the new demands of technology is not easy.

AZ When can a museum be defined as successful?

EAM Attendance figures are the primary indication of a successful institution but a museum has many audiences and stakeholders who may view this success in different ways. One of the MCA's goals is to support Australian artists in an international context. This can be judged by the increasing interest in Australian art from international curators and the inclusion of Australian artists in major exhibitions overseas. It is also crucial that the quality of the art experience is maintained and that the museum does not simply provide blockbusters to gain audiences. Through careful programming the MCA aims to present better known artists alongside artists that may require more time investment and deeper engagement with the work. This introduces new audiences to a broad range of contemporary art. Another key factor indicating success is building a reputation for excellence which allows visitors, sponsors and investors to trust that the brand will continually deliver successful events and quality experiences. The museum attracts a large proportion of return visitors and a high proportion of younger visitors who respond to the museum as a social space. Building this reputation has also had a positive impact on securing and retaining sponsors and individual donors. As a contemporary museum, the support of artists is critical and the museum's reputation for responding to the needs of artists is a key factor in its success.

AZ *At the intersection of artistic direction and business development, how do you assess the potential success of a particular exhibition?*

EAM Each exhibition is planned within an annual context that takes into consideration the different audiences and the range of artistic practice. Exhibitions are not considered in isolation and a number of factors are taken into account. The curatorial team regularly meets to discuss the program, identify areas of interest, suggest particular artists or themes and debate the merit of proposals that have been sent to the museum by artists or galleries. The proposed annual program is analysed with input from the marketing and education staff to ensure a balance of exhibitions and potential audiences. Unlike a private museum, publicly funded institution should embrace a diversity of viewpoints to reflect contemporary practice. As the names of the artists are unknown, it is often hard to predict the audience response which reinforces the desirability of a diverse programme.

AZ *In terms of measuring success, and not just in terms of counting visitors, what are some of the other indicators or metrics you use to gauge how well you're performing?*

EAM We measure success in a number of ways. We have targets in our strategic plan for all the key areas but we are more interested in how we measure the level of engagement. Numbers of visitors we convert to members for example. Repeat visits, popularity of public programs, recommendations to others, press articles and blog mentions and website traffic are a few indicators. We undertake visitor surveys which delve into motivation as well as the quality of the experience. We rely on our front of house staff to encourage visitors to give us feedback, positive and negative, to which we always respond. We have also established a number of formal mechanisms for consultation: an Artists Advisory Group, an Aboriginal and Torres Strait Islander Advisory Group, a Teachers Council and the Director's Circle (of general supporters). All of these groups give vital feedback in key areas and ensure that the museum stays in touch with its constituents. Demand for touring exhibitions in Australia and internationally and the museum's ability to secure major artists are also indicators of success. Attracting international curators and collectors to Australia and arranging for them to visit galleries and studios are important measures of the museum's role as a promoter of Australian art internationally. In relation to building new audiences, the museum's long term commitment to projects in Western Sydney is measured by the number of partnerships which lead to opportunities for artists to engage with groups who are not regular gallery goers. The museum's reputation among artists is another crucial measure of success. The MCA Australia prides itself on working closely with artists to ensure the best possible installation of their work. We have had countless positive comments from the many local and international artists who have participated in exhibitions. Part of the success is due to the MCA's staff—many of whom are practising artists themselves. Another contributing factor to the artist experience is the MCA's ability to be flexible to their needs. This in part is because we are an independent organisation that is quick to embrace and encourage artistic experimentation. We have also worked on projects that seek to demonstrate how art and artists can contribute to business development and innovation. Evaluation plays a key role in all our socially engaged projects.

AZ According to your experience as a museum director, what are the most important levers affecting the museum's excellence?

EAM The visitor experience has been essential to the success of the MCA. By focusing on providing an accessible and enjoyable experience, the MCA has been able to open art up to a wide demographic. Not by changing the art we show but by changing the context in which it is shown. The MCA provides a welcoming environment for people to explore the complex world of contemporary art. We make challenging art accessible to broad audiences, not by 'explaining' art but by providing the kind of information that curators get from dialogue with artists. The balance of the program is critical—with exhibitions that focus on the needs of the artist balanced with exhibitions of wider popular appeal. Digital technology offers opportunities to deepen the visitor engagement, with visitors encouraged to access information about the artists before, during and after a physical visit to the galleries. Ultimately though, any museum's success must be gauged principally by its program and its reputation among its peers.

AZ What led you to choose this profession?

EAM Until I was 16, I wanted to study music. Then my maths teacher told me this was a shocking waste of a good brain! I ended up at Edinburgh University to study languages but quite by chance discovered Art History and fell in love with it. I went on to a post-grad diploma at Manchester University but found to my frustration that the curatorial studies program was more concerned with connoisseurship than public engagement. My first job was as curator/driver of the Scottish Arts Council's Travelling Gallery, a bus which was converted into a mobile exhibition space. I drove exhibitions on board the bus to remote areas of Scotland where there were no galleries and in winter we toured the major cities, reaching people who may have had little opportunity or indeed inclination to go to art galleries. I got to know artists, which sparked my interest in the contemporary. This experience of working with artists and being in direct touch with the audience inspired a life-long passion to break down the barriers that prevent people engaging with contemporary art.

AZ What inspires you and motivates you to be in this field, atop a non-profit arts institution?

EAM My career mantra has been to work closely with artists to bring their work to a broad audience. I never cease to be inspired by artists and delighted by the ways in which audiences of all backgrounds respond. I believe that art can change lives. Taking the MCA from near bankruptcy to being regularly voted Sydney's favourite attraction has been challenging but immensely rewarding. I am fortunate to work with a team of very talented and highly committed people and building a supportive board has also been critical. I am not a fan of expanding buildings, preferring to focus on programming, but for a variety of practical reasons we had to undertake a renovation. The MCA reopened to the public in 2012 after a major building renovation and transformation. What is most rewarding is to see so many people in the galleries, looking at art, talking to our staff, and taking part in workshops in the new National Centre for Creative Learning. The museum really is a social hub—our programs for teenagers are packed out. There is a huge public interest in contemporary art. The redevelopment admirably answers our brief to make the building more accessible and enjoyable to visit, a social experience where informal learning is as important as formal. Most important of all, artists are at the heart of all we do. As well as exhibiting, we employ artists as educators, as installation crew and as front of house staff. Our late night events are curated by artists. I'm now focusing on building the national and international standing of the MCA Australia to secure its place among the best contemporary art museums in the world and to increase the profile of the many wonderful artists who live and work here.

Julia Peyton-Jones

Julia Peyton-Jones became Director of the Serpentine Gallery in 1991, where she is responsible for commissioning and showcasing the groundbreaking Exhibition, Education and Public Programmes as well as the annual architecture commission, the Serpentine Gallery Pavilion, which she conceived in 2000. Under the patronage of Diana, Princess of Wales, the Serpentine completed a £4 million renovation in 1998. Since then visitor numbers have increased six-fold up to 1.2 million in any 1 year. In 2014 the Serpentine Sackler Gallery opened, renovated by Pritzker Prize winning architect Zaha Hadid. This is a platform for established and emerging artists and provides an expanded programme that runs in tandem with the programme at the Serpentine. Julia Peyton-Jones is a Senior Fellow of the Royal College of Art (RCA), the Royal Institute of British Architects (RIBA) and is an Officer of the Most Excellent Order of the British Empire (OBE). She is also a professor at University of the Arts, London. Before joining the Serpentine, she studied painting at the RCA, worked as an artist, lectured in fine art at Edinburgh College of Art and was a Curator at the Hayward Gallery.

Alessia Zorloni As a leader of a non-profit arts and culture institution, what are some of the unique challenges you face?

Julia Peyton-Jones One of the biggest ongoing challenges that we face is fundraising. We are fortunate to have a number of loyal individual, corporate and not-for-profit institutional supporters. However, the Serpentine receives just 15% of its income from public funding and has to raise more than £6 million per year to maintain free admission to the public.

AZ When could a museum be defined as successful?

JPJ There are a number of ways to measure the success of an institution. Critical acclaim and a positive response from both the public and the press are key indicators. Strong visitor numbers are another yardstick and being recognised as pioneering within the field together with enjoying an international reputation are similarly very important.

AZ At the intersection of artistic direction and business development, how do you assess the potential success of a particular exhibition?

JPJ Over and above a positive public and the press response, feedback from our peers in the arts is also very important. Attendance is another important indicator and, last but not least, a satisfied artist, architect or designer is central to the success of any exhibition.

AZ In terms of measuring success, and not just in terms of counting visitors, what are some of the other indicators or metrics you use to gauge how well you're performing?

JPJ Another indication that we are succeeding is in other words the loyalty of our visitors—how often they come back, visit the Bookshop, buy our limited editions, and so on. Do members of the public, as well as our peers in the art world, make it a priority to visit the Serpentine even if they don't already have an interest in the artist (or artists) whose work is on view? Do our visitors believe in the vision that drives the programme? To measure this, we regularly invite visitors to fill out questionnaires to judge their reception of the Gallery. Externally, the institutions that we are involved with, such as Arts Council England and other Trusts and Foundations who support the Gallery, have such measuring systems in place. Artistic assessors from these institutions periodically visit the Gallery and the results are immensely valuable in calibrating the Gallery's performance.

AZ According to your experience as a museum's director, what are the most important levers affecting a museum's excellence?

JPJ A stable board and strong vision are key to ensuring a Gallery's excellence. Supportive funders are central to enabling an institution to put on its groundbreaking exhibitions, architecture, design, education and public programmes. A strong sense of purpose needs to be shared by everyone involved to enable an institution to truly excel. From the artist/architect, to the board of trustees, curators, funders, as well as each member of staff, everyone involved must have a shared commitment to the institution and its foundational ideals. Excellence as their foremost aspiration and the passion and dedication required to achieve this goal.

AZ What led you to choose this profession?

JPJ Ever since I was a child I have always had a passion for art. Originally I trained as an artist and moved from making my own work and curating my own shows, to joining a public gallery to work in their exhibitions department.

AZ What inspires you and motivates you to be in this field, atop a non-profit arts institution?

JPJ A desire to communicate to the widest possible public the importance of art, architecture, design and public programs is the central driving force that motivates me each and every day. The Serpentine Gallery motto, taken from Gilbert and George's popular maxim, is 'Art for All' and this belief that the arts and culture sit at the core of our society inspires everything we do.

James Bradburne

James Bradburne is an Anglo-Canadian architect, designer, museologist and specialist in informal learning. He has designed World Expo pavilions, science parks and international art exhibitions. He was educated in Canada and in England, graduating in architecture with the Architectural Association and taking his doctorate in museology at University of Amsterdam. Over the past 20 years he has produced exhibitions and organised research projects and conferences for UNESCO, national governments, private foundations and museums in many parts of the world. He was Head of Design and Education for newMetropolis (now NEMO), the Dutch National Science and Technology Centre, Director General of the Museum für Angewandte Kunst (applied art), Frankfurt, and Director General of the Next Generation foundation, which he created for the owner of LEGO to promote creativity, learning and play. From 2006 to 2014 he was the Director General of the Fondazione Palazzo Strozzi, the organisation that transformed the

Palazzo Strozzi in Florence into the city's most dynamic cultural centre. Since 2015, James Bradburne has been Director of Milan's Pinacoteca di Brera.

Alessia Zorloni *As a leader of a non-profit arts and culture institution, what are some of the unique challenges you face?*

James Bradburne None of the challenges I face are unique. The key challenge facing the institution I direct is to preserve the autonomy of the Board, which means keeping the pressures of public and private partners in balance. The Board's autonomy, and its trust in its professional staff, is indispensable to implementing a coherent cultural strategy over the medium-to-long term. A second key challenge is to retain an ideal mix of funding streams (public, private, earned revenue) in a very difficult economic climate. A third challenge is to find ways to motivate and support the learning and growth of all the professional staff, despite the very different contractual relationships with the institution.

AZ When can a museum be defined as successful?

JB A museum is successful when, in the words of Nelson Goodman, it functions *"as an institution for the prevention of blindness in order to make works work. Works work when, by stimulating inquisitive looking, sharpening perception, raising visual intelligence, they participate in the making and re-making of our worlds"* This means that success can only be measured in terms of impact on the user, not in terms of attendance or revenue. The museum is a fundamental part of our shared culture, and contributes best when used most. The quantitative measures best suited to museums are repeat visits and time spent in the museum.

AZ How do you assess the potential success of a particular exhibition, given the need to balance artistic direction and business development?

JB In a sense this is a false dichotomy, like the false opposition expressed by the word 'edu-tainment'. An exhibition has to fulfil three criteria: (1) create new scholarship (2) conserve and restore artworks and (3) transform visitors. An exhibition is a success if it can show it fulfils these three criteria. It is taken as given that the cost of an exhibition should not exceed its revenues from all sources. There should be no need to compromise the quality of an exhibition due to the demands of business development. It is a sure recipe for failure to have a business development strategy that is in opposition to the educational/cultural strategy.

AZ In terms of measuring success, and not just in terms of counting visitors, what other indicators or metrics do you use to gauge how well you are performing?

JB The key quantitative measures of success are: (1) number/increase of repeat visits (2) amount of time spent in the exhibition and with individual works of art

(3) the diversity of the publics reached. A museum is obliged to create the maximum cultural value for the investment.

AZ *According to your experience as a museum director, what are the most important factors affecting a museum's excellence?*

JB The most important factor that affects a museum's ability to aspire to excellence is autonomous, independent governance. Excellence in a museum depends on consistent leadership, vision, trust, patience and unflagging attention to the end-user's experience.

AZ *What led you to choose this profession?*

JB In a sense the profession chose me. I have spent my life trying to find ways to better support self-initiated, self-directed and self-sustained learning, learning done for its intrinsic pleasure not extrinsic rewards. The museum is the ideal institution in which to experiment with creating settings in which someone can discover that 'the life of the mind is a pleasure'.

AZ *What inspires you and motivates you to work in this field?*

JB The belief that in some small way the work we do can transform someone's life.

AZ *And if you were to give advice to collectors interested in opening and managing a private museum, what would you tell them?*

JB Despite the pressures of the economy, they will be doing culture—not business. The impact of investment in culture—like education—can only be fully measured after decades. They should never be misled by short-term thinking. The key is to innovate in the service of the end-user, not to try to fulfil the needs of the existing market. As Henry Ford said, '*if I had asked my customers what they wanted, they would have said a faster horse.*' Steve Jobs just said: '*stay hungry, stay foolish*'.

References

Anderson, M. L. (2004). *Metrics of success in art museums*. Los Angeles: The Getty Leadership Institute.
Anderson, M. L. (2007). Prescriptions for art museums in the decade ahead. *Curator The Museum Journal*, 50(1), 9–17.
Carnegie, G., & Wolnizer, P. (1996). Enabling accountability in museums. *Accounting, Auditing and Accountability Journal*, 9(5), 84–99.
Cresswell, J. W. (2007). *Qualitative enquiry and research design: Choosing among five approaches*. Thousand Oaks, CA: Sage.

Dainelli, F. (2006). I nuovi standard per l'accreditamento dei musei americani. In B. Sibilio (Ed.), *Un modello di misurazione delle performance dei musei* (pp. 20–38). Roma: Aracne.

de Bruijn, H. (2002). Performance measurement in the public sector: Strategies to cope with the risks of performance measurement. *International Journal of Public Sector Management, 15*(7), 578–594.

Falk, J. H., & Sheppard, B. (2006). *Thriving in the knowledge age: New business models for museums and other cultural institutions.* Lanham, MD: AltaMira Press.

Finocchiaro Castro, M., & Rizzo, I. (2009). Performance measurement of heritage conservation activity in Sicily. *International Journal of Arts Management, 11*(2), 29–40.

Fox, H. (2006). *Beyond the bottom line: Evaluating art museums with the balanced scorecard.* Los Angeles: The Getty Leadership Institute.

Gilhespy, I. (1999). Measuring the performance of cultural organizations: A model. *International Journal of Public Sector Management, 2*(1), 38–52.

Goodyear, M. (1990). Qualitative research. In R. Birn, P. Hague, & P. Vangelder (Eds.), *A handbook of market research techniques* (pp. 229–248). London: Kogan.

Jalla, D. (2001). *Il museo contemporaneo.* Torino: Utet.

Kaplan, R., & Norton, D. (1992). The balanced scorecard: Measures that drive performance. *Harvard Business Review, 70*(1), 71–80.

Kaplan, R. (2001). Strategic performance measurement and management in nonprofit organizations. *Nonprofit Management & Leadership, 11*(3), 353–370.

Kaplan, R., & Norton, D. (2000). Having trouble with your strategy? Then map it. *Harvard Business Review, 78*(5), 167–176.

Koster, E., & Falk, J. H. (2007). Maximizing the external value of museums. *Curator The Museum Journal, 50*(2), 191–196.

Kvale, S. (1995). The social construction of validity. *Qualitative Inquiry, 1,* 20–42.

Matthews, J. (2008). *Scorecards for results: A guide for developing a library balanced scorecard.* Westport, CN: Libraries Unlimited.

McMaster, B. (2008). *Supporting excellence in the arts. From measurement to judgement.* London: Department for Culture, Media and Sport.

Orr, R. (1973). Progress in documentation: Measuring the goodness of library services: A general framework for considering quantitative measures. *Journal of Documentation, 29*(3), 315–332.

Paulus, O. (2003). Measuring museum performance: A study of museums in France and the United States. *International Journal of Arts Management, 6*(1), 50–63.

Porter, M. (2006). *Strategy for museums.* Boston: Harvard Business School.

Sibilio Parri, B., & Dainelli, F. (2009). Accountability level in museum communication via web: An international comparison. In *Proceedings of AIMAC 2009 10th International conference on arts and cultural management.* Dallas: Southern Methodist University.

Turbide, J., & Laurin, C. (2009). Performance measurement in the arts sector: The case of the performing arts. *International Journal of Arts Management, 11*(2), 56–70.

Weil, S. (2002a). *Are you really worth what you cost, or just merely worthwhile? And who gets to say?* Los Angeles: Getty Leadership Institute.

Weil, S. (2002b). *Making museums matter.* Washington, DC: Smithsonian Institution Press.

Weil, S. (2005). A success/failure matrix for museums. *Museum News, 84*(1), 36–40.

Weinstein, L., & Bukovinsky, D. (2009). Use of the balanced scorecard and performance metrics to achieve operational and strategic alignment in arts and culture not-for-profits. *International Journal of Arts Management, 11*(2), 42–55.

Celebrity Effect in the Contemporary Art Market

Alessia Zorloni and Antonella Ardizzone

1 Introduction

There are no established rules underpinning the evaluation of works of art. Fluctuations in prices are continuous and unpredictable, because they are conditioned by a series of variables that are able to contradict all the possible scenarios (Besana 2003). It is not surprising that Baumol (1986) describes the prices of works of art as a "floating crap game". This is due to the fact that prices are not anchored to any objective element and therefore can unpredictably fluctuate based on unobservable changes in consumer tastes (Zorloni 2013). Criteria determining the value of works of art may relate to the artist and to his work. With reference to the first criterion, an important element is constituted by the artist's reputation, which consists of the persona he adopts, the wider movement of which he is an expression, and his nation of origin. Personal reputation is extremely important, generating a very high value for works of art by artists considered stars and a trash market for those of doubtful authenticity, which can be similar in appearance to authentic works. Reputation is built from the information that art historians, critics, curators and art dealers provide; this information results in the creation of the artist's brand (Zorloni 2005).

In the world of contemporary art, as pointed out by Thompson (2008), branding activities have led to the creation of strong brands, ranging from art dealers to museum brands, and from auction house brands to collector brands, not to mention of course artist brands. With the decline of traditional judgment criteria, which are based on technical quality and are therefore verifiable on parameters dictated by the academies, the assessment of artistic production, particularly contemporary

---

A. Zorloni • A. Ardizzone (✉)
IULM University, Milan, Italy
e-mail: alessia.zorloni@iulm.it; antonella.ardizzone@iulm.it

production, has begun to depend more and more on refined market strategies, by making the added value deriving from the brand of the creator progressively more important than the intrinsic value of his work. The valuation of painters such as the African American Jean-Michel Basquiat, who died from an overdose, the graffiti artist Keith Haring, who died from AIDS, or Jeff Koons, a former partner of a porn star he elected as his muse, has risen proportionally to the provocations or myths that artists have created around themselves. As Koons himself theorized, in a world where everything is based on money, price makes an artwork.

Artists' income has been addressed by Rosen (1981) from a theoretical point of view, and by Adler (1985) from an empirical point of view. Rosen's Superstar model explains artists' income as a function of their talent. The purpose of the model is to explain why the relatively few artists who earn enormous sums of money dominate the market through the activities they undertake.

This model has been utilized by Adler (1985) to explain why the art consumer is not prone to a varied consumption, but prefers to focus on a few great artists. Also according to Adler, the existence of celebrities does not derive from the differentiation of talent, but from consumers' need to have a common culture and symbols to share. The creation of a star, that is the transformation of an artist into a symbol, begins when each consumer randomly selects a new artist to add to his basket from a group of equally talented artists. The initial advantage allows the selected artist to become popular, and because consumers need a culture and symbols to share, other consumers in turn will start to become interested and to purchase the artist's works of art.

Edgar Morin (2005) has traced the source of the star system to the beginning of the last century when the first group of film companies was formed in Hollywood, competing to conquer the domestic market and to confirm their place on the international one. Today this system also prevails in the visual arts industry, especially in the contemporary art market (Zorloni 2011; Quemin 2013).

In the era of marketing, entertainment and seduction, the economic exploitation of notoriety, in the context of mass production and ubiquity of the mass media, has given rise to a sort of "celebrity economy" (Turner 2004), characterized by three specific aspects. For artists, creators and personalities who are part of the star system, the difference in their compensation is often vastly greater than the difference in talent; the exploitation of glory extends beyond their original field of competence; the results, sometimes obtained more by chance than talent or specific training, are self-perpetuating (Benhamou 2002).

Based on this evidence, this study examines the way the contemporary art market works. Section 2 explains in detail the influence of network externalities and positive feedback on the contemporary art market. Section 3 presents the results of empirical research that, considering the theoretical positions outlined above, has the objective of identifying whether the art market is a winner-take-all-market subject to network effects. The last section offers general conclusions.

2 How Collectors Influence the Global Art Market

There are a number of markets where a large part of consumer spending ends up in the pockets of a small number of producers, while the majority of the producers earn little or nothing (Frank and Cook 1995). Although there is usually more than one winner, figuratively speaking the "winner takes all", as Robert Frank and Philip Cook wrote. Contemporary artists operate in a "winner-take-all" market. There are thousands of contemporary artists all over the world offering high quality works, but only a few earn big incomes, while the vast majority cannot even earn a basic living from their works (or earn not enough to live by their work). According to Artprice (2015) 68 % of global auction revenue from contemporary art is generated by 100 artists and 35 % by just ten artists. The price inflation is thus continuing for the same *"trophy brands"* that inspire both generosity and ferocious competition in collectors. As pointed out by Abbing (1989), this happens because people have a "limited star capacity". People tend to remember the relevant details of only a limited number of products, such as product names or an author's name. Other than the influence of the limited star capacity, network externalities also contribute to the emergence of the "winner-take-all" market.

It is possible to assume that the demand for contemporary works of art is characterized by indirect demand-side network externalities[1]: the collectors' utility—and thus willingness to pay—depends on the number of prestigious and influential collections the artist is already part of. A product (or technology) is said to exhibit network externalities when, for the individual buyer, the value of the product depends on the number of users who consume the same product (Varian 2003). For instance, if being the only collector of an artist can increase the private utility (the pleasure derived from admiring a painting), the social utility, on the other hand, grows as more famous collectors appreciate and share interest in the same artist.

The influence of network externalities on demand can be defined and represented using Leibenstein's model (1948). This model allows us to estimate the demand function for a contemporary artist:

$$Q_{d,i} = f(P_i, n_a), \quad \frac{\partial Q_{di}}{\partial P_i} < 0, \quad \frac{\partial Q_{di}}{\partial n_a} > 0. \tag{1}$$

where n_a represents the total number of collectors, P_i is the price and Q_i is the quantity demanded of a product i (Fig. 1).

If $n_a = n_0$, $Q_{di} = f(P_i) \Rightarrow$ corresponds to D_0, $n_a = n_1$, $Q_{di} = f_1(P_i) \Rightarrow D_1$.

---

[1] In economics and business, a network effect (also called network externality or demand-side economies of scale) is the effect that one user of a good or service has on the value of that product to other people. When a network effect is present, the value of a product or service is dependent on the number of others using it. Fax, telephone, email and software applications grow in value with an increasing network of users.

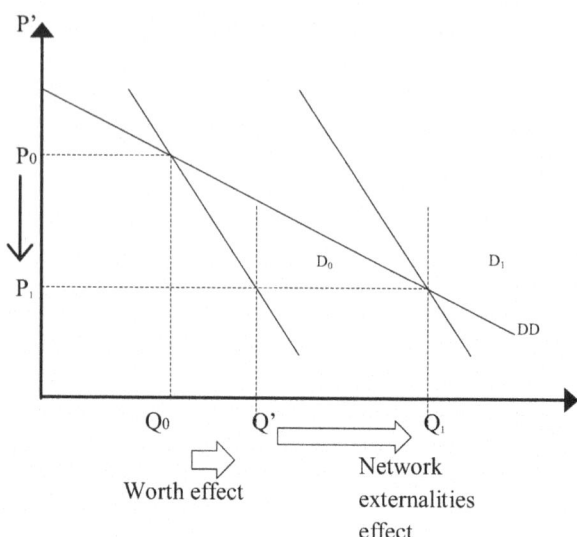

Fig. 1 Network externalities in the contemporary art market. *Source*: Zorloni 2013

For, $n_a = n_1$, with, $n_1 > n_0$, the demand curve shifts from D_0 to D_1 and so on, until the increase of collectors causes the devaluation of the image of the artist and thus the emergence of a snob effect, i.e. negative externalities. The demand curve for collectors—namely the relationship that connects each hypothetical level of price to the quantity that buyers are willing to buy—is obtained by considering the worth effect and the externality effect for each price. For example, if the price falls from P_0 to P_1, the quantity of works of art demanded by collectors increases from Q_0 to Q' (worth effect): the appreciation of the artist by new collectors ($n_1 - n_0$) causes a further increase of quantity demanded from Q' to Q_1 (externality effect). This occurs because as the circulation of works of art in the network of renowned public and private collections increases, an increasing number of individuals will be encouraged to adopt the product, making the artist even more attractive to additional collectors and triggering the self-reinforcing effect (celebrity effect) defined above.

This celebrity effect is the result of the new collectors' common practice of reducing search and information costs by only purchasing recognized works or those by famous artists. By doing so, new buyers can rely on preferences established by previous successful buyers, hence reducing the risk and insecurity inherent in relying on their own taste. These risk-reducing techniques tend to reinforce the celebrity effect in the art market, whereby the works of the most famous artists are the most demanded and achieve the highest prices in the market, while emerging artists face high barriers to entry (Zorloni 2013).

In markets with network externalities, like the contemporary art market, competition appears to be particularly fierce at the initial stage because the achievement of critical mass, triggering positive feedback, can lead to almost monopolistic positions with the inevitable consequence of informally creating reputational barriers to entry. Not only is the artist's talent and ability to innovate of great importance, but also the speed at which he grows, since the first artists who reach critical mass will conquer the entire market. In these competitive dynamics, expectations play an important role: the simple belief that a given artist will become the star of the market may cause an increasing number of critics to talk about him, media to cover him and collectors to buy him, making him indeed become the market celebrity. In this case, in fact, it is not necessarily the most valuable artist that achieves success: a minor artist can also succeed if there are wide expectations that this may occur. So, if an artist is willing to conquer a market with network effects, the most critical challenge lays in triggering positive feedback (Zorloni 2011).

In this market a pivotal role is also played by the "economy of attention" (Franck 1998). According to Franck, attention, and thus fame, in the cultural world is an economy working along the same lines as capitalism. The curator/investor (also the museum director or the gallery owner) acts as a financial investor and lends his property (his exhibition space and his fame) to an artist from whom he expects a return on his investment in the form of more attention (reputation, fame, etc.). Therefore, the relationship between the gallery owner and the artist relates to that between the investor and the entrepreneur. The investor puts his money into companies from which he expects to gain rewards. This is always a mixed bag, where just a few artists succeed and pay for the investment in others who are lower achieving.

3 Research Methodology

Considering the theoretical positions outlined above, this section shows the results of empirical research conducted in order to verify the way the art market works and to identify a correlation (if any exists) between artists' notoriety and some of the variables suggested by the literature (Frey and Pommerehne 1989; Throsby 1994; Menger 2014). In particular, according to the literature review on artistic success and art market (Galenson 2002; 2005; 2006; Bull 2011), we have formulated the following research hypotheses:

HP_1: *The contemporary art market is a winner-take-all market subject to network effects, whereby "the strong become stronger and the weak become weaker";*
HP_2: *The artist's international prestige increases with the number of public and private institutions that have decided to buy and include in their collection at least one work by the artist;*
HP_3: *The contemporary art market is driven by the "economy of attention", whereby turnover increases with notoriety.*

To verify the research questions, the authors analysed a sample including the top 155 contemporary artists and photographers in the world in 2011, according to the ranking published by Artfacts.[2] Since 1996, the British company Artfacts has developed a model classifying artists with respect to their degree of celebrity called "Artist Ranking". The aim of the "Artist Ranking system" is to arrange artists by their exhibition success and define those who got more attention at an international level, and thus more visibility. Therefore, the database only includes artists who exhibit at international level. The Artist Ranking has been built in this way because only artists that are common to several countries will be very important and will therefore create a sort of sign or universal symbol (considered as a prototype). The final score describes the degree of recognition of an artist, and thus the strength of their brand within the contemporary art system. The Artfacts score is calculated through assigning a reputation score to cultural institutions. Institutions gain reputation based on their past exhibition activity. This reputation (in points) is applied to their exhibitions. An artist exhibiting in this institution receives these points. The final score is calculated using an algorithm taking into account the artist's solo shows, the reputation of the exhibitor and the number of countries where the artist has been exhibited.

Data provided by Artfacts about the most famous contemporary artists in the world were integrated with data provided by Artprice.[3]

3.1 Data Collection

To test the research hypotheses, the study has taken the following variables into consideration:

1. "Artfacts score" (AS): an index of the artist's visibility or notoriety level. This variable is used as a proxy for the artist's cultural success. It is calculated weighting the number of "solo shows" (exhibitions) in respect to the "importance" of the exhibitor and the number of countries in which the artist has been exhibited;
2. "Change in visibility" (Variation of Artfacts score—CV): the increase or decrease in the artist's visibility. It is expressed by the absolute difference in points earned by Artfacts with respect to the previous year;
3. "Artist's living status" (L): dummy variable indicating if the artist is living (1) or not (0);
4. "Number of galleries" (NG): the number of galleries representing the artist and selling his works;
5. "Number of collections" (NC): the number of public and private institutions that have decided to buy and include in their collection at least one work by the artist;

---

[2] http://www.artfacts.net/it/home.html.

[3] Artprice is the world leader art market information provider, producing one of the most valuable data sets to study the art market from an economic and financial perspective. http://www.artprice.com/.

6. "Turnover" (T): the artist's annual sales value in US dollars in the secondary market (auctions). This variable is used as the most important proxy for the artist's economic success;
7. "Top Sale" (TS): the historical price record reached by an artist in the secondary market in US dollars);
8. "Number of lots sold" (NLS): the number of items or quantity exchanged in the secondary market;
9. "Unsold" (NS): the percentage of unsold items;

All the variables refer to the year 2011 (except "number of collections" and "number of galleries" which refer to the entire artist's career). Data pertaining to the score and the score variation of the most famous contemporary artists were collected from the database Artfacts.net, as well as data relating the "artist's living status", "number of galleries", and "number of collections".

"Turnover", "top sale", "number of lots sold", and "percentage of unsold items" were collected from the Artprice.com database. Combining data from these two sources, the total sample is made of the top 155 world contemporary artists.

First of all, we used a correlation matrix to understand simple linear correlation among the variables collected. Then the research hypotheses were tested using multiple linear regression models. The Standard Ordinary Least Square technique has been applied, as well as a test for multicollinearity (VIF Test) and homoscedasticity.[4]

3.2 Results

To verify HP_1 (the contemporary art market is a winner-take all market), the authors tested the following two models:

$$(1) ASi = \alpha + \beta(CVi) + \gamma(Li) + \delta(NGi) + \eta(NCi) + \lambda(Ti) + \mu(NLSi) + \sigma(NSi) + \varphi(TSi) + \varepsilon i$$

where the artist's visibility depends on change in visibility, artist's living status, number of galleries, number of collections, turnover, number of lots sold, percentage of unsold items, and top sale price.

Even using cross-sectional data and not panel data, according to results, HP_1 is accepted. Table 1 shows that, in our sample, the artist's visibility (or cultural success) increases in line with change in visibility, number of collections, and turnover. This indicates that the most visible artists, that is, those who are more

---

[4] A test for multicollinearity is applied to all the regressions in the paper. Results are included in the tables. If not specified in the text, all the statistical tests are significant. Homoscedasticity has been evaluated using the scatter plot of the standardized residuals (*zresid) against the standardized predicted values (*zpred). There are some outliers, as expected. SPSS has been used to perform the quantitative analysis.

Table 1 Ordinary least squares regression of artists' notoriety, most famous contemporary artists in the world, 2011

Dependent variable: Artfact score (or artist's visibility/notoriety)

	Model 1			Model 2			
	Unstandardized coefficient β	Standard error of β	Standardized coefficient		Unstandardized coefficient β	Standard error of β	Standardized coefficient
(Constant)	2729.972	1508.800		(Costant)	614.966	995.631	
Change in visibility	3.497**	1.009	0.168	Change in visibility	3.500**	1.010	0.169
Living	2532.641**	930.719	0.132	Living	3299.378**	919.619	0.172
N. galleries	−54.149	36.923	−0.129	N. collections	191.207**	16.713	0.662
N. collections	218.483**	20.453	0.757	Turnover	7.205E-5**	0.000	0.177
Turnover	0.000**	0.000	0.340				
N. Lots sold	−0.682	5.389	−0.010				
Unsold (%)	−30.804	37.706	−0.042				
Top sale	0.000	0.000	−0.196				
N. of osserv. (N)	155 (8)			155 (4)			
F statistic (df)	0.00			0.00			
R-squared	0.830			0.816			
Adj R-squared	0.689			0.665			

Data sources: Artfacts.net and Artprice.com

Notes: model 1: all the VIF < 3.622; Model 2: all the VIF < 1.502; *p < 0.005; **p < 0.01

often invited to show their works in the most important museums around the world, have a greater chance of being selected again by other museums, as predicted by the "winner-take-all" theory. This result empirically supports Rosen's superstar model (Rosen 1981) and the first research hypothesis, according to which a positive feedback in the contemporary art market leads to an international predominance of a few artists in the most important cultural venues, with the subsequent creation of high entry barriers. Moreover, market success (turnover) shows a linear influence on an artist's cultural success (visibility). The artist's score shows a negative linear relation with living status (higher notoriety if the artist is living): there is no "death effect" for the top contemporary artists, because there are many famous living artists in the sample of the top 155.

The model explains 83 % of the total variance, it is significant (Prob. F = 0.00), and there is no heteroscedasticity and multicollinearity (VIF < 3.56 for all the variables).

$$(2)\,AS_i = \alpha + \beta(CV_i) + \gamma(L_i) + \delta(NC_i) + \lambda(T_i) + \varepsilon_i$$

In model 2 the insignificant variables of model 1 are removed. R-squared does not significantly change: the model explains 81 % of the total variance (and adjusted R-square is high too). According to the analysis of the standardized beta values, the most influential variable on artists' visibility is the number of collections (0.66); change in visibility (0.17), turnover (0.17), and living status (0.17) have the same relative influence. Therefore, model 1 also tests and confirms HP_2: the artist's international prestige increases with the number of collectors that decide to include a works of art in their collection. This occurs because as the circulation of works of art in the network of renowned public and private collections increases, an increasing number of new buyers will be encouraged to include the artist in their collections, making the artist even more attractive to additional collectors and triggering the self-reinforcing effect (celebrity effect).

To verify if turnover is explained by visibility (HP_3), the following model has been tested:

$$(3)\,T_i = \alpha + \beta(AS_i) + \gamma(CV_i) + \delta(NLS_i) + \eta(TS_i) + \varepsilon_i$$

This model explains 86 % of total variance. HP_3 is accepted: turnover is linearly correlated to notoriety and its variation (negatively). As expected, it also depends on quantity sold, and top sale price. This is due to the fact that artists reaching the highest prices get access to a wider market and to higher average quotations, in virtue of self-reinforcing effects (Table 2).

The last data analysis pertains to the relationship between financial success and cultural success. Single regression (OLS) between turnover (used as a proxy for financial success) and the Artfacts score or notoriety (used as a proxy for cultural success) shows a strong cubic relationship (R square = 0.63; Sig. F = 0.00); the more notoriety increases, the more turnover increases in a cubical way. Even excluding the five outliers in the dataset, the results do not significantly change and

Table 2 Ordinary least squares regression of turnover, most famous contemporary artists in the world, 2011

Model 3			
	Unstandardized coefficient β	Standard error of β	Standardized coefficient
(Constant)	−9179327.062	1578976.32	
Artfacts score	526.766**	121.48	0.214
Change in visibility	−5313.547*	2249.070	−0.104
N. Lots sold	53637.405**	8126.964	0.323
Top sale	1.650**	0.143	0.553
N. of osserv. (N)	155 (4)		
F statistic (df)	0.000		
R-squared	0.860		
Adj R-squared	0.739		

Data sources: Artfacts.net and Artprice.com
Notes: VIF < 1.40; *p < 0.005; **p < 0.01

the relation stays cubical. Thus, cultural success, determined by notoriety, strongly increases financial success (HP$_3$). The scatterplot makes clear that some artists are overvalued and others are undervalued (the straight lines in the graph are median values for financial success and cultural success). The overvalued contemporary artists are in the upper left quadrant: they have high financial success but low cultural success with respect to the first half of artists taken into consideration in this study. Some examples are Enrico Castellani and Agostino Bonalumi. The undervalued artists are in the lower right quadrant: they have high cultural success but low financial success. Some very visible artists, such as Sol LeWitt, Marcel Broodthaers, Thomas Ruff, and Marcel Duchamp, who do not have huge turnover, should have had a higher value on the basis of the preferences expressed by cultural institutions. These artists, together with many others, may represent a very good investment opportunity for the future. Nevertheless, it is necessary to point out that the majority of the artists placed in the lower right quadrant belong to younger generations with respect to those lying in the upper right quadrant. This may explain lower market quotations. If fame, notoriety, or even the simple interest of public institutions, dealers, museum directors and curators—here all included in the score that the artists received from Artfacts—proves a good indicator, some artists may have more interesting performances in the coming years. On the contrary, those artists who were valued more than would be expected on the basis of the interest expressed by the critics (that is to say, positioning in the upper left quadrant) may start declining in the future or, in any case, enjoy weaker revaluations with respect to those in the lower right quadrant. Nevertheless, it is worth noting that, in the contemporary art market, aesthetic value and subsequent monetary value is greatly influenced by temporary fashions. This is due to the fact that historians and operators in this market have not yet been able to establish what is valuable and will last in the future (Fig. 2).

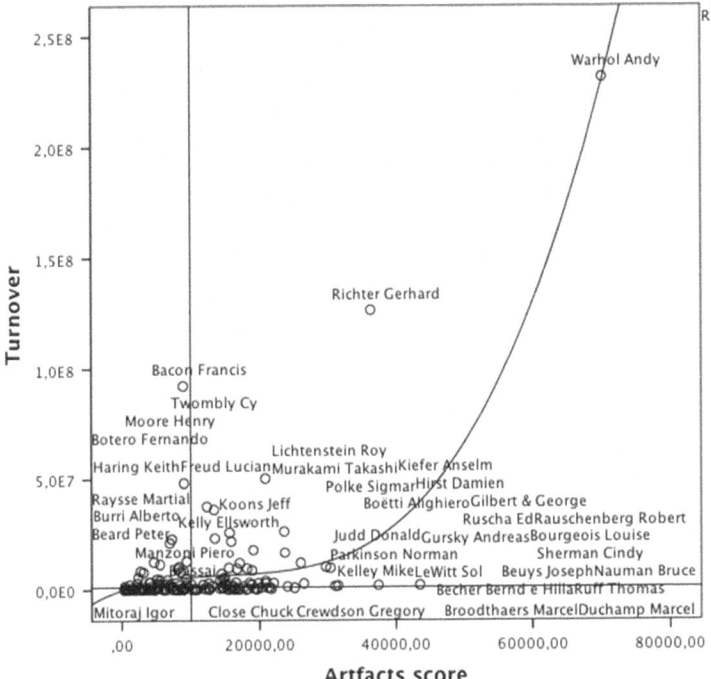

Fig. 2 Cultural success and financial success matrix, 2011. *Data sources*: Artfacts.net and Artprice.com

4   Conclusion

This paper represents a first attempt to empirically verify how the contemporary art market works. Going back to the research hypotheses, it is possible to draw some conclusions on the basis of the empirical evidence based on the 155 most famous contemporary artists in the world.

HP_1: The contemporary art market is a winner-take-all market subject to network effects, whereby "the strong become stronger and the weak become weaker".

HP_1 has been confirmed in our sample. An artist's cultural success is highly correlated to his exposition (the number of collections), the variation in notoriety with respect to the previous year, living status and turnover. This indicates that the more an artist is exhibited (in private and public collections), the more his notoriety increases and notoriety increase boosts the chance to be selected again by other museums. Thus, the analysis empirically supports Rosen's superstar model (1981) and the hypothesis that a positive feedback in the market of contemporary arts leads to extreme situations, characterized by the international predominance of a few artists in the most important cultural venues with the subsequent creation of high entry barriers.

HP₂: The artist's international prestige increases with the number of public and private institutions that have decided to buy and include in their collection at least one work by the artist;

HP₂ is also confirmed. Cultural institutions' decisions to include a work of art in their collections influence notoriety, making the artist even more attractive to additional collectors and accelerating the process of mainstream adhesion. This celebrity effect tends to reinforce the same artists in the art market.

HP₃: The contemporary art market is driven by the "economy of attention", whereby turnover increases with notoriety;

Franck's economy of attention theory is confirmed by data analysis; the more the art system (cultural institutions, critics, curators, gallery managers, and collectors) invests in an artist, the more he sells his works, and the more his turnover increases. Since turnover is correlated to visibility, the market success of an artist is explained by his cultural success, which is fostered by exhibitions in cultural institutions. Thus, the results of this research verify the density dependence phenomenon put forward by Adler (1985).

Finally, analysing the relationship between financial success and cultural success, it was found, as expected, that each strongly enhances the other.

This study has a number of limitations. Panel data (data in different years) instead of cross-sectional data (data collected by observing the artists in the same year) would be more useful to test for network effects and would allow a deeper examination of competitive dynamics in the contemporary art market. In addition, the data are from a relatively small sample of contemporary artists. Having a huge number of less famous artists would give stronger results.

This is only a first attempt to empirically study the contemporary art market. A lot more empirical analysis should be done in the future to test the mainstream theory and to achieve a deeper knowledge of the way in which the contemporary art market works.

References

Abbing, H. (1989). *Ean Economie Van De Kunsten*. Groningen: Historische Uitgeverij Groningen.
Adler, M. (1985). Stardom and talent. *American Economic Review, 75*(1), 208–212.
Artprice. (2015). *The contemporary art market report 2015*. Saint Romain au Mont D'Or: Artprice.
Baumol, W. (1986). Unnatural value: Or art investment as floating crap game. *American Economic Review, 76*(2), 10–14.
Benhamou, F. (2002). *L'économie du star-system*. Paris: Odile Jacob.
Besana, A. (2003). *L'arte in chiave economica*. Milano: Led Edizioni.

Bull, M. (2011). The two economies of world art. In H. Jonathan (Ed.), *Globalization and contemporary art* (pp. 181–185). Massachusetts: Wiley-Blackwell.

Franck, G. (1998). *Ökonomie der Aufmerksamkeit*. München-Wien: Carl Hanser Verlag.

Frank, R. H., & Cook, P. J. (1995). *The winner-take-all society*. New York: Free Press.

Frey, B., & Pommerehne, W. (1989). *Museus and market: Explorations in the economics of the arts*. Oxford: Basil Blackwell.

Galenson, D. (2002). Quantifying Artistic Success. *Historical Methods, 35*(1), 5.

Galenson, D. (2005). *Who are the greatest living artists? The view from the auction market*. NBER working papers series no. 11644. Cambridge: National Bureau of Economic Research.

Galenson, D. (2006). Do the young British artists rule. *World Economics, 7*(1), 175–184.

Leibenstein, H. (1948). Bandwagon, Snob and Veblen effects in the theory of consumers' demand. *The Quarterly Journal of Economics, 64*(2), 165–201.

Menger, P. (2014). *Economics of creativity*. Harvard: Harvard University Press.

Morin, E. (2005). *Star*. Minneapolis, MN: University of Minnesota Press.

Quemin, A. (2013). *Les stars de l'art contemporain*. Paris: CNRS Editions.

Rosen, S. (1981). The economics of superstars. *American Economic Review, 71*(5), 845–858.

Thompson, D. (2008). *The $12 million stuffed shark: The curious economics of contemporary art*. New York: Palgrave Macmillan.

Throsby, D. (1994). The production and consumption of the art: A view of cultural economics. *Journal of Economic Literature, 32*(1), 1–29.

Turner, G. (2004). *Understanding celebrity*. London: Sage.

Varian, H. (2003). *Intermediate microeconomics*. London: W.W. Norton & Company.

Zorloni, A. (2005). Structure of the contemporary art market and the profile of Italian artists. *International Journal of Arts Management, 8*(1), 61–71.

Zorloni, A. (2011). Lo star system nel mercato dell'arte contemporanea. *Economia della Cultura, 3*, 275–288.

Zorloni, A. (2013). *The economics of contemporary art. Markets, strategies and stardom*. Heidelberg: Springer.

Deepening Business Relationships Through Art

Alessia Zorloni

1 Introduction

Since the turn of the new millennium, the global luxury industry has increasingly looked to the art world for inspiration. Some of the larger luxury brands have incorporated the fine arts directly into their products, inviting individual artists to collaborate. For instance, the French fashion house Louis Vuitton regularly commissions contemporary artists to reinvent the brand's most iconic handbags and supports art museums and art projects like the Espace Culturel Louis Vuitton Paris or the Louis Vuitton Young Arts Project London, a partnership between five of London's leading art institutions (Baumgarth et al. 2014). Likewise, Montblanc uses art in its brand communication by awarding cultural prizes and launching artist-related special editions; many luxury brands such as Salvatore Ferragamo, Brioni and Breguet invest in artistic patronage in various fields such as contemporary art, heritage, dance, film, and photography (Chailan and Valek 2014). Moreover, several of the industry's leading luxury brands, including Prada, Trussardi, Hermès and Cartier, have begun investing in and supporting the fine arts through the establishment of their own art foundations dedicated to the collecting and presentation of contemporary art. These examples illustrate that the competitiveness and economic value of many products and services are increasingly strongly related to a company's capacity to incorporate the quality and features which characterise and underpin works of art. From a business perspective the idea is not to create artworks, but to infuse the artful energy that distinguishes works of art into their products and services. A number of examples can be provided from diverse industries. For instance, car manufacturers such as Ferrari, Lamborghini, Maserati and Aston Martin pay great attention to artistic aspects of their products, from design to materials and other components, which as works of art can affect

A. Zorloni (✉)
IULM University, Milan, Italy
e-mail: alessia.zorloni@iulm.it

clients' experiences. Arts can also be considered a fundamental component of the success of Italian home furnishings companies such as Alessi, Artemide, Cassina, Flos, B&B Italia, Cappellini and many others (Gilmore et al. 2009). As a result, in today's highly competitive business context many companies are therefore starting to position themselves at the intersection of commerce and arts (Bangle 2001). This study introduces a framework to show how successful brands take advantage of the unique characteristics of the arts and lays the foundations for a series of case studies analyses exploring the links between fine arts and fashion brands. Section 2 reviews the literature on arts-corporate collaborations. Section 3 examines in detail the use of culture as a marketing lever and the practice of integrating art into branding and marketing activities; Section 4 presents a global perspective on the involvement of fashion houses in contemporary art and explores the opportunities that arts-luxury brands collaborations can offer. The last section offers general conclusions.

2   Literature Review on Arts-Corporate Collaborations

In the last few years, many authors have discussed the potential benefits of engagement with art and culture for the business world in general, and some researchers have developed frameworks to classify different types of arts-corporate collaborations (Darso 2004; Schiuma 2011; Kastner 2014; Lindenberg and Oosterlinck 2011; Baumgarth et al. 2014; Chailan and Valek 2014). Schiuma (2011) proposes a holistic framework, suggesting that arts-corporate collaborations can offer valuable opportunities to respond to organizational challenges, management problems and business performance issues. In this regard, arts-corporate collaborations have the potential to develop competencies and communication skills and give important impulses to the organization as a whole. Another research branch follows an external perspective by exploring the benefits of arts in marketing and communication. Many authors have analyzed corporations' motivations to create and enhance corporate art collections (Martorella 1990; Witte et al. 2009; Wu 2002; Kottasz et al. 2007; Lindenberg and Oosterlinck 2011). Martorella (1990) identified three main reasons and motives for companies collecting art. Buying art serves as a communication vector of the brand image a company wants to transmit and as relevant tool of corporate philanthropy. Exhibiting art pieces in a building is also intended to contribute to the cultural and intellectual education of the collaborators, at the same time promoting open-mindedness and creativity. In addition, art collections are also an investment enabling risk diversification. More recently, the approach devised by an active bank on a truly global level has been investigated by Kottasz et al. (2007). Based on interviews with 14 senior executives at Deutsche Bank, the analysis shows that the development of the company's corporate identity was the main motivation behind the creation of the art collection. In particular, the role of the collection is to transmit an image of prestige and exclusiveness. Even though financial institutions have often developed their collections to communicate an idea of exclusiveness and elitism, art collections can nowadays help promote other perceptions and lead to positive associations with attributes such as dynamism or innovation, thus strengthening a company's positioning. Banks also promote their collections by organizing public and private events. These events can be seen as a relational marketing tool used to establish a sustainable privileged relationship with stakeholders by involving them in ethical and social actions lead by the company (Rosé et al. 2006). For instance, Degroof Bank, Ethias and ING often organize events and private parties where both clients and artists are invited and where the artworks of their respective collections are exhibited (Lindenberg and Oosterlinck 2011). Boche (2010) refers to the interaction between brands and the arts using the term "Artketing" and highlights the heterogeneous approaches by which luxury brands incorporate art within their communication activities. In this regard, the author distinguishes art collaborations at the corporate level (e.g. foundations, corporate collections, art patronage and sponsored exhibitions) from those at the brand level (e.g. co-created products in the form of limited editions). Against this background, arts-luxury brands collaborations can be interpreted as a co-branding of a luxury brand with a contemporary artist, a piece of art or an art institution. A review of the relevant literature suggests that the practice of integrating art into branding and marketing activities has been in existence for over a century (Bogart 1995). In the early part of the twentieth century, American companies first sought to commission or buy artwork for advertising purposes, as in the case of the Atchinson, Topeka and Santa Fe Railroad (Adamson 1994). Artistic advertising campaigns expanded in the 1930s, with companies such as Steinway & Sons and The Container Corporation of America commissioning artists to illustrate their brands. Subsequently, a tradition of commissioning artists to create advertisements to promote and to enliven a company began with American companies such as Steinway, Dole, and many others. In the book *Artists, Advertising, and the Borders of Art*, Bogart (1995) describes the history of artists being commissioned for commercial advertisements. Similar efforts to use art as a way of branding are seen today, with more emphasis than ever before being placed on art as a luxury commodity used to represent a brand. This has become especially prevalent in the luxury industries. According to Baumgarth et al. (2014), arts-luxury brands collaborations constitute a recurrent approach in the international luxury goods industry: around 16 % of luxury brands are currently, or have previously been, involved in collaborations of this kind. In most cases luxury brands cooperate with the visual arts (74 %) and these collaborations are predominately characterized by a limited duration (80 %). Analysis of the frequency distribution over time reveals that, even if the concept of arts-luxury brands collaborations does not represent a totally new phenomenon, this practice has grown in popularity since 2008 (Kastner 2014). The empirical study of Baumgarth et al. (2014) proves that arts-luxury brands collaborations do not represent a uniform strategy, but become manifest in three distinct types: arty limited edition, philanthropic collaboration and experimental collaboration. The different types of arts-luxury brands collaborations are undertaken for divergent reasons: the re-emphasis of exclusivity and scarcity for the arty limited edition, the attainment of social legitimization and recognition for the philanthropic collaboration, and the generation of creativity, newness and additional brand content for the experimental collaboration.

3 Integrating Art into Branding and Marketing Activities

Arts in business can be a powerful means to develop an organisation and to increase its capacity to create value. As a consequence, artists and businesses are discovering the benefits of developing partnerships (Schiuma 2009). There are a number of key reasons for engaging in cultural partnerships. For many companies, it is simply the case that there is a natural fit between their brand and the arts. For others, the attraction is that the arts are forward-thinking and mould-breaking. It is beneficial to be associated with these qualities that commercially translate into the perception of being trend-setting. According to Chin-Tao Wu (2002), a peculiar form of collaboration between art and business occurs when companies make their spaces available to host public exhibitions and cultural events, or when companies give life to exhibition spaces that they manage themselves within their own working environments, thus becoming included alongside art galleries and museum spaces in lists of artistic events compiled by the specialized press. In this way, art can become a communication strategy that strongly characterizes corporate image, able to enrich a company's products and brand with spiritual values. On the communication front, the realization of an artistic project may have different purposes. It can set the firm apart from the competition and position it uniquely, as in the case of Absolut Vodka, whose product personality has become inseparable from contemporary art. More than 10 years' partnership with some of the most creative and well-known contemporary artists, who one by one have been asked to work on the now famous Absolut bottle, has transformed the product into a real object of experimentation (Zorloni 2013). Cultural investment can assist with launching new products through the direct collaboration of artists in studying and creating new product lines. This is the case with LVMH, which over the past 14 years has developed a multifaceted sponsorship strategy targeted at culture, collaborating with Takashi Murakami, Richard Prince, Yayoi Kusama and Jake and Dinos Chapman to produce limited-edition Louis Vuitton goods. These co-branding collaborations have resulted in increased audience numbers for arts organizations hosting Takashi Murakami, Richard Prince, Yayoi Kusama and Jake and Dinos Chapman exhibitions and increased revenues for Louis Vuitton. In contrast to Louis Vuitton, which maintains its contemporary relevance by periodically inviting artists to reinterpret their products, Hermès favours purely artistic collaborative projects in which its products and the artist's presentation of them engage in a dialogue. In 2008, the Austrian artist Erwin Wurm created a series of incongruous and witty photographs, entitled *Monde Hermès*, depicting people engaging with Hermès products in the style of his *One Minute Sculpture*. These photographs were conceived purely as artistic works and not as eventual promotional material, and were exhibited in Hermès stores alongside surreal sculptures such as a mirrored leg dressed in clothing and shoes (Smith et al. 2013). Cultural investment is also seen as being helpful for brands that are entering a new market and need to gain the interest and attention of new targets. This is the case of ZegnaArt, that has partnered museums in India, Turkey and Brazil to improve its international visibility and to attract a younger audience to the brand.[1] Finally the realization of an artistic project can maintain the loyalty of existing customers by providing a positive brand experience. Illy is an example of a company that has chosen to communicate its values through the creative potential of art. Since 1992, its ambitious project concerning the coffee it produces has involved some of the most significant contemporary figures, of the calibre of James Rosenquist, Mimmo Paladino, Sandro Chia, Jeff Koons and Robert Rauschemberg. In this way the product has been rendered recognizable, presented as expressing an idea of taste and refinedness. The Illy collection of cups and saucers, which are only on sale for short periods, and in limited series, have become true collectors' items, with the capacity to immediately identify the product with the image projected by the company (Zorloni 2013). The execution of a cultural project needs to be easily understood by the target audience and must reflect the style or values of the brand. Within the visual arts scene it is possible to identify three macro-categories to which specific values correspond; the latter are required to be consistent with the identity, mission, objectives and target of the sponsoring company (Bondardo 2004). These categories are:

Ancient Art includes artistic expressions related to ancient painting and traditional plastic arts. A company that chooses to invest in this area transmits values that speak of universality and tradition and focuses on a mode of communication allowing the company to reflect the prestige of works of art by great masters, or the authority of the cultural institution supported. In terms of investment, the company must have a medium-high budget, which can be translated into sponsorship, partnership or corporate collections initiatives.

Contemporary Art a language including artistic expressions of contemporary culture is attractive to companies that have a limited budget and wish to communicate values that speak of modernity, openness, courage, and tolerance of diversity. A company that chooses to invest in this area demonstrates attentiveness to young emerging artists and more generally to the evolution of trends in the expressive and therefore social field, testifying to its ability to look ahead.

Photography increasingly considered a form of contemporary art, photography is able to communicate with a larger and more diversified audience. Indeed, unlike contemporary art, it is a form of expression that can be appreciated without sophisticated knowledge of the field. A company that chooses to invest in this area conveys values that speak both of realism and poetry. Projects can range from the simple sponsorship of an exhibition, to the promotion of a contest, to editorial production, to the realization of multimedia installations (Table 1).

---

[1] http://www.zegnart.com/.

Table 1 Art and characteristics of the offer system

	Contemporary art	Photography	Ancient art
Values expressed	Openness, dynamism, innovation	Sophistication, style, class	Durability, reliability, stability
Personality	Advanced, dynamic, trendy	Modern	Classic, traditional
Opportunity	Launch of new products	Positioning on new markets	Corporate campaign

Source: personal elaboration

4 Arts-Fashion Brands Collaborations

Since the turn of the new millennium, the fashion luxury industry has increasingly looked to the art world for inspiration. Some of the larger fashion brands have taken a philanthropic approach, building relationships with artists by establishing foundations in support of the arts, or by funding projects and exhibitions independent of their own businesses. Other brands have incorporated the fine arts directly into their products, inviting individual artists to collaborate (Smith et al. 2013). One of the first collaborations between fashion and the arts date back to the 1920s and 1930s when Italian designer Elsa Schiapparelli worked with Surrealists such as Jean Cocteau and Salvador Dalì to generate new creative ideas for her clothing designs. Later, in the 1960s, Yves Saint Laurent designed a collection of clothes inspired by Piet Mondrian, printing Mondrian's famous multi-coloured rectangles onto his dresses. Yves Saint Laurent was also noted as using Van Gogh and Picasso's paintings as inspiration for various jackets and gowns exclusive to the line. However the collaboration between fashion and the arts can be considered a relatively young phenomenon that was only triggered in 1997 when Marc Jacobs initiated several high-profile collaborations with contemporary artists. In order to explore the adoption of arts within the fashion industry we will use a conceptual framework based on two organizing dimensions: the frequency with which organizations link themselves to the arts and the role of arts within the organization.

Frequency Arts-fashion brands collaborations can be either limited or unlimited in terms of duration. They can take on the form of temporary projects, which are designed in such a way that their end is foreseeable, or are organized so that their particular raison d'être does not imply their imminent end and may signal a long-term marketing strategy, of which the arts are a constituent and identity-forming part. This attribute shows the extent to which arts collaborations are initiated randomly or, in contrast, represent a long-term strategy pursued by the luxury brand (Kastner 2014). In terms of duration, there are three main forms of arts collaborations: art intervention, art project, and art programme (Schiuma 2009).

Business Purpose A work of art can play different roles within an organization and can be adopted for diverse business purposes. When a business supports the arts apart from its core offerings, either through financial contributions (direct giving, sponsorships) or non-financial support in various capacities (serving on boards), the business embraces art as a cause (Gilmore et al. 2009). On the other hand, when a company uses various art concepts or specific artistic projects to enhance the performance of their business enterprise, art acts as a marketing tool. To clarify both the typology and the specific characteristics of arts-fashion collaborations, we outline prototypical cases for each dimension.

4.1 Art Intervention

An intervention is the kind of art collaboration performed within a limited time frame, usually from 2 to 3 weeks, and it works towards a specific operative goal. This kind of initiative tends to take the form and function of a workshop or a commission of a work of art. Spearheaded by Doris and Donald Fisher's commitment to contemporary art, in 2008 the Gap commissioned, 13 artists, including Chuck Close, Jeff Koons, Kiki Smith, Cai Guo-Qiang, Barbara Kruger and Sarah Sze, to design limited edition t-shirts. The Gap worked in close partnership with the Whitney Museum of American Art and Art Production Fund to create the collection with the 13 artists, who were all previous Whitney Biennial participants, and financed a nationwide, 2-week advertising campaign to support the initiative during the 2008 Whitney Biennial.[2]

4.2 Art Project

An art collaboration takes the form of a project when the duration of an initiative is characterised by a set of integrated and coordinated interventions, planned and programmed over a period of time to achieve a business performance objective. The focus of a project tends to be the production of an output; that is, the realisation of a work of art that is either tangible or intangible in nature. This is the direction in which Hugo Boss has been moving, having sponsored a contemporary art prize since 1996. Now in its 12th year, the Hugo Boss Prize is a $100,000 grant and solo exhibition at the Guggenheim New York that is awarded to a mid-career contemporary artist. The purpose of the award is to bolster the Hugo Boss image and brand within the arts community and appeal to the customer with an interest in luxury, art and in aesthetic values. The close relationship between art and fashion is increasingly reflected in the built environment. Luxury fashion brands now regularly

---

[2] http://gapinc.com/content/gapinc/html/media/pressrelease/2008/med_pr_Gapartisteditions051508.html.

collaborate with award-winning architects to create unique retail stores, art museums and temporary structures to exhibit their goods. Chanel is an example of a company that has chosen to communicate its values through the creative potential of art and architecture. In 2008, Karl Lagerfeld commissioned architect Zaha Hadid to create a futuristic exhibition pavilion to exhibit 20 artists' tributes to the 50th anniversary of Chanel's 2.55 quilted handbag. Chanel Mobile Art began its tour in 2008 with stops in Hong Kong, Tokyo, and New York. Following the tour, the exhibition was dismantled and Chanel donated Hadid's mobile art pavilion to the Arab World Institute in Paris, where, since 2011, it has been used to showcase contemporary art from Arab countries.

4.3 Art Programme

When the initiative has a plurality of objectives and considers a set of different projects, although ascribable to the same strategic goal, the art collaboration takes on the nature of a programme. For Louis Vuitton, the use of art can be evident in select areas of a business and permeates the entire enterprise as an overall business model. Over the past 14 years, LVMH has developed a multifaceted sponsorship strategy targeted at culture with notable initiatives such as the restoration of the North Wing of the Palace of Versailles and the LVMH Young Artists Award. However, LVMH's most high-profile arts engagements are the collaborations with Takashi Murakami, Richard Prince and Yayoi Kusama to produce limited-edition Louis Vuitton goods. Its involvement in the arts intensified when in 2006 it opened a new art space, the Espace Louis Vuitton, on the seventh floor of its building on the Champs-Elysees in Paris, where it holds regular exhibitions of mostly contemporary art three times a year. With the opening in 2015 of the Louis Vuitton Foundation for Creation designed by Frank Gehry in Paris's centrally-located Jardin d'Acclimatation, LVMH is pushing the boundaries of art and fashion further than anyone else has so far dared to do. Unlike its commercial competitor Louis Vuitton, which has centred most of its art activities in Paris, the luxury house Hermès, although based in Paris, has devoted its energy and art resources to its Asian stores. It has specifically designed built-in art and cultural facilities within the shopping complex of its two flagship stores, Maison Hermès in Tokyo (opened in 2001) and in Seoul (2006). This includes in both cases a cutting-edge art gallery and an exhibition space. While the Tokyo store, designed by renowned architect Renzo Piano, has an extra facility, *Le Studio Hermès*, for film screenings, the Korean store has initiated the Hermès Prize for Contemporary Korean Art (Wu 2010). Unlike Louis Vuitton, the artwork in the exhibitions at Hermès galleries possesses no connection to the Hermès brand, as the engagement of Hermès with the arts is about patronage, not marketing or co-branding.

4.4 Art as a Cause

A work of art can play different roles within an organization and can be adopted for diverse business purposes. When a business supports the arts apart from its core offerings, either through financial contributions (direct giving, sponsorships) or non-financial support in various capacities (serving on boards), the business embraces art as a cause (Gilmore et al. 2009). Such embracing of the arts serves the cause of both the arts and the business. In France, the company that is by far the most committed to contemporary art is Cartier, whose foundation possesses a collection of more than 1000 works by 300 artists, covering all media. Founded in 1984 by Dominique Perrin with the aim of promoting contemporary art in all its variety, the Cartier foundation is completely financed by the company of the same name, with an annual budget of around €4.6 million. On average it organizes around five exhibitions and purchases 15 new artworks per year. The collection attracts around 100,000 visitors yearly and contains works by Arman, César, Barceló, Barney, Orozco, and Sugimoto (Zorloni 2013). One distinct element of the Cartier collection, compared to other private collections, is the importance that the Cartier Foundation attaches to commissioning their own artworks. This commissioning, very often related to exhibitions that are to be held at the Foundation, can consist of a single work, a series of works or an entire exhibition, such as that by the American artist Sarah Sze. There is no link between the artworks commissioned by or in the foundation's collection and the Cartier brand. The brand is only alluded to in the organization name.

4.5 Art as a Marketing Tool

Finally, when a company uses various art concepts or specific artistic projects to enhance the performance of their business enterprise, art acts as a marketing tool. One company that has managed to make investment in art a cardinal point of its marketing strategy is Montblanc. The Montblanc Cultural Foundation has sponsored the Philharmonia of the Nations and the Prix Montblanc Award for classical music since 1995, alongside the 'New Voices Award' for singers, the Young Directors Project (a competition for theatre directors as part of the Salzburg Festival since 2002), and the Montblanc Arts Patronage Award since 1992. Art activities have also been incorporated into Montblanc's business practices. In 2002, Montblanc started its corporate collection of contemporary art, the Montblanc Cutting Edge Art Collection, which comprises more than 180 works. The idea was to commission international artists to interpret the Montblanc's logo using their own visual vocabulary, and thus to make the collection truly unique. The Montblanc Cutting Edge Art Collection is usually showcased at the company's Headquarters in Hamburg, at the Montblanc Pelleteria in Florence, and the Montblanc watch manufactory in Le Locle. There, the artworks are exhibited in the production areas, hallways, conference rooms, as well as in the cafeteria, and in the lobby. Montblanc has also arranged cultural events such as classical music

	Business purpose	Cultural purpose
Long-term commitment	Business collaboration	Foundations
Short-term commitment	Entertainment	Art Patronage

Fig. 1 Art positioning matrix. *Source*: personal elaboration

recitals, lectures, readings and theatrical performances for their employees in Hamburg. Another benefit that the 800 employees receive is the Montblanc Cultural Card which entitles them to an 80 % discount on any classical music or theatrical performance in Hamburg, a very substantial discount and an incentive designed to encourage their employees to become regular art-goers (Wu 2010). In order to assess the varying levels of engagement between fashion brands and culture, we have devised the Art Positioning Matrix. It has been built on the dimensions of the scale of commitment and business purposes (Fig. 1).

This matrix shows varying levels of engagement between brands and culture. These are:

- *Entertainment.* Business uses the arts for entertainment, either by giving employees benefits such as tickets for selected shows, performances and arts exhibitions in their leisure time, or by inviting artists into the company for performances at annual meetings, customer events or special occasions. This method is relatively easy to implement and requires no long-term commitment.
- *Business collaboration.* Business collaboration is established through a classic business relationship base between the artist and the brand. The artist commits to creating a product or a line for the brand for a generally determined time period and receives remuneration in recompense.
- *Art Patronage.* Patronage is the support, encouragement, privilege, or financial aid that an organization or individual bestows on another. Patrons operate as sponsors. Sponsorship of artists and the commissioning of artwork is the best-known aspect of the patronage system; in the history of art, arts patronage refers to the support that kings or popes have provided to musicians, painters, and sculptors. Many luxury brands such as Salvatore Ferragamo, Brioni or Breguet invest in artistic patronage in various fields such as contemporary art, heritage, dance, film, or photography (Chailan and Valek 2014).

- *Foundations*. A foundation is a legal category of nonprofit organizations that will typically either donate funds and support, or act as the source of funding for its own charitable purposes. A foundation's objective is the creation of general interest with a non-profit goal. Due to the strict parameters for its associated fiscal privileges, creating a foundation is complex and thus automatically implies long-term vision (Chailan and Valek 2014). World-renowned luxury brands such as Cartier and Louis Vuitton have created foundations.

At each level there is full commitment to and recognition of artistic input into the brand. However, the scale of commitment increases as the collaboration moves beyond mere entertainment or product enhancement. Daring sponsorship or the creation of an art foundation or museum represents a massive commitment from the brand. Correspondingly it can help to establish the brand within national or indeed international culture.

5   Conclusion

The aim of this study has been to examine the heterogeneous approaches by which luxury brands incorporate art within their communication activities. In this regard, this study has introduced a framework to show how successful brands take advantage of the unique characteristics of the arts and lay the foundations for a series of case studies analyses exploring the links between fine arts and fashion brands. The description of selected cases presented in this paper has shown that arts-fashion brands collaborations are both a popular and recurrent approach in the international fashion industry. Fashion houses' involvement in art can take various forms: firstly, by sponsoring art exhibitions at museums, including those that display clothes designed by celebrity designers; secondly, by organising contemporary art prizes administered by the companies, as with the Hermès Art Prize in Korea or the Hugo Boss Art Prize; thirdly, by providing gallery spaces managed by the companies or their associated foundations, such as the Cartier Foundation for Contemporary Art or the Hermès galleries in Tokyo and Seoul; and lastly, by establishing contemporary art collections, assembled by the companies or their foundations, for instance the Cartier Foundation for Contemporary Art or Montblanc's Cutting Edge Art Collection at its headquarters in Hamburg (Wu 2010). The close relationship between art and fashion is increasingly reflected in the built environment. Luxury fashion brands now regularly collaborate with award-winning architects to create unique retail stores, art museums and temporary structures to exhibit their goods. These architectural commissions are part of a wider twenty-first century trend in which large luxury fashion houses, such as Louis Vuitton, Chanel, Hermès, Gucci, Cartier and Montblanc are increasing their involvement in the art world both financially as patrons and creatively as collaborators (Smith et al. 2013). It can be concluded that, in the case of fashion brands, the practice of integrating art into branding and marketing activities is an important strategic brand management tool but does not represent a uniform strategy. However, some patterns were observed and these have enabled us to categorize the collaborations using two dimensions: the frequency with which organizations link themselves to the arts and the role of arts within the organization. The analysis resulted in the delineation of four main types of collaborations between fashion brands and art: entertainment, business collaboration, art patronage and foundations. However, the identified typology is only the first step towards a deeper understanding of collaborations between the arts and fashion brands. Further research projects could broaden the current view on arts collaborations by analyzing, for example, consumer perceptions of arts-luxury brands collaborations.

References

Adamson, J. (1994). *Art at the office: Corporate collecting in America, 1898-1994*. KPMG Peat Marwick Collection of American Craft Catalogue.

Bangle, C. (2001). The ultimate creativity machine: How BMW turns art into profit. *Harvard Business Review, 79*(1), 47–55.

Baumgarth, C., Lohrisch, N., & Kastner, O. (2014). Arts meet luxury brands. In B. Berghaus, G. Mueller-Stevens, & S. Reinecke (Eds.), *The management of luxury*. Philadelphia: Kogan Page.

Boche, G. (2010). *The artketing age of luxury*. Accessed March 23, 2015, from http://fblog.futurebrand.com/the-artketing-age-of-luxury/

Bogart, M. (1995). *Artists, advertising, and the borders of art*. Chicago: The University of Chicago Press.

Bondardo, M. (2004). Vademecum per investire in arte. In Osservatorio Impresa e Cultura (Ed.), *Impresa e arti visive*. Pavia: Ibis.

Chailan, C., & Valek, I. (2014). Preserving luxury exclusivity through arts. In B. Berghaus, G. Mueller-Stevens, & S. Reinecke (Eds.), *The management of luxury*. Philadelphia: Kogan Page.

Darso, L. (2004). *Artful creation: Learning tales of art in business*. Copenhagen: Samfundslitteratur.

Gilmore, J., Mermiri, T., & Pine, J. (2009). *Beyond experience: Culture, consumer and brand*. London: Arts & Business.

Kastner, O. (2014). *When luxury meets art. Forms of collaboration between luxury brands and the arts*. Wiesbaden: Springer Gabler.

Kottasz, R., Bennet, R., Savani, S., Mousley, W., & Ali-Choudhury, R. (2007). The role of corporate art collection in corporate identity management: The case of Deutsche Bank. *International Journal of Arts Management, 10*(1), 19–31.

Lindenberg, M., & Oosterlinck, K. (2011). Art collections as a strategy tool: A typology based on the Belgian financial sector. *International Journal of Arts Management, 13*(3), 4–19.

Martorella, R. (1990). *Corporate art*. New Brunswick, NJ: Rutgers University Press.

Rosé, J., Barthe, N., & Le Moigne, J. (2006). *Responsabilité sociale de l'entreprise: pour un nouveau contrat social*. Bruxelles: De Boeck.

Schiuma, G. (2009). *The value of arts-based initiatives*. London: Arts & Business.

Schiuma, G. (2011). *The value of arts for business*. Cambridge: Cambridge University Press.

Smith, M., Kubler, A., & Guinness, D. (2013). *Art/fashion in the 21st Century*. London: Thames & Hudson.

Witte, A., Dijksterhuis, E., Tegenbosch, P., Knoop, R., Hartog Jager, H., & Braak, L. (2009). *Corporate collections in the Netherlands*. Rotterdam: Nai Publishers.

Wu, C. (2002). *Privatising culture: Corporate art intervention since the 1980s*. London: Verso.

Wu, C. (2010). Catwalk to culture: How the fashion industry values art. In *UNESCO's Second world conference on arts education*. Seoul: UNESCO.
Zorloni, A. (2013). *The economics of contemporary art. Markets, strategies and stardom.* Heidelberg: Springer.

The Art Collector Between Private Passion and Philanthropy

Patrizia Sandretto Re Rebaudengo

1 Introduction

The collections I have chosen to include in this chapter are of different types: private collections, museum-collections, collections that operate under the legal status of a Foundation, be it civil, corporate or, in Italy, of banking origin. The study of their diversity in history, size, type, purpose and accessibility, allows me to propose and outline, in this introduction, a new form of contemporary art collecting. I will dwell in particular on three factors I think are distinctive of this new identity, which is already visible and active in the public sphere: the end of the anonymity that is traditionally associated with the private collection; participation in the life of art through the production of works; and the choice of connecting the collection to an exhibiting space that is open to visitors.

My approach to this matter is situated, it is the result of my own experience as a collector and president of Fondazione Sandretto Re Rebaudengo, which I founded in 1995 along with my family, and whose 20th year of activity we celebrated in 2015.[1] My viewpoint is the result of my familiarity with a particular community, and is shaped by direct knowledge of the national and international art scenes, and by being a member of the committees of major museums, such as the International

---

[1] For an in-depth account of the story and activity of the Collection and of the Foundation, I recommend referring to *Bidibidobidiboo. Works from Collezione Sandretto Re Rebaudengo*, Skira, Milan 2005 (Italian and English); Achim Borchardt-Hume (edited by), *Think Twice. Twenty Years of Contemporary Art from Collection Sandretto Re Rebaudengo*, catalogue of the exhibition, London, Whitechapel Gallery, September 25 2012—September 8 2013, Fondazione Sandretto Re Rebaudengo, Whitechapel Gallery, 2012; *Große Gefühle. Von der Antike bis zur Gegenwart/ Deep Feeling. From Antiquity to Now*, catalogue of the exhibition, Krems, Kunsthalle, 10 March—30 June 2013, Verlag für moderne Kunst Nürberg 2013.

P. Sandretto Re Rebaudengo (✉)
Fondazione Sandretto Re Rebaudengo, Via Modane, 16, Turin, Italy
e-mail: psrr@fsrr.org

Council of New York's MoMA and of London's Tate Gallery, the Leadership Council of New York's New Museum and the Advisory Committee for Modern and Contemporary Art of the Philadelphia Museum of Art. In these contexts I had the opportunity to meet and get to know a great number of collectors, exchange ideas with them, visit their collections, exhibiting spaces and foundations, and study their acquisition strategies and different cultural attitudes.[2]

While relationships among the actors of the art system are undoubtedly marked by competition, it is also true that there are exchange networks based on affinities and common goals, especially outside the sectors that are more oriented towards market and speculation. My imprint is deeply influenced by the fact that I belong to a collective history, that of collecting in my city. Ida Gianelli reconstructed this history in the exhibition *Collezionismo a Torino*, which she curated in 1996 in the rooms of Castello di Rivoli Museo d'Arte Contemporanea, where she was director at the time.[3] Of the six collectors invited I was the youngest, in terms of age and of collecting history, since I had only begun acquiring works 4 years before, in 1992. The works I chose to exhibit, all by women artists (Vanessa Beecroft, Mona Hatoum, Cindy Sherman and Rosemarie Trockel, among others[4]), were representative of trends that were atypical with respect to the local tradition, dominated by Arte Povera and Transavanguardia. They provided a gender-themed point of view and a glimpse of the main emerging scenes, revealing the farsightedness of Gianelli's exhibition, which introduced viewers to an open, dynamic and, above all, plural *genius loci*.

I continued to believe in the importance of plurality and debate, and this led me to personally engage in the building of associations with a proper formal status. In 2008 I was among the founders of FACE—Foundations of Arts for Contemporary Europe, along with the Ellipse Foundation of Cascais, Portugal, La Maison Rouge—Fondation Antoine de Galbert of Paris, Magasin 3 Stockholm Konsthall of Stockholm, and DESTE Foundation of Athens. The purpose of this group, which was officially launched and presented in Brussels in the buildings of the European Parliament, is to provide exchange among institutions which belong to its five member states, and which possess a contemporary art collection as well as

---

[2] Since 2014 I have been conducting interviews with collectors for "How To Spend It", Italian edition published by "Il Sole 24 Ore" of the "Financial Times" magazine. Collectors I have interviewed include: Dakis Joannou, Ingvild Goetz, Juan and Pat Vergez, Uli Sigg, Fusun Eczacibasi, Thomas Olbricht, Francesca von Habsburg, Myriam and Amaury de Solages, Paloma Botin, Norah and Norman Stone, Sevda Elgiz.

[3] The exhibition included works from the collections of Gemma De Angelis Testa, Eliana Guglielmi, Corrado Levi, Marcello Levi, Marco Rivetti and my own collection. I. Gianelli (ed.), *Collezionismo a Torino*, catalogue of the exhibition, Rivoli (TO), Castello di Rivoli Museo d'Arte Contemporanea, February 15—April 21 1996, Charta, Milan 1996.

[4] In addition to the artists mentioned, the show featured works by Angela Bulloch, Katharina Fritsch, Dominique Gonzalez-Foerster, Zoe Leonard, Eva Marisaldi, and Andrea Zittel. See I. Gianelli, *Collezionismo a Torino* ...cit., pp. 68–77, 80.

an exhibition space open to the public.[5] I value this model greatly, and I have tried to introduce it in my country, starting with a discussion of public and private policies in matters of culture, and to adapt it to the Italian situation: in September 2014, in Turin at Fondazione Sandretto Re Rebaudengo, we founded the Comitato Fondazioni Arte Contemporanea, of which I am President, and which includes 15 Foundations that operate on the whole national territory, from East to West, from North to South.[6] Conceived as a network to share our missions, methodologies, strategies and critical issues, the Committee first of all undertook to initiate a dialogue with the Public sector, which in June 2015 led to the signing of a Memorandum of Understanding with MIBACT—Ministero dei Beni e delle Attività Culturali e del Turismo, the Italian Ministry of Cultural Heritage and Activities and Tourism.

Today the "new central role" of collectors, their strategic position in the art sector, is an accepted fact: "new actors (...), have moved—in the space of a few years—from a somewhat snobbish attitude, an almost hidden, backstage activity, to center stage", as we read in the introduction to *Collezionare contemporaneo*, a collection of interviews with 40 Italian and foreign collectors, edited in 2008 by Andrea Bellini,[7] now director of the Centre d'Art Contemporain Genève. Aside from the vogue and spectacular associated with it, I think the centrality of this role points to a process of transition, whereby the collection moves from the traditional private domain to a dimension of social visibility, which results in the collector becoming a public figure. A true metamorphosis, if we think of the set of ideas that

---

[5] FACE produced an important exhibition, based on the sharing of all collections under the title *Investigations of a Dog. Works from the FACE collections*, which travelled to all five collection locations between October 2009 and October 2011. The show was the result of a joint curatorship, which brought together the artistic directors, and other professionals, of all five foundations: Nadja Argyropoulou (DF), Alexandre Melo (EF), Francesco Bonami and Irene Calderoni (FSRR), Paula Aisemberg and Noëlig Le Roux (LMR), Tessa Praun (M3).

[6] Comitato Fondazioni Arte Contemporanea, founded in Turin on September 22, 2014, consists in Fondazione Brodbeck (Catania), Cittadellarte-Fondazione Pistoletto Onlus (Biella, Turin), Fondazione Giuliani per l'Arte Contemporanea (Rome), Fondazione Memmo—Onlus (Rome), Fondazione Mario Merz (Turin), Fondazione Antonio Morra Greco (Naples), Nomas Foundation Onlus (Rome), Fondazione Pastificio Cerere (Rome), Palazzo Grassi—Punta della Dogana—Pinault Collection (Venice), Fondazione Antonio Ratti (Como), Fondazione Pier Luigi e Natalina Remotti (Camogli, Genua), Fondazione Sandretto Re Rebaudengo (Turin), Fondazione Spinola Banna per l'Arte (Poirino, Turin), Fondazione Nicola Trussardi (Milan), Fondazione VOLUME! (Rome). President: Patrizia Sandretto Re Rebaudengo, Fondazione Sandretto Re Rebaudengo; Vice President: Giovanni Giuliani, Fondazione Giuliani per l'Arte Contemporanea; board of directors: Maurizio Morra Greco, Fondazione Antonio Morra Greco, Beatrice Trussardi, Fondazione Nicola Trussardi, Martin Bethenod, Palazzo Grassi—Punta della Dogana—Pinault Collection; General Secretary: Riccardo Rossotto, R&P Legal.

[7] The introduction, entitled *La nuova centralità del collezionista tra passione, speculazione e spirito messianico*, appears in A. Bellini (ed.), *Collezionare contemporaneo*, jrp/ringier, 2008, p. 4. Published in coincidence with the 15th edition of Artissima, the volume reflects the international policy of the Turin art fair and of its host program for 200 top collectors, who visit each year from all over the world.

have come to characterize the centuries-old tradition of bourgeois collecting, such as secrecy, possessiveness, anonymity, protection of the identity of the owner and of the owned works and objects. This transformation is the product of a process that developed in the past decades, and has its roots in the expansion of the art scene, and in the higher spatial and temporal concentration of events like biennials and fairs which, has art historian Julie Verlaine noted, have changed the geography of art and its market, leading to a new conception of the relationship between collectors and gallery owners.[8] Starting from the 1970s in Europe (with Kunstmarkt Köln in 1967, followed in 1968 by Prospect in Düsseldorf, and then Art Basel in the spring of 1970), again according to Verlaine, fairs have brought about a radicalization of the 'contiguity effect',[9] in that they free the acquisition of art from the local markets and spread it across a global, intensive and highly specialized space, which also ultimately functions as a stage, a place where decisions, choices, contacts and transactions achieve public resonance. Significantly, it is precisely in this space that contemporary art collectors have spoken up, when asked to talk about themselves, to exchange views with their peers, and to reflect, along with curators and museum directors, on the trends, phenomena and changes of contemporary art—as can be seen from the list of topics proposed each year at the *Collectors Focus* promoted by Art Basel in its three locations: Basel, Hong Kong and Miami Beach.[10]

While the modern art collector participates in cultural life by granting loans to exhibitions (and even today prefers to remain anonymous), the paradigm of involvement that characterizes major collectors of contemporary art is the support they give to the production of works, especially when the artists participate in exhibitions organized in institutional and public venues. The Biennials and Documenta Kassel are the most prestigious settings for this type of sponsoring, since they guarantee acknowledgement and international notoriety to collectors, linking their image to an idea of active patronage. This patronage takes the form of participation in the careers of artists, to the process of creation and production of works and,

---

[8] Julie Verlaine, *Femmes collectionneuses d'art et mécènes de 1880 à nos jours*, Hazan, Malakoff Cedex 2013, p. 217. The author provides a historical overview of collecting from a gender perspective, with thematic sections and a focus on women collectors, from Isabella Stewart Gardner to younger generation figures. Julie Verlaine dedicated one chapter of her book to me, reconstructing my story under the title *Patrizia Sandretto Re Rebaudengo. Instituer l'art contemporain*, pp. 255–263.

[9] *Ibidem*.

[10] *Collectors Focus* is part of the *Conversations* program organized by Art Basel in its three venues, Basel, Hong Kong and Miami Beach. Addressed to major collectors, each year it focuses on different topics, some of which are rather specific like *Collecting New Media* (Basel 2013), while others pertain more to the global system, such as *Asia's New Private Institutions* (Basel 2012), *The Asia Pacific Region* (Hong Kong 2013), *Trans-Pacific Collecting* (Hong Kong 2015), *Art Basel Miami Beach and South Florida: A Decade of Transformation* (Miami Beach 2011), *Latin America: The Collector as Catalyst* (Miami Beach 2010); yet other ones are strategic and general, such as *Patronage and Politics* (Basel 2011) and *Cross Cultural Colleting* (Hong Kong 2014), or concentrate on significant figures, as in the case of the Conversation in *Honor of Giuseppe Panza di Biumo* (Basel 2010).

more generally, it presupposes a direct engagement in the cultural world, through various project typologies and expressions, and should have a positive effect on society. The role of producer is one of the key elements in creating an updated map of the mechanisms and relationships that govern the sophisticated, multi-faceted ecosystem of art: if we just take a look at the colophons and tables of contents of major exhibition catalogues, we will realize how collecting and private foundations occupy a strategic position next to public and government bodies, businesses, corporations, banks, academic and research institutions involved in the production of works. A true constellation, in which the traditional boundaries between public and private have become less clear-cut, in what Verlaine describes as 'porosity' of several missions, which however share one common ambition—that of promoting art and artists.[11] The most recent example of this (chronologically) is the 56th Venice Biennale, curated by Okwui Enwezor, where this collective effort, revolving around individual works and national Pavilions, reached a significant degree of complexity—and I would like to emphasize the fact that Fondazione Sandretto Re Rebaudengo was part of this system along with, among the other interviewees, the Aïshti Foundation—Tony and Elham Salamé Collection of Beirut.[12]

The third factor in the evolution of collecting is interwoven with the creation of exhibiting spaces that are open to the public. The range of solutions here is very broad, and the present collection of ten interviews is meant to reflect this variety, documenting the missions and strategies that lead to the various typologies. The exhibition is often a point of entry, or a starting point. In my own experience, even before I instituted Fondazione Sandretto Re Rebaudengo and opened its two permanent venues of Guarene d'Alba and Turin, I felt the need to test the validity of my choices in the display itself. The earliest exhibitions, in 1995, gave me a chance to clarify and consolidate the focus lines that guided my interests back then: I was attracted to an emerging scene, and the result was *Arte inglese oggi nella raccolta Re Rebaudengo*, which was first displayed in an industrial space near Torino, and then at the Galleria Civica in Modena.[13] I was also attracted to the photography medium as reworked by artists, and this was explored in *Campo*, an open show at the Corderie dell'Arsenale in Venice,[14] curated by Francesco Bonami, who then went on to become artistic director of my Foundation.

---

[11] Julie Verlaine, *Femmes collectionneuses…* cit., p. 221.

[12] See *La Biennale di Venezia. 56. Esposizione Internazionale d'Arte. All the World's Future*, edited by Okwui Enwezor, exhibition catalogue, Marsilio Editori, Venice 2015. Fondazione Sandretto Re Rebaudengo, Turin, contributed to the production of the work of Jason Moran and Jason Moran & Alicia Hall Moran (p. 616) and to the Italian Pavilion, curated by Vincenzo Trione (Vol. 2, p. 96); the Aïshti Foundation—Tony and Elham Salamé Collection, Beirut—Lebanon, contributed to the works of artists Jumana Emil Abboud (p. 604), Mounira Al Solh, Walead Beshty (p. 605), Inji Efflatoun (p. 610), Isa Genzken (p. 612), Joana Hadjithomas & Khalil Joreige (p. 613).

[13] *Arte inglese oggi nella raccolta Re Rebaudengo Sandretto*, exhibition catalogue, Modena, Palazzina dei Giardini, Galleria Civica di Modena, May 21—July 30 1997, Mazzotta, Milan 1997.

[14] *Campo*, Venice, Corderie dell'Arsenale, Turin, Sant'Antonino di Susa, September 19—December 30 1995, Malmö, Malmö-Konstmuseum, February–March 1996, Allemandi & C., Turin 1995.

The display is the typical way of opening the collection to possible interpretations, in a twofold direction: one which centers on the involvement of curators, and another one which looks at the relationship with visitors. The collection continues to produce meaning in the 'mental space' of those who have built it, to use Enea Righi's vivid image. It is a 'material biography' of its (male or female) author, as Julie Verlaine noted.[15] At the same time, it can become an extraordinary source of experiences, reflections and shared projects. The structures produced by an individual undertaking—collections, private museums, foundations—tend to mirror the personality and interests of their creators, in terms of both artistic specialization and organization, good practices and reception of visitors, which are taken as a playfield for experiments that in some cases are more innovative, flexible and dynamic than those taking place in the public sector. So, while in Fondazione Sandretto Re Rebaudengo the theme of education has an absolutely central role, as have cultural mediation and professional training, the Salsali Private Museum—SPM of Dubai hosts a specially designed collectors center; the Rubell Family Collection of Miami promotes internship programs and partnerships with local schools, while in Italy, in Turin, Fondazione per l'Arte Moderna e Contemporanea—CRT acquires works to be added to the permanent collections of GAM—Galleria Civica d'Arte Moderna e Contemporanea di Torino and of Castello di Rivoli Museo d'Arte Contemporanea, and promotes programs aimed at developing the local art system with projects on education, professional training and artist mobility.

As the gallery owner, and great collector Ingvild Goetz wrote: "I believe that the private collection, if one feels the responsibility to make it publicly accessible, should take on the role that museums can no longer maintain. (...). A museum should bring together representative works, while a collector can present a concept—and it is interesting to show this concept to the public."

The questions I asked in the following ten interviews[16] are formulated in such a way as to shed light on the evolution of collecting, which still revolves around the conceptual, and formal, public/private pair. My intent is to document, through significant experiences, the ethics, approaches, and structures, through which the ideas of passion and philanthropy express and manifest themselves today. I have used a single question list, with a few variations depending on the interviewee, or to follow the topics that emerge from the discussion, welcoming with equal interest both complex narratives and short, concise answers.

---

[15] Julie Verlaine, *Femmes collectionneuses...* cit., p. 255.

[16] Interviews have been taken in 2015.

2 Enea Righi Collection

Enea Righi was born in 1956 and lives in Bologna. He works in a major industrial group as an Executive Vice President, and is a member of the Board of Directors in several companies associated to the Group. He has been a collector for 30 years now, and was a member of the Administrative Board of the Modern and Contemporary Art Museum of his city. Interview with Enea Righi.

Patrizia Sandretto Re Rebaudengo *When and why did you start collecting art?*

Enea Righi I cannot remember ever being particularly fond of collecting. I have always had a pragmatic approach to life, even during adolescence, which did not leave much room for an intimate relationship with objects. It was only later that I became curious about the intrinsic value of the art object, the need to have an intimate exchange with it, and the desire to possess it.

PSRR *What is the main focus of your collection? Is it organized according to specific subjects (chronological, thematic, by medium or trend, etc.) or does it grow with no particular constraints?*

ER My collection did not originate in any specific idea, but grew naturally along with my taste and personal experiences. Today I can identify a clear, coherent line, which revolves around such themes as the body, identity, and political and social engagement. However, I find it limiting to build a collection around a theme, partly because art is a life experience, and as such cannot be reduced to a single topic. This is why my collection is developing on its own—by increasing the number of works for each single artist, on the one hand, but also by paying special attention to young artists from emerging countries, and finally by rediscovering the work of historical artists who were forgotten by the art market, but have now luckily been rescued by some young curators. This choice may have something to do with my tendency to shy away from speculation and the frustrating oversupply of mediocre artists. This attitude is part of my personality.

PSRR *Some people maintain that the need to collect has to do with the affirmation of one's own self, and therefore a collection expresses the personality of the collector. Do you agree?*

ER A collection should represent the collector's vision, and if it has to survive in the long run it should be the compendium of a personal take on history. If it's not so, then the collection becomes nothing but a sort of anonymous catalog, just irresponsible, pointless accumulation.

When I have the pleasure of visiting a private collection, what I want to do is find the spirit of those who have built it, find it even in the mistakes, I want to feel the same emotions as them. Unfortunately, this only happens rarely.

PSRR *Do you also commission works? How would you describe your relationship with the artists whose works you collect, or whom you have asked for works?*

ER I believe in the role of the collector as an active protagonist at this moment in history, which sees the public sector retreat in favor of the private sector, especially in the domain of economy. Whenever possible, I choose to collaborate with the public system, in particular with the institutions whose projects are more attuned with my way of looking at art. This has resulted in a series of past projects, and others which are still in progress, and which have started a real partnership with young curators and museum directors. What I do is I simply share a project I like. I am not interested in exercising any power in art. My role is simply to support institutional projects or events such as Documenta or the Biennials, so I do not commission works directly from the artists.

On the other hand, I am not at the forefront of the art scene with a foundation of my own, because I do not believe in it would not have a positive impact on the level of culture, so I prefer to invest in the public system, which today is going through a crisis, because it invests more on the soul of citizens than on their actual, everyday needs.

PSRR *Do you select the works personally or with the help of an art advisor?*

ER I am not interested in collecting works based on the choices of an art advisor or curator, or because they feature prominently in specialized magazines. It is just a collection of works that cannot find a new interpretation other than the idea of the artist who created them.

PSRR *In what kind of space is your collection displayed or stored?*

ER The space for a collection is a mental space, it has nothing to do with logistics. Limitations in space are limitations in collecting. What was important in my case was the relationship I have established with various museums, which gave me the opportunity to overcome this issue through deposits, and to agree long-term loans. The collection was exhibited in museums in Italy and France so far, next up is a show in Venice. I can tell you the title in advance: *Quand fondra la neige ou ira le blanc*, where white, or blank, is intended and a concept, in relation to a collection, so the question is: "What will be left of a collection in the future, when our day and age will have ended?". On this topic I will have a famous sixteenth century art historian write the introductory text, in order to understand what is left today of all the private collections that had been built in such a disciplined, enlightened way in that period.

PSRR *Which are your terms for lending works for exhibitions or museum deposits?*

ER As I have already mentioned, given my relationship with museums I always loan works if the concept of the exhibition interests me. The terms I set are the usual insurance covering guarantees, a condition report, and air conditioning. If the project is particularly bold, I can take risks, too, as in the case of a show inside a prison that had been closed for 30 year in France, in Avignon, where climatic and environmental conditions were obviously not controllable. I love daring projects, if the end justifies them. It turned out that the show attracted 100,000 visitors, and not all of them were art enthusiasts, but also people who did not know about it and were intrigued by the idea of visiting an unusual space. This, too, is a smart way of encouraging people to approach contemporary art.

PSRR *What do you think about donating to museums?*

ER I have never thought about it. I think the Italian law does not make it easier since there are no tax breaks for donors. We'll see what the future holds, but I am still relatively young to consider this.

3 Sigg Collection

The Sigg Collection is the foremost and most comprehensive collection of Chinese contemporary art in the world, consisting of some 2,200 works dating from its beginnings in 1979 to today, across all media. Its purpose is to mirror the short history of Chinese contemporary art, since there is no such collection either in Mainland China or outside. In 2012, 1,463 works were donated and 47 works sold to M+ Museum of Visual Arts in Hong Kong. Interview with Uli Sigg.

Patrizia Sandretto Re Rebaudengo *When and why did you start collecting art?*

Uli Sigg As a student I got quite involved in contemporary art through a very knowledgeable friend, who took me along to exhibitions and talks. This was a revelation to me, after having grown up with some art from nineteenth century Romantic realism in our home, of which I never really took notice. A friend of a friend of mine went bankrupt—so I decided to buy, with my scarce funds at the time, one of his surrealist paintings by a local Swiss painter. To accept myself to now be a collector happened much later, when living in China.

PSRR *What is the main focus of your collection? Is it organized according to specific subjects (chronological, thematic, by medium or trend, etc.) or does it grow with no particular constraints?*

US In the nineties, upon renewed analysis of the Chinese art scene, I realized that nobody, neither institutions nor individuals, were collecting its contemporary art production in any other but a random way. So I decided for myself to close this gap that existed in the biggest cultural space of our world—what actually a national institution ought to do, but never did: to collect in a systematic way, mirroring the art production since 1979, the beginning of contemporary art in China, and across all media. For the encyclopedic nature of my collection, the works I choose must document something Chinese artists were concerned with at a certain moment in time. It therefore does not have to appeal to my personal taste. Still we cannot deny that subjective criteria also enter the validation process. Does the work have an adequate form? Should it rather be a video than a painting? Should the artist write a text rather than simply show us a small fragment of a lofty concept? Does the work have intensity, a certain energy, however calm it may appear, can it surprise us? And so on.

PSRR *Some people maintain that the need to collect has to do with the affirmation of one's own self, and therefore a collection expresses the personality of the collector. Do you agree?*

US Not in my case: it is much more based on my analysis that this collection just had to be done by someone, to preserve somewhere the ability to read the storyline of the history of Chinese contemporary art. And then collecting is one of my three ways to access China—besides that of a businessman setting up the first joint venture between China and the West, and the one provided by being a diplomat. And it is the most rewarding one when exploring my ultimate study object, which is China.

PSRR *Do you also commission works? How would you describe your relationship with the artists whose works you collect, or whom you have asked for works?*

US Where I at times may also be involved in the creative process together with the artist, such as a large, computer-designed painting with the artist Feng Mengbo, where we jointly tried to recreate the tradition of landscape painting in an innovative way, so that a nontraditional audience could be enticed into taking a new look at what they consider things hopelessly past.

PSRR *Do you select the works personally or with the help of an art advisor?*

US The major part I bought directly from artists, as I know probably more of them in person than anybody else. This becomes increasingly difficult since more and more artists are now bound contractually to galleries, so I now have to use also these conventional channels.

PSRR *In what kind of space is your collection displayed or stored?*

US Currently a major part is stored in Switzerland in a facility built for my needs, waiting for the completion of the M+ Museum in Hong Kong in 2018; many works are continuously travelling to various exhibitions; minor parts of course are in my home.

PSRR *Which are your terms for lending works for exhibitions or museum deposits?*

US Decisions regarding the works donated to M+ are now with the Museum, even though I still must physically handle the collection for them. As to my remaining part, I loan freely as I did promise when I bought from the artists, provided professional display standards are met.

PSRR What do you think about donating to museums?

US This has been the route for me to go. Already when putting together the collection I had the intention of bringing it back to China. After lengthy negotiations with Beijing, Shanghai, and the Ministry of Culture, I decided for the new museum M+, to be built in Hong Kong. It will be a world class institution, larger than MoMA or Tate. I am a fan of public institutions—in the end they will be the ones to last and they are not hostage to the taste and stamina (or lack thereof) of a single collector.

4   La Gaia Collection

La Gaia Collection has its beginnings in the early Eighties, born from the passion for art of Bruna and Matteo Viglietta. There are over 1,000 works of art in La Gaia Collection. The central part covers art from the early twentieth century through to the 1950s to then continue with a more remarkable group of works from the 1960s to the present day. These works of art have been collected without criteria or order, favouring no particular movement, creative approach, medium or generation, if not personal taste. La Gaia Collection's exhibition space is in Busca, Piedmont, Italy. Interview with Bruna and Matteo Viglietta.

Patrizia Sandretto Re Rebaudengo When and why did you start collecting art?

Bruna and Matteo Viglietta We started in the mid-1970s, when we began visiting art galleries, we were curious and interested in a world we did not know at all. With humility and eagerness to learn, we started collecting nineteenth and early twentieth century art, and then moved closer and closer to contemporary art, which today is our only interest as collectors.

Before that we used to collect carpets, glass objects, Vuitton chests… we have always loved to surround ourselves with beautiful things. With art we found that the idea of beauty and craftsmanship were no longer enough for us. We wanted to go further, get in touch with pure creativity, and address the issues of our time.

PSRR When did you decide to create your own museum? What are the main activities in it?

BMV The collection grew over time, and when there was no longer enough room on the walls and floor of our home, we started to fill a warehouse with crates. The stuff in the warehouse, too, grew disproportionately, along with our frustration for not being able to see and experience the works we had acquired. So we decided to create a space where we could finally display the works. The building is huddled against a hillside, on top of which stands our house. We wanted it to be as close as possible to where we live, so as to really be able to live immersed in our works: the two buildings are separated only by a stone alley.

The size is 3,400 square meters, which initially seemed far too big to be filled, but in fact turned out to be totally inadequate to contain our whole story as collectors, which has been going on for 40 years now! This is why we completely redesign the spaces each year, so that we can take new works out of the crates or reopen old ones, always trying to create a dialogue between past works and recent acquisitions.

Our museum, or so everybody calls it—now even we have started to think of it as such—is a completely private entity. We have never thought about turning the collection into a foundation, because we have always wanted to have total control over our choices and activities. We feared that a foundation would have somehow betrayed our freedom of action and even, maybe, the deeply instinctive and passionate nature of our collecting. This does not mean that our space is closed an inaccessible. On the contrary, there are many school classes that come and visit us, and we always welcome with great pleasure artists, curators, collectors and gallery owners. We are particularly proud of schools. It is very exciting for us to try and communicate with young people, stimulating their curiosity about a subject that is never even touched on in high school, stuck as we are in ministry curricula that hardly cover Pop Art. Sometimes these young people from academies, high schools and art schools do not come to us with great expectations, but we are sure that, when they leave, they will take home an unforgettable experience, regardless of whether they loved or hated what they saw and learned.

PSRR *What motivates two private collectors to enter the public sphere, share their own works with the community, spend time, energy and financial resources to support and promote art internationally?*

BMV I think what motivates us is again the need to share and discuss things, to avoid getting stuck in a self-referential discourse, which would ultimately turn out as unproductive. Contemporary art lives in the present time and feeds on it. How can we even think about not sharing it with the largest possible public? No doubt there is also a narcissistic side to this, although we are actually hardly interested in showing off. The opposite is true, and our natural shyness and the fact that we are no socialites, have not helped us in our career as collectors. Showing up at every opening can certainly help to consolidate your relational capital, which can be spent in negotiations, or can turn out to be helpful when you want to purchase works by very popular artists, as galleries usually require a sort of 'pedigree' of collectors (to make sure the collection itself is worthy of the work at hand). So the fact that we have always had little visibility was sometimes a drawback, which we had to overcome by establishing closer relationships with the professionals in the art system, so that they would understand that we had a genuine interest in the works and had no desire whatsoever to speculate on them.

PSRR *Why have you chosen to create a museum of your own, instead of donating your works to an already existing museum?*

BMV We chose to create our own museum because we have developed a sort of addiction to our collection. We cannot imagine having come this far and parting with works that have had such a special meaning for us, in each season of our life together. To us it would be like asking a mother to part with her son. Our relationship with the works is very intimate and, inevitably, very possessive. To say the truth, though, we would share part of our collection with some major Italian museums, even in the form of long-term loan. Only the circumstances have not been favorable enough so far. What it all comes down to is that our country certainly is no role model in these matters. Just think of Panza di Biumo and his story, which is still paradigmatic of this.

PSRR *What is the relationship between the collection and the museum?*

BMV As we mentioned, the collection is one, and our museum is the space where it resides, with a different display each year. We are the collection and the collection is entirely ours, there are no foundations, or other legal entities.

PSRR *Does the museum commission works from artists? And if so, does it produce works for its own exhibitions, or also for exhibiting events abroad? How would you describe your relationship with the artists whose works you collect, or whom your museum asks to create works, or invites to produce an exhibition?*

BMV Throughout the years we have received many proposals for sponsoring exhibitions, individual artist projects, biennials... Some of these we have accepted with great enthusiasm, as when we produced the monumental work of Gerard Byrne for the past edition of Documenta in Kassel. On that occasion we were motivated by our deep admiration for the curator, Carolyn Christov-Bakargiev, and for the artist, whom we already knew, since one of his video works was already in our collection. We did not know exactly what kind of work he would have come up with, but we trusted him completely and so made a 'blind' investment in this project. At the end we were completely satisfied with the result.

Other times we have produced individual works within a personal exhibition, as in the case of a video installation by Rä di Martino, for her solo show at the Museion in Bolzano, last year. On that occasion the artist contacted us directly and we purchased a work on a project basis, so as to allow her to make it, by compensating for budget limitations.

Yet other times we have supported artists for a long time. It is the case of the Masbedo, whom we met 13 years ago in Madrid and, after buying their first major video installation, we decided to help them regardless, without even analyzing each one of their projects, given the friendship we had with them. Our relationship with artists is primarily human. We appreciate creativity and genius, but in the end it all boils down to the person as a whole. So throughout the years the artists we have become close to are people who share a similar way of relating to life. By this I don't mean we share the same vision, but rather a positive, collaborative attitude, one that privileges substance over appearance, is direct and uninterested in society and public relations.

PSRR *Do you ever seek the help of curators and art advisors for exhibitions and for identifying works to include in your collection?*

BMV As we mentioned, our collection is us, both of us who, in the past 40 years, have pursued our own way in the research and knowledge of art, often choosing works instinctively, without mediation, without being influenced by the artist's CV or the list of collectors who had already included them in their collections. Because of this, our collection would never need an external advisor to guide us in making acquisitions, as is common today. Our collection reflects every inch of who we are, our weaknesses and idiosyncrasies, our contradictions and dark sides, so to speak. It is us, for better and for worse. Maybe we have made mistakes, but we achieved all of this with our efforts and in complete independence. Everyone who visits us can feel this, and I think they view it positively. They say that you can sense the authenticity of our experience, the sincerity of our evolution, the genuineness of our insane passion.

Thirteen years ago, when we started working on the museum project, we realized that we would indeed need help. So we found Eva Brioschi, a young art historian from Turin, who began by working on the archiving of works and has stayed with us ever since, accompanying us with her discreet presence. Eva takes care of displays under our direction, and in collaboration with Manuela Galliano, who has been our registrar for 7 years now. Last but not least, our 21-year-old niece Lucia, who is still uncertain about what to do in her future, comes to the collection on a regular basis to start 'breathing' the air of the art world. We'll see: the proof of the pudding is in the eating...

PSRR *What are the main problems that a non-profit organization faces in our Country?*

BMV Well, we are rather untypical. We are not exactly an institution, but a completely private organization, and as such we have never asked nor received anything from public administrations. What we would certainly like to see is a reduction in art taxation. Considering we are going through a global crisis, and given the government's draconian cuts to cultural budget, many artists and gallery owners are in deep trouble, not least because we have the same tax rate for art as for any other commodity. In the past few days the French government (which already applies a rate of just 7 % on any commodity, compared to our 22 %) has decided to lower the taxable income for artworks to just 5 %. This difference obviously makes our country a lot less competitive than our French cousins who, as usual, are proving to be much more farsighted than we are.

PSRR *Do you usually lend works for temporary or museum exhibitions? What are your loan terms?*

BMV We do loan works, but first we have to consider the cultural value of the exhibition project, and the security standards of the applicant institution. Our terms have to do with such aspects as the choice of the insurance company and of the company in charge of transport (with some of them we had permanent damage so we no longer work with them). Sometimes, when it comes to installing particularly complex works, we ask that the job be entrusted to Attitudine Forma (the team that mounts installations for Castello di Rivoli Museo d'Arte Contemporanea, Turin's GAM—Galleria Civica d'Arte Moderna e Contemporanea and other major museums). Other times we ask for a courier, for instance when we lent a 1964 painting by Vija Celmins, which went to Madrid last year, escorted by our Manuela.

5   Salsali Private Museum

Ramin Salsali was born in Tehran in 1964, he studied economics, strategic management and marketing with a focus on Industry Design, in Germany and England. He founded a specialized consulting company for innovative and green technologies for application in the field of the petrochemical industries. Later, he entered into real estate development with particular focus on the preservation of historical buildings. In November 2011, Ramin Salsali opened his private museum in Dubai. Salsali Private Museum (SPM) is the first Private Museum for contemporary art in the region. It shows Salsali's collection and hosts travelling exhibitions from around the world. Salsali's mission is to contribute to the development of art, culture and creative communities, support artists and promote the culture of collecting. Interview with Ramin Salsali.

Patrizia Sandretto Re Rebaudengo *When and why did you start collecting art?*

Ramin Salsali I always liked to collect. Art is my passion. It goes back to my childhood, when I started to collect toys. Not only my toys, but also the toys of my friends and brothers. My first collection consists in 800 Matchbox cars, which I have collected up to today! In my teenage years, I started collecting old Iranian stamps. Art followed at the age of 21, while I was studying in Munich. The first paintings I acquired were by Kiddy Citny, an artist and musician, who painted the Berlin Wall. Those pieces of the Wall are displayed today in public places in Berlin and in Museums.

PSRR *When did you decide to create your own museum? What are the main activities in it?*

RS Creating a museum for contemporary art was always one of my dreams. After the financial crisis in 2008 all projects such as Dubai Museum (Architect Rem Koolhaas) or Guggenheim (Frank Gehry) or National Museum (Norman Foster), or Louvre (Jean Nouvel) were postponed, so I decided to take the initiative and establish the first private Museum in the region, hoping that others would follow this path. Why should we always wait for the Government to promote such projects, while Dubai and the UAE accommodate the wealthiest Families and corporations? The main activity of the Museum is to display my collection while hosting other collections each year, and collaborating with other institutions such as Guggenheim/Deutsche Bank and Rolls Royce, to name a few.

PSRR *What motivates a private collector to enter the public sphere, share his own works with the community, spend time, energy and financial resources to support and promote art internationally?*

RS I believe in the social responsibility of all individuals and corporations to contribute to the development of creativity in their communities, by sharing an art collection with the public. Sharing a collection with a wider range of viewers is a pleasure. I hope it will have an impact and motivate others to follow in the same footsteps.

PSRR *Why have you decided to create your museum instead of simply donating your works to an already existing museum?*

RS First of all, my intention was to create a cultural institution in a city I admire for its development and positive impact on its inhabitants. Furthermore, due to the lack of a public museum, it was not possible to create a private-public partnership. Finally we need to support Art and Culture as part of our Eco-System, by going public.

PSRR *What is the relationship between the collection and your museum?*

RS Each piece in my collection is special and has a memory attached to it. My collection is not engineered, as some are, it is not an investment. I personally know many of the artists in my collection and their work continues to inspire me, and I want to share this passion with the public.

PSRR *Does the museum commission works from artists? And if so, does it produce works for its own exhibitions, or also for exhibiting events abroad? How would you describe your relationship with the artists whose works you collect, or whom your museum asks to create works, or invites to produce an exhibition?*

RS Yes! SPM has commissioned many art works and projects to the artists. Some of them have been shown in solo and group shows, such as Reza Derakshani, Amir Hossein Zanjani, Pantea Rahmani and Hazem Harb. As a collector and co-curator, I have a very close and, if necessary, critical relationship with my artists. I visit them in their studios or host them in my museum, turning it into their studio. However, I try not to interfere into their creative process.

PSRR *Do you ever seek the help of curators and art advisors for exhibitions and for identifying works to include in your collections?*

RS I rarely do, and only if I believe in their integrity. Some of them are little dictators and I like my freedom!

PSRR *What are the main problems that a non-profit organization faces in our Country?*

RS Lack of necessary support by governmental organizations. For example one of the most important measures would be to waive custom duties.

PSRR *What goals does your institution pursue and what are your criteria to evaluate its achievements?*

RS First I consider SPM as a catalyst for the evolution of the cultural process in the region.
    The difference between a private and a public museum is that a private museum enjoys maximum freedom to design its own program while a public museum is subject to restrictions in its creative process. A private museum can offer programs that a public museum would and could not do. The Salsali Private Museum sees itself as a cultural base and platform for both new and well-established collectors, and acts as a catalyst in breeding a new generation of collectors.
    We advocate support for collectors. SPM is indeed the first center for collectors in the world. We provide them with a whole range of free services.

PSRR *Do you usually lend your works to other museums for temporary exhibitions? What are your terms for a loan?*

RS Yes. We cooperate with other cultural entities such as museums. Of course we evaluate the program and the concept of each show, and get in touch with curators to understand the framework of our cooperation.

6 Collezione Maramotti

Collezione Maramotti is a private contemporary art collection which opened to visitors in 2007: it is located in the historical headquarters of Max Mara company, in Reggio Emilia. The permanent collection can be visited with free admission and upon booking, according to the wishes of the founder Achille Maramotti. It comprises a relevant selection of more than 200 works representing only a portion of the collection put passionately together in 40 years. The collection includes mostly paintings, but also sculptures and installations, made from 1946 till the present day, and presents pieces from the most significant artistic trends both in Italy and abroad from the second half of the twentieth century. More than 120 artists are represented with important works which at the time of their creation and acquisition had introduced elements of substantial innovation and experimentation in artistic research. For the most part, twenty-first-century works are not included in the permanent collection: specific exhibitions are dedicated to them in the rooms set for temporary shows, spaces where projects commissioned to international artists are also regularly exhibited. The artworks created for these exhibitions are acquired by the Collection, with the aim of merging acquisition policies with public showing. Interview with Marina Dacci, Director.

Patrizia Sandretto Re Rebaudengo How did you arrive at the decision to make the Collezione Maramotti an exhibition centre open to the public? And what was the driving force behind this project?

Marina Dacci Achille Maramotti began collecting contemporary art in the Sixties, and in the late Seventies had already indicated his desire to open up it to the public, for the pleasure of sharing it. Previously, the iconographic collection was not located in a single place: it was scattered between private homes, company offices and various storage facilities, though there had always been a lively, ongoing proclivity to exhibit new acquisitions in order to show them to employees (especially the creative staff) at the factory.

The family embraced this legacy, and the right opportunity came along when the Max Mara company moved to a new site, freeing up the spaces of the first plant, which dated back to the Fifties: this offered a way of bringing together the works as an organic whole in a place that had housed them in rotation since the beginning of the collection process. So there is also a reason that we could call "sentimental", since the space takes on a spirit of memory. Another significant factor is this family's approach to collecting art. It involves neither a compulsive appetite for possession nor a close connection to the idea of financial investment, but rather a sort of magnificent obsession with discovering something new and the pride and pleasure of sharing it. Once acquired, no work has ever been given away or sold, and I believe this demonstrates the strong ties between the works and the life story of the collector. So there's a certain approach to collecting, a sentimental factor, a logistical motivation and an integrated cultural use. There are multiple answers.

PSRR *What are the Collezione Maramotti's activities on the contemporary art scene?*

MD There are also multiple activities. Some are visible to the public and others are "back office", but just as important. We aren't a *Kunsthalle*, but since we have a major collection to manage and a large space that I would call akin to a museum (it has a permanent collection and also presents temporary projects and shows in an ongoing fashion), our activities are naturally carried out at different levels. They start with the conservation and maintenance of the works in collaboration with the appropriate professionals, then there's the question of loans, of keeping databases on the iconographic, bibliographic and archival resources, of the insurance, and of everything that has to do with asset management. The library is very important for us because we try to keep up with the activities of the artists that figure in the collection (who are quite numerous), continuing to add volumes and artist books: the latter are treated as works in their own right.

Moreover, there's the entire process of filing the materials that constitute the historical record of the interactions between the Collection and the artists in our archive. One shouldn't overlook the management of the space, which covers about 10,000 square metres, and the professional training of the staff that works there. Then there are myriad activities related to organization and communication, vis-à-vis the press (website, press folders, newsletters), visitors (access, visits), and the artists we work with (production of the shows and the connected books). Specifically, handling communication for a museum-like space means deciding how to compose and convey content through press folders, through the site and social networks, and through one-on-one contact. In a word: presenting our cultural identity in a coherent, consistent fashion. And then there is the production of the works, which is a considerable part of our responsibilities, because we never present "package" exhibitions; instead, we decide on the project with the artist, commissioning and underwriting the production of works and collaborating on the development of the show all the way to its installation, in addition to which there is the preparation of the catalogue or book to accompany the exhibition and the video to document it. Because every project is accompanied both by a documentation video and by a book, which before being handed over to the publisher for printing and distribution is conceived in-house by us with our graphic designer and with the artist.

The collection presents itself in a natural way to the outside world by making the permanent exhibit open to the public through prebooked visits, accompanied by dedicated museum personnel who act as "narrators" telling stories about the Collection. In addition to commissioned exhibitions and projects, we also organize open storage exhibitions in which we thematically show works in the collection that are not on permanent view; we produce events focused on the relationship between dance and the visual arts, with major site-specific performances in our spaces; we curate an annual show as part of Fotografia Europea, the photography festival held here in Reggio Emilia that is now in its tenth year; we collaborate on the Max Mara Art Prize.

Moreover, we occasionally organize exhibitions with material from our archive and library.

PSRR *How does the acquisition process work? Do you prefer to acquire finished pieces or to commission them?*

MD The projects we realize are commission-based, and end with the acquisition of the works for the permanent collection. This is another approach that is used alongside the acquisition of individual works through traditional channels (artist's studio, galleries, fairs, auctions).

With these projects, there's a "carte blanche" idea: we aren't buying an object, we're investing in the energy and explorations of an artist who is considered interesting for the Collection, without knowing beforehand what the final outcome will be. This is definitely a more organic and interesting way to build the collection. Our interactions with the galleries who represent the artists differ according to the type of agreement that the artists have with them. There are artists who are more closely bound by contract, and in this case we work through the gallery for the financial transaction, as is appropriate; others are free to take on projects independently and have direct transactions with us. We respect the rules of the market, and work in consonance with how the artists handle their relationship to the market and to their galleries.

PSRR *What is the relationship like between the MaxMara fashion label and the Collezione Maramotti?*

MD This collection belongs to a family, it's not a brand collection. Max Mara provides the exhibition space free of charge and allocates an annual quota to fund its activities (according to the programming and the management costs that are estimated each year), which makes it possible to provide services and activities to the public for free, but the company has no hand whatsoever in artistic decisions. For those there is an informal board made up of three siblings (the children of the founder Achille Maramotti) and a staff who works directly with them, on everything from the choice of the artists to the realization of shows and events.

The sole link between the company and the collection is the family, a subject that plays a double role: as collectors opening up a private space to the public, and at the same time, as owners of the company. And then there are the connections/collaborations between the company and the Collection. The most important is the Max Mara Art Prize for Women, a biennial award to support female creativity, for which Max Mara works in partnership with the Whitechapel Gallery and the Collezione Maramotti.

PSRR *So this is why even for the name of the collection, the reference chosen was not Max Mara but Maramotti*

MD Of course. Max Mara is a true empire and people tend to connect the art collection directly to the company brand. We ourselves give Max Mara a certain visibility by putting the company logo on our publicity materials, because in the end, that's where the financial resources supporting our activities come from. But that's very different from blending the identities together when it comes to the cultural aspect.

PSRR *And why is the prize named "Max Mara", on the other hand?*

MD The prize has a very different history, dating back to before the collection was opened to the public. It dates back to 2005, whereas the collection was opened at the end of 2007; the prize is biennial and is now in its fifth edition. It was established because the company wanted to offer opportunities for professional growth and connection to women artists, giving the winners a 6-month residency in Italy to help them get to know our culture and develop an artistic project.

At the time, a choice was made regarding the subject entrusted with ensuring artistic quality in the process of selecting candidates and awarding the prize, settling on the Whitechapel Gallery for a number of reasons: the historical characteristics of the gallery, which had been supporting female creativity since the Seventies, and the fact that Whitechapel is a highly reputable name in the contemporary art world. The jury panel changes with each edition, and its members are women with different professional roles in the art world (collectors, critics, journalists, gallery owners, artists). One does not apply for the prize; the jurists must present a selection of names they find particularly interesting and whose work they know in depth. The artists are not particularly young, but are usually mid-career: they've already travelled a clear path, but are not yet fully established artists. They have to be residents of the UK, but can be of any nationality. Once the winner is named, the Collection springs into action. The artist gets a 6-month residency in Italy, and we have the task of facilitating her contact with Italian culture, suggesting residency sites for the project, providing tutorship in the system of interaction and assisting with research aimed at the realization of the project. The project concludes with a double show at the Whitechapel Gallery, and with the Collection acquiring the work.

PSRR *What led the Maramotti family to decide against setting up a foundation?*

MD The legal form of a foundation has its advantages and disadvantages. On the one hand, a foundation can request and receive public funding, on the other it is subject to public supervision of its finances, and must balance its budget. In its operation, it must create the economic and financial conditions necessary to access outside funding. Since the Maramotti family was interested in preserving complete autonomy and independence regarding the Collection's management choices and financial decisions, it chose not to be bound by the legal restrictions of a foundation. So a limited company was set up and entrusted with managing and developing its assets. This company obviously has a budget, which is based on a provisional estimate made each year in accordance with the artistic programming. The company does not have a true commercial identity (it does not sell tickets and does not sell products or services): rather, it produces a cultural program that is underwritten by the family and by Max Mara. The budget that is assigned does not include artistic acquisitions, since the works are purchased directly by the collectors and then given to the company to manage. This choice allows for maximum freedom and fluidity in art acquisitions, which can vary from year to year without the need to balance the budget.

PSRR *What is your attitude about lending the works to other museums?*

MD We naturally have no problem lending works that are in storage rather than in the permanent collection. For instance, we recently loaned pieces to the MAGA in Varese and to the Musée de Saint-Etienne for the Gianni Caravaggio show, a work by Gennari to the Museo Marino Marini in Florence, and a video installation by Beatrice Pediconi to the Sequences festival in Reykjavik.

For works shown in the permanent collection, the situation is different: we only lend those for particularly important exhibitions, like those of the Guggenheim, the New Museum, Tate Gallery, or the Philadelphia Museum of Art, to name a few. Professionalism in handling and managing the works on loan is a delicate issue, and being moved is always stressful for artworks. Moreover, the permanent exhibition was carefully designed, and when all the selected works are present it offers viewers a complete vision of the collection's history.

PSRR *For the conservation of the works, do you have an in-house staff or do you rely on outside services?*

MD We perform two types of operations on works: routine maintenance and special maintenance, which means actual restoration. For routine maintenance, we have created a "dusting manual" for our own cleaning staff, and then our restorer cyclically checks up on the state of conservation, both of the works on view and those in storage. For special maintenance (restoration), we have our own lab where our trusted restorers work for the simpler operations. We take the works to outside labs only in special cases when some particular technology is required, so as not to stress the pieces.

PSRR *Have you ever sold a work from the collection?*

MD Never a single work. That's another unique characteristic of this collection. Achille Maramotti truly started it out of passion in the Sixties, and never thought of art as a form of investment. There are very important historic works that have now acquired a significant value, but also works by artists who never really took off on the market yet were important to him in his development as a collector, and are therefore considered sacrosanct.

7   Falckenberg Collection

Since 2001, the Falckenberg Collection has been based at Phoenix-Hallen in Hamburg's Harburg district. In 2007, Harald Falckenberg acquired one of the buildings and had architect Roger Bundschuh convert it into a spacious exhibition hall for his collection. Since January 2011 the Falckenberg Collection has become part of Deichtorhallen Hamburg. The Falckenberg Collection includes about 2,000 works of contemporary art, with an emphasis on German and American contemporary art of the last 30 years. Interview with Harald Falckenberg.

Patrizia Sandretto Re Rebaudengo When and why did you start collecting art?

Harald Falckenberg 1994.

PSRR When did you decide to create your own institution?

HF 1994.

PSRR What motivates a private collector to enter the public sphere, share his own works with the community, spend time, energy and financial resources to support and promote art internationally?

HF Both reasons are relevant for me.

PSRR Why have you decided to create your institution instead of simply donating your works to an already existing museum?

HF In larger international museums the collections die in the depot.

PSRR What is the relationship between the collection and your institution?

HF The collection and the exhibition space are privately owned by me, but lent until 2023 to the state-owned exhibition hall Deichtorhallen, which is now responsible for the exhibitions, with me only as consultant.

PSRR Is your institution involved in the production of new works? And if so, does it produce works for its own exhibitions, or also for exhibiting events abroad?

How would you describe your relationship with the artists whose works you collect, or whom your institution commissions new works, or invites to produce an exhibition?

HF No production, but bigger installations in cooperation with the artist.

PSRR *Do you ever seek the help of curators and art advisors for your exhibitions and for identifying works to include in your collection?*

HF Curators, yes, if necessary. Art advisors, no.

PSRR *What are the main problems that a non-profit organization faces in your Country?*

HF The budgets granted by the government become smaller and smaller, thereby lowering the quality of shows.

PSRR *What goals does your institution pursue and what are your criteria to evaluate its achievements?*

HF The goal is to show international exhibitions, independent, sometimes with and sometimes without works from my collection.

PSRR *Do you usually lend your works to other museums for temporary exhibitions? What are your loan terms?*

HF Lend, yes. We normally charge 500 euro for our work involved.

8   Rubell Family Collection

The Rubell Family Collection (RFC) was established in 1964 in New York City, by its founders Donald and Mera Rubell. In Miami, Florida, since 1993, the RFC is exhibited within a 45,000-square-foot repurposed Drug Enforcement Agency confiscated goods facility, and is publicly accessible. The Contemporary Arts Foundation (CAF) was created in 1994 by Don and Mera with their son Jason. The Foundation maintains an internship program and an extensive artwork and exhibition loan program to international museums. Its ongoing partnership with Miami-Dade County Public Schools enables thousands of schoolchildren to visit and engage with the Foundation every year. Interview with Donald and Mera Rubell.

Patrizia Sandretto Re Rebaudengo When and why did you start collecting art?

Donald and Mera Rubell 1964. We were in Europe playing tennis tournaments and started going to galleries in Paris and found that more interesting than the tennis.

PSRR When did you decide to set your foundation? Which are its main activities?

DMR 1993. We have exhibitions open to the public, as well as special tours for school groups. In addition we travel 2–4 exhibitions from the collection to other institutions every year. We also have the largest contemporary art library south of Washington DC which we make available to students and scholars. There is also an internship program, which accommodates up to 24 students per year.

PSRR What makes a private collector enter in a public dimension, sharing his/her works with a larger public, spending time, energies and financial resources for supporting and promoting contemporary art at an international level?

DMR We are lucky to have been offered many of the best works of various artists, and felt obligated to share them with the general public. In addition, both of our children majored in art history and in both cases the version of art history which they were taught ended with Andy Warhol. We thought it important that they would be exposed to the vitality and great meaning of contemporary art. Also, it is great fun.

PSRR Why did you decide to create your foundation instead of simply donating your works to an already existing museum?

DMR If we were to donate our work to an institution like MoMA or the Whitney Museum of American Art, no matter how important the work, only a very few would see the light of day at any given time. Someone once said the best collection of modern art is at MoMA and the second best was in their storage.

PSRR What is the relationship between the collection and your foundation?

DMR All the work we show is either owned by the collection or the institution.

PSRR Is your institution involved in the production of new works? If so, are these productions destined only to your exhibitions or to other institution's displays too? How would you describe your relationship with the artists whose works you collect, or to whom your institution commissions new works, or whom you invite to participate in your exhibitions?

DMR Although it is rare that we commission new work, we decided this year to commission work by five artists to celebrate our fiftieth wedding anniversary. We acquire all the works we commission, and afterward these works are often included in our travelling exhibitions, or loaned individually to support exhibitions organized by other institutions. Since we deal primarily with young artists or artists whose work we have already collected, we generally find it very useful to know the artists.

PSRR Do you seek the help of curators for your exhibitions? Do you avail yourself of art advisors for implementing your collection?

DMR All of our exhibitions are curated in house with the participation of our son Jason, our director Juan Valadez and Mera and me. We do not use, and have not used, advisors.

PSRR Which are the main difficulties that a non-profit institution has to face in your Country?

DMR Paying for it.

PSRR Which are the goals your institution sets itself, and the criteria you utilize to value its achievements?

DMR Our goal is to obtain the best art possible and then expose it to an ever-enlarging public.

PSRR Do you usually lend your works to other museums for temporary exhibitions? Which are the conditions you consider necessary to allow the loan?

DMR As I mentioned, we loan 2–4 entire exhibitions per year, as well as anywhere from 50 to 200 individual pieces per year. All pieces are lent only with the approval of the artists and only if we are comfortable with the institution to which we are lending the piece.

9 The Aïshti Foundation

The Aïshti Foundation—Tony and Elham Salamé Collection was created by Tony Salamé in Beirut, Lebanon, in 2005 and aspires to become an institution dedicated to contemporary culture, from art and design to architecture and performance. As globalization becomes the norm, the Foundation accepts the challenge of contextualizing exchanges between cultures, from East to West. The purpose is to collect, exhibit and preserve art, and to conduct visual research on an international scale, while focusing on the Middle East and on living artists whose work is key to define this particular moment in contemporary art.

The Aïshti Foundation—Tony and Elham Salamé Collection will also offer public programs in arts education at an international standard.

The Foundation's collection consists of approximately 2,000 works, ranging from painting and sculpture to drawing, video and new media. With over 150 artists, the collection includes many works that are representative of the first decade of the twenty-first century, from 2000 to 2010. Interview with Tony Salamé.

Patrizia Sandretto Re Rebaudengo *When and why did you start collecting art?*

Tony Salamé I started collecting at university, but back then it was old books, rugs and stamps. Over time, my interests evolved to include contemporary art. I officially began collecting in 2005.

PSRR *When did you decide to create your own foundation? What are the main activities in it?*

TS In addition to exhibitions, the Foundation will support young artists through research programs, sponsorships, artist residency packages and contributions to activities related to international exchange in the art field.

PSRR *What motivates a private collector to enter the public sphere, share his own works with the community, spend time, energy and financial resources to support and promote art internationally?*

TS The pleasure of sharing my passion with the public was the main driving force—that and the desire to give back to the community. So many other international foundations have demonstrated a positive impact in their communities, setting the example for an organization like ours.

PSRR *Why have you decided to create your foundation instead of simply donating your works to an already existing museum?*

TS In Lebanon, there is no museum or institution to donate the collection to. Creating the concept from scratch is much more complicated, and I never shy away from a challenge—in fact, it's something I look forward to overcoming.

PSRR *What is the relationship between the collection and the foundation?*

TS The collection is the core of the Foundation, and it will be the main focus of our activity.

PSRR *Does the foundation commission works from artists? And if so, does it produce works for its own exhibitions, or also for exhibiting events abroad? How would you describe your relationship with the artists whose works you collect, or whom your Foundation asks to create works, or invites to produce an exhibition?*

TS It's important to me that the Foundation is not only part of, but contributes to, the industry. We will invite artists to produce works on-site, as part of our artist-in-residence program or for specific exhibitions. Those works will be loaned to other institutions at their request. Many of the initial artists we plan to work with are friends, which makes it easy to invite them to participate in things like exhibitions or curated rooms.

PSRR *Do you seek the help of curators and art advisors for exhibitions and for identifying works to include in your collection?*

TS In the past, I was overseeing the collection because it's something I'm passionate about. Now that it has grown so substantially, we seek help from curators and advisors to enhance it.

PSRR *What are the main problems that non-profit organization faces in your Country?*

TS In Lebanon, we don't have non-profit art institutions. We are funding the project from our business, but there are difficulties—like extremely high taxes and a lack of government incentives (like tax breaks) for cultural initiatives like these.

PSRR *What goals does your institution pursue and what are your criteria to evaluate their achievements?*

TS Our primary goals are to create a discourse and to encourage a creative exchange, within the art world and with those outside it. They're quite difficult goals to measure in quantitative terms.

PSRR *Do you usually lend works for temporary or museum exhibitions? What are your loan terms?*

TS Yes, we lend our works to museums, particularly those in the U.S. It allows us to support artists, their shows and the museums, and of course maintain a dialogue with those institutions.

10 Daimler Art Collection

The Daimler Art Collection started in 1977 and has since then developed a clear profile that has been built up steadily and systematically. Today the Collection represents an important spectrum of major twentieth century art developments and it extends right up to the present day: Examples of abstract art range from the avant-garde tendencies associated with the German Bauhaus movement and classic modernist art, Concrete Art, Constructivism and post-1945 Art Informel, the European Zero movement, Minimalism and Conceptual art, Neo Geo, post-minimalism and conceptual tendencies within international contemporary art, car-related art, international photography, video art and public sculptures. The Daimler Art Collection reflects a commitment to art as a full part of Daimler's self-image and cultural profile. Interview with Dr. Renate Wiehager, Head of the Daimler Art Collection, Stuttgart/Berlin, Germany.

Patrizia Sandretto Re Rebaudengo *To what do you attribute the passion for art that led Daimler to become a renowned collector and promoter of contemporary art in Berlin through the Daimler Art Collection?*

Renate Wiehager One has to distinguish between the contentual and curatorial goals of the collection and its goals in terms of communication and education. In contentual and curatorial terms, we try to give the collection a clear and recognizable orientation in art history terms without imposing too many stylistic restrictions. Our collection comprises about 2,600 works by 700 international artists and focuses on twentieth-century abstract avant-garde art right up to the art of the present day: from artists of the early era who were students of Adolf Hölzel in Stuttgart circa 1910 (such as Willi Baumeister and Oskar Schlemmer) to the Bauhaus, constructive and concrete tendencies, European post-war abstract art and the Zero avant-garde movement, minimalist/conceptual art and Neo Geo and their predecessors, right up to the present day. Besides we constantly building up collection areas around international photography and video art, commissioned artworks, car-related art as well as public sculptures. With regard to communication and educational goals, we have been consistently expanding the formats of the exhibitions that we present since 2001: three themed exhibitions are staged every year at our Berlin public exhibition space, Daimler Contemporary, accompanied by shows with the collection in international public museums. Our one or two temporary themed exhibitions with guided tours for company employees at the Stuttgart-Möhringen venue per year have been supplemented by temporary visits by the collection to other Daimler venues or also in the Mercedes-Benz Museum. For some time now, we have also been staging themed exhibitions in the public museums in the Stuttgart region. All company employees and their children are invited to tour all of these exhibitions, and this means that we are reaching an audience both within the company and among the wider public. At the same time, we have also staged by-request exhibitions in certain German museums, in locations such as Würzburg and Kiel and we started a world tour in 2003.

PSRR *When did Daimler start collecting and why?*

RW The Daimler Art Collection was founded in 1977. Until 2000 it was curated by Hans J. Baumgart, whereas since then it has been headed by me. The main goal of the collection from the beginning is communicating and offering cultural knowledge via implementing twentieth century and contemporary international art in areas of daily work and life.

PSRR *Who is the legal owner of the Daimler Art Collection?*

RW The art collection is part of the holdings of the company, as is the Daimler Art Department a regular part of the Daimler structure.

PSRR *How is the collection curated? Does it have its own staff? How many full-time employees does the Daimler Art Collection have?*

RW We are a team of one curatorial expert and four organizational assistants. Next to that, and related to our exhibition program, there are external art historians working part-time for the collection and we also have interns who support us.

PSRR *Do you research before acquiring art?*

RW The collection's substantial acquisition activities require long-term planning. So yes, I do a lot of research before acquiring art. I'm always up to date about the contemporary art scene, I travel a lot, visit exhibitions, galleries, art museums and meet artists in their studios. We observe the artists and their development for some time before acquiring their artworks for our collection. For specific themed exhibition series, e. g. "Minimalism in Germany" and "Conceptual Tendencies 1960 to today"—and, in particular, for the acquisition of art from a different cultural context—we undertake a lengthy period of preparation, involving intensive academic research, studio visits etc. (in China's case, this took 10 years).

PSRR *Do you usually buy or prefer commissioning?*

RW Most of the artworks in the collection are acquisitions, but our collection concept also includes a small number of commissioned artworks. Some relate to the company's product and some are part of the sculpture and wall paintings collections. One indicator of the future in this respect—and also an indicator of the early international direction taken by the art collection—was the commissioning of a series of artworks from Andy Warhol in 1986 to celebrate the 100th anniversary of Daimler-Benz AG. Since the 1980s, commissions to design and realize location-specific artworks have gone to Max Bill, Heinz Mack, François

Morellet, Walter De Maria, Ben Willikens, Sylvie Fleury, Gerold Miller, Natalia Stachon, Pietro Sanguineti, Patricia London, Franz Erhard Walther, Jan van der Ploeg and other artists. We also support younger contemporary artists. For example, for the 'Conceptual & Applied' exhibition series at Daimler Contemporary Berlin in 2014, we asked Martin Boyce, Leonor Antunes and Luca Trevisani for a space-related commissioned work.

PSRR *Some say a collection is a portrait of the collector and express his personality. Do you agree?*

RW I have curatorial oversight of all acquisitions and exhibitions; including the details of the artworks' hanging—one reason for this is that the Daimler's art collection also suits my preferences as a curator. So partly I would agree, but the main decisions regarding acquisitions and exhibitions are rooted in the nearly 40 years of the history and main tasks of the Daimler Art Collection. And moreover, I'm also working with a young team that brings in ideas as well.

PSRR *When can a corporate collection be defined as successful?*

RW Of course, it is most important, to be visible in the art scene, which means to reach people, who are interested in art and to have substantial numbers of visitors, but also to make a contribution to the scientific research in art history. In addition to the continuous expansion of the collection through purchases, we publish a lot. The Daimler Art Collection has a clear art scientific profile that has been built up steadily and systematically, which is almost unique in the context of corporate collections. The Daimler Art Collection's surefire "recipe for success" was to put trust in an independent, distinctive mixture of work by internationally well-known artists and more peripheral work, whilst bringing younger, less well-established approaches into a dialogue with internationally-discussed contemporary artists. This was combined with a strategy of offering support to art activities that have previously had a low profile in the art system. This provides an opportunity for exciting contrasts—something that is not always possible in museums that are required to present an established "canon".

PSRR *How do you assess the potential success of an exhibition?*

RW Due to the fact that we don't really advertise our exhibition space in Berlin, we are dependent on the fact that our visitors 'promote' our exhibitions by recommending them to colleagues and friends. So the number of visitors is a quite good indicator regarding the success of our exhibitions. As the Daimler Art Collection is a corporate collection a second main focus is to attract the curiosity of colleagues internally at the company and to cause them to look beyond the horizons of their working environments. Feedback from leading representatives of the international art world and press and internet reviews is equally important for us.

PSRR How many exhibitions does Daimler Art Collection organize each year?

RW The number is variable. In the Daimler Contemporary in Berlin, we are organizing 2–3 exhibitions per year. Additionally, we organize one or two themed exhibitions with guided tours for company employees and external groups at the Stuttgart-Möhringen venue per year. Besides that we have also been staging themed exhibitions in public museums in Stuttgart region. In 2003, I started the Daimler Art Collection's world tour, which began with a preliminary overview at the Museum für Neue Kunst/ZKM Karlsruhe, followed by major exhibitions in Detroit, Singapore, Tokyo, South Africa, South America and Vienna. So on average you could say six to eight exhibitions take place every year.

PSRR What was the total number of visitors in 2014?

RW The total number of visitors at Daimler Contemporary Berlin was approximately 30,000. Moreover, around 10,000 employees, guests and partners visited our thematic exhibitions internally in Stuttgart, in the MAC—Museum Art & Cars in Singen, as well as in other smaller venues. In 2013 in total, including internal/external exhibitions in Germany and the world tour of the collection, the number of visitors went up to approximately 150,000.

11   Fondazione per l'Arte Moderna e Contemporanea–CRT

Fondazione per l'Arte Moderna e Contemporanea—CRT was born in 2000, as an operating entity of Fondazione CRT, a foundation of banking origin (Fondazione CRT: current assets amounting to about 3.6 billion euro, expenditures amounting to about 75 million euro a year in three main sectors, including impact investing: art and culture, research and education, and welfare). It was instituted with the purpose of consolidating the Turin urban art system through the purchase of works to add to the permanent collections of Turin's GAM—Galleria Civica d'Arte Moderna e Contemporanea and Castello di Rivoli Museo d'Arte Contemporanea. In the past few years, in addition to the purchase of works, Fondazione per l'Arte also committed itself to supporting and promoting a series of professional training programs, as well as exhibiting, education and communication projects.

Interview with Massimo Lapucci, General Secretary, Fondazione CRT, Turin, Italy. Massimo Lapucci is a member of the Management Committee of the EFC (European Foundation Center), and a member of the Board of the EVPA (European Venture Philanthropy Association).

The Art Collector Between Private Passion and Philanthropy

Patrizia Sandretto Re Rebaudengo In 2015 Fondazione per l'Arte Moderna e Contemporanea—CRT celebrated 15 years of activity. What are the main stages in the development of your cultural project?

Massimo Lapucci In the course of its activity, Fondazione per l'Arte Moderna e Contemporanea—CRT has carried out acquisition campaigns that have focused on Arte Povera, Transavanguardia, 1950s painting and, more in general, on Italian art since the 1950s, and then increasingly turned its attention to the international scene. Of particular strategic importance are the purchases we make each year at Artissima, which is a good occasion to meet the foreign art scene, and also an opportunity for visibility that attracts tourists as well as people working in the sector. Today the Collection of Fondazione per l'Arte Moderna e Contemporanea—CRT, with its 740 works, is one of the most important collections of artworks in Europe, and allows both the GAM—Galleria Civica d'Arte Moderna e Contemporanea and Castello di Rivoli Museo d'Arte Contemporanea (to which we have granted the works on an extended loan) to interact with the most important contemporary art museums in the world, and this in turn helps make Turin a unique pole of attraction for contemporary art lovers. The recent appointment of Carolyn Christov-Bakargiev as director of both GAM and Castello di Rivoli is meant to boost this attractiveness: Christov-Bakargiev was strongly supported for her ability to facilitate contact between the Turin territory and a more international network. For 15 years now, the development of the Collection has been the top priority of the Foundation. Since May 2009, however, in addition to carrying on with the purchase of works, Fondazione per l'Arte CRT has also started designing and creating actions and projects for the development, enhancement and efficiency of the Turin-Piedmont system of Modern and Contemporary Art, by supporting the creative offer on the territory and constantly interacting with the institutions.

PSRR Since its inception, the orientation of the Collection has been one of sharing. Its purpose is to be visited by the public and to enrich the collections of the two main museums on the territory: the GAM—Galleria Civica d'Arte Moderna e Contemporanea, in Turin, and the Castello di Rivoli Museo d'Arte Contemporanea. It therefore constitutes a role model in the collaboration between Public (as institution but also as all types of public, i.e. the addresses of the cultural offer) and Private. What are the strong points of this collaboration, and what are the main issues?

ML The Collection belongs to Fondazione per l'Arte Moderna e Contemporanea—CRT, but ever since its beginnings there has been a will to make it directly available to the GAM and Castello di Rivoli museums, and hence to citizens in general. The spirit has always been one of building a legacy which is not meant to be admired and kept in a private building, but can be experienced by anybody. The digitalization and publishing of works on digital platforms is another step in this direction, i.e. to try to extend as much as possible the possibility to experience contemporary art. The beginning of 2013 saw the start of the R'accolte project, supported by the Ministry of Cultural Heritage and Activities and Tourism and organized by ACRI, Associazione di Fondazioni e di Casse di Risparmio spa, to bring together on one website all the art masterpieces collected by the Italian foundations of banking origin in past years, making as many as 9,000 works available online. Since 2014, the Collection of Fondazione per l'Arte Moderna e Contemporanea—CRT also joined the Google Art Project, the technological platform of the Google Cultural Institute which allows to explore thousands of artworks from the most important museums worldwide. Access is entirely free, and users have a variety of available tools and options.

The fact that we have supported this kind of projects confirms the nature of Fondazione per l'Arte Moderna e Contemporanea—CRT as a private subject that works towards giving public access to a unique heritage, and collaborates with the public sector to develop the cultural offer in Turin and Piedmont, in ever closer synergy with the institutions, and with constant participation in the programs of local cultural politics. The public/private synergy, when it is based on collaboration and the pursuit of a common goal, holds great potential, as Italy is also currently redesigning its legislation and structures to give a stimulus to private investment in culture, as is the case with the Art Bonus.

PSRR *More recently the Foundation has broadened the scope of its mission. In addition to the Collection, you have undertaken a series of support actions aimed at developing the local art system. What are the guiding principles of this project?*

ML Fondazione per l'Arte Moderna e Contemporanea—CRT has chosen to serve the needs of the cultural system and of the community, trying to encourage cultural projects and optimize (financial and non-financial) resources, without interfering in the project-related and organizational decisions, but only, if need be, providing assistance and financial support. In collaboration with the other actors operating on the territory, it has identified four specific lines of intervention: "Education", "Professional training", "Accessibility and system events", and "Promotion and communication". Each line is addressed by means of innovative system projects that strive to optimize resources and costs, complementing the main, classic policy of work acquisition. In the Education line, our support to Progetto Zonarte consolidates our collaboration with Artissima, also reinforcing the synergy among the different institutions involved. In the Professional training line, the Foundation supports Progetto RES.O', a one-of-a-kind in Italy, which aims at promoting the mobility of Italian and foreign artists. The Foundation also supports the Campo project, a study course for young Italian curators offered by Fondazione Sandretto Re Rebaudengo. In this way we have created a strong network of cultural institutions dedicated to providing young artists with a comprehensive education. The Accessibility line sees Fondazione per l'Arte Moderna e Contemporanea—CRT support specific, chosen system initiatives, such as Artissima, Paratissima, Ouverture, which involve most institutions working on the territory and have an impact on them. Finally, in the field of Communication Fondazione per l'Arte is committed to support Progetto Contemporary Art Torino Piemonte, a

communication program for Sistema Arte Contemporanea developed by the City of Turin in collaboration with all the entities and institutions operating in the contemporary art sector.

PSRR *Fondazione per l'Arte Moderna e Contemporanea—CRT is without doubt a highly innovative model of cultural patronage. What other forms of patronage and philanthropy are necessary for the good functioning of a cultural ecosystem?*

ML I think we are increasingly going towards a more widespread kind of patronage, which sees the involvement of multiple institutions, but also an active role on the part of local communities, which are often called upon to decide which projects to support through innovative systems such as crowdfunding, which is a sort of true shared ownership. In their action to support culture, the new forms of philanthropy should combine investment with participation. This is encouraged by mechanisms of fiscal subsiding such as the recent Art Bonus act, which makes cultural spending more advantageous, and applies both to natural and legal persons. The challenge now is one of experimentation and innovation—finding new solutions to problems, but also, above all, finding new opportunities. This also emerges very clearly from international, especially European, trends, both in the more traditional institutions and foundations (the so-called grant makers), and in those that use "philanthropy 2.0" operating models, such as venture philanthropy or impact investing. Both categories share a desire to redefine and renew their missions, which they feel is something urgent and of capital importance. This leads to new avenues being opened up by civil society actors—and hence also for foundations of banking origin, which, as private financers with a strong social commitment, also have great responsibility towards society and its growth. This growth must be supported in two ways: by making the most of the heritage of our Country (a crucial goal), and by having the courage to seek out, and select, projects that are high-quality and highly innovative.

Appendix: Private Museums and Their Founders

Sonia Pancheri

Saatchi Gallery

The Saatchi Gallery opened in October 2008 in the 70,000 sq. ft. Duke of York HQ building, located in central London on Kings Road, Chelsea. The building represents an ideal environment for displaying contemporary art, with very large well-proportioned rooms and high ceilings. The Saatchi Gallery occupies the entire building with space for educational facilities, a bookshop and a café. The Saatchi Gallery aims to provide an innovative forum for contemporary art, presenting work by largely unseen young artists or by international artists whose work has rarely or never been exhibited in the UK. Many artists shown at the Saatchi Gallery were unknown when first exhibited, not only to the general public but also within the commercial art world. Several of these artists have subsequently been offered shows by internationally galleries and museums. In this way, the Saatchi Gallery also operates as a springboard for young artists to launch their careers. Free admission to all shows, including temporary exhibitions, is part of the Saatchi Gallery's aim to bring contemporary art to the widest audience possible. When the Saatchi Gallery first opened over 30 years ago it was the only British gallery with a dedicated interest in contemporary art hosting works by new artists. The audience, however, has built steadily over the years and the visitors to the King's Road building now exceed 1.5 million per annum, with over 2,000 schools a year organizing student visits.

Charles Saatchi

Charles Saatchi, born in 1943, is an Iraqi-British advertising executive who is known as one of the most important post-war art collectors in Britain. Born to a wealthy family, by the age of 18 he had begun working as a copywriter in the advertising business. In 1970, together with his younger brother, he founded Saatchi & Saatchi. In 15 years the company, which is now part of a larger conglomerate, became the largest advertising firm in the world. In the early 1980s Saatchi began spending millions on contemporary art: he collected in particular American minimalists artists, such as Donald Judd, Dan Flavin, and Sol LeWitt. His activities were closely monitored in the art world and he had a considerable impact on the fortunes of several artists, such as Damien Hirst. In 1985 he opened the Saatchi Gallery in London, in order to display his collection. He patronized the Young British Artists (Trecey Emin, Chris Ofili, Ron Mueck, Jenny Saville, Sarah Lucas) and in 1997 he co-curated the popular *Sensation* show at the Royal Academy of Arts in London. His interest in contemporary art has helped London to become the leading centre in the field. Saatchi's success has not left him without critics: his buying power and consumerist approach towards art is considered a distortion of market values. Saatchi is no longer the dominant art figure that he used to be in the late 1990s, but he is of course recognized as a major philanthropist through his commitment in Saatchi Gallery.

Lyon Housemuseum

The Lyon Housemuseum, located in Melbourne, displays selected works from the Lyon Collection of contemporary art that includes paintings, sculpture, large scale installations and video art by many of Australian leading artists. In 2000 Corbett and Yueji Lyon built the institution, developing the concept of *housemuseum* to accommodate their family and their collection. The Lyon Housemuseum was designed by Corbett Lyon and his architectural firm; in 2010 the building won the Australian Institute of Architects Harold Desbrowe-Annear Award for Residential Architecture and was exhibited at the World Architecture Festival in Barcelona. The design interweaves and juxtaposes conventional domestic and museum typologies to create a scenographic landscape for the display of artworks and for the daily living needs of the family. Through the juxtaposition of art and living the Housemuseum challenges conventional perceptions of *public* and *private*. The Lyon Collection was established in 1990 by Corbett Lyon, who invested in young Australian artists who were his contemporaries. After 25 years, the collection includes works by many of Australia's most recognised artists including Howard Arkley, Patricia Piccinini, Callum Morton, Daniel von Sturmer, and Shaun Gladwell. The Lyon Housemuseum is open for public viewing by appointment and offers educational tours, programmes for students and sponsors an annual series of lectures and talks on art and architecture. In 2012, Corbett and Yueji Lyon established the Lyon Foundation to provide a permanent guardian for the collection, which has been enriched with over 40 major works from the family's private aggregation.

Appendix: Private Museums and Their Founders

Corbett Lyon

Corbett Marshall Lyon, born in 1955, is an Australian architect and academic who lives and works in Melbourne. He is well known as an art collector and patron. He is co-founder and director of Melbourne architectural firm Lyons, established in 1996. His firm is a leader not only in major commercial projects, but also in cultural, institutional and urban design fields. With partners, he has designed many award-winning institutional and public buildings in Australia. Lyon is a leading expert in the design of buildings involving multiple stakeholder input and he has pioneered Lyons' design methodologies, which engage clients actively in the design and planning process. In 2007, he was appointed a Professorial Fellow at the University of Melbourne and in 2009 was made Visiting Professor in Architectural Design in the University's School of Design. He is one of Australia's leading collectors, patrons and commentators on contemporary art and has participated in numerous forums on art and architecture in Australia and overseas. He is a Trustee of the National Gallery of Victoria and a member of the Victorian Government's Design Review Panel. With his wife Yueji, he has developed the Lyon Collection since 1990. In 2000 he started to conceive the Lyon Housemuseum, a hybrid residence and art museum, which displays his own collection and makes it available for public viewing.

de la Cruz Collection

The de la Cruz Collection, privately funded by Carlos and Rosa de la Cruz, offers an overview of international contemporary art. Since 2009 it has been located in a new contemporary art space: a 30,000 sq. ft. building in the Design District of Miami, designed by John Marquette. The building serves as an extension of the founders' home, where for over 25 years they have shared artworks with the public. The primary purpose of this space is to promote education and awareness of the visual arts. In order to serve local schools, educational programmes have been established. These include lectures and classes, artist-led workshops, docent-led tours, scholarship opportunities and travel initiatives to serve both teachers and students. Students are encouraged to visit the spaces and to apply for internship positions. In order to create a cross-disciplinary platform for artists and audiences, lecture series are concentrated on creating public awareness of art history and the de la Cruz Collection provides artist residencies to support the local art scene. Miami artists are invited to propose ideas for temporary site-specific installations and experiential artworks using non-traditional practices that are exhibited throughout the year. Projects commissioned by the collection have been exhibited outside of Florida at institutions such as the Philadelphia Museum of Art.

Rosa and Carlos de la Cruz

Rosa and Carlos de la Cruz are two of the Miami area's most prominent art collectors. Both Rosa and Carlos were born in Cuba and left their country as teenagers because of Castro's veer towards communism. They arrived in the United States in the 1960s, where they first lived in Philadelphia while Carlos was finishing his masters at Wharton before moving for a few years to New York. They subsequently lived in Madrid before returning to the USA, settling in Miami in 1975. Nowadays, Carlos is a chairman of $1 billion-per-year business empire that includes Coca-Cola. The passion of collecting has always been in Rosa's family: her father was an architect in Havana who collected paintings, ensuring that she was exposed to art. Rosa and Carlos first started collecting with decorative purposes. They now have an excellent contemporary art collection, including works by Christopher Wool, Peter Doig, Felix Gonzalez-Torres. Though the de la Cruzes have previously donated art to other institutions, such as MoMA, the couple had no reservations in creating their own art institution. The couple considers the art space open to the public as an extension of their home. Rosa and Carlos de la Cruz hope to use their considerable resources to elevate Miami from its status of once-a-year art attraction, during the week of Art Basel Miami, to a true contemporary art capital.

Glenstone Museum

In September 2006, Glenstone opened to the public, inviting visitors to discover a new kind of museum. Glenstone Museum seamlessly integrates art, architecture and landscape into a serene and contemplative environment. Glenstone is hidden among the rolling hills of Potomac, Maryland, on a former foxhunting estate of 150 acres that has been gently reshaped and restored into an ideal setting for quiet aesthetic contemplation. The core of Glenstone Museum is the collection of postwar art of Mitchell Rales. It is a very personal project that, since 1990, has been driven by the pursuit of the highest quality artworks that impact the way of thinking of modern and contemporary art. Rotating exhibitions are hosted in the galleries of the main building designed by Gwathmey Siegel & Associates Architects, while monumental outdoor sculptures are permanently exhibited in a landscape designed by Peter Walker and Partners. The collection concentrates on critical moments in an artist's career. Artists represented include Willem De Kooning, Joseph Beuys, John Baldessari, Dan Flavin, Felix Gonzalez-Torres, Jasper Johns, Ellsworth Kelly, Barbara Kruger, Bruce Nauman, Jackson Pollock, Robert Rauschenberg, Richard Serra, and Cy Twombly. Glenstone Museum also makes works from its collection available on loan to public institutions throughout the United States and abroad. Glenstone sustains an active acquisitions programme, with a commitment to the growth of a collection of modern and contemporary artists of the highest order throughout the lifetimes of its founders. In order to visit Glenstone Museum, guests must schedule an appointment as the institution is open by reservation.

Mitchell Rales

Mitchell Rales, born in 1956, is an American businessman and a collector of modern and contemporary art. Rales was raised in a Jewish family; his father was a humble yet successful businessman active in a philanthropic found. Mitchell Rales is co-founder and director of the Danaher Corporation conglomerate, a large company headquartered in Washington D.C., globally active in the design, manufacturing, and marketing of industrial and consumer products. In collaboration with his wife Emily Wei Rales, an art historian and curator, Mitchell Rales has established Glenstone Museum, which presents exhibitions of their collection of art and installations. Art has brought Mitchell Rales out of shadows: the museum has led him to bend his policy of non-engagement with the public and grant occasional interviews. As proof of his discretion, it is noteworthy that the name of the museum does not refer directly to its founders, but to a local toponym. Mitchell Rales and his wife did not establish the institution for a self celebration; indeed, they hope that Glenstone Museum will be a destination for all who seek meaningful encounters with art, architecture, and nature for many years to come. Mitchell Rales is currently on the board of the National Gallery of Art in Washington D.C. and is a former board member of the Hirshhorn Museum.

Fondation Louis Vuitton

In 2006, at the behest of Bernard Arnault, the LVMH group created the Fondation Louis Vuitton within the policy of art and culture patronage developed by the Group over the last 20 years. The project was made possible through the corporate patronage of LVMH and the Group's companies, and the values shared by the people of LVMH and its shareholders. Designed by the American architect Frank Gehry, the building opened in October 2014. The unique and emblematic structure appears like an immaculate white iceberg next to the Jardin d'Acclimatation in the Bois de Boulogne, the famous park on the west side of Paris. Though respectful of a history rooted in French culture of the nineteenth century, Frank Gehry dares to use the technological achievements of the twenty-first century, opening the way for pioneering innovation. His architecture combines tradition and visionary daring with new design processes: each stage of construction pushed back the boundaries of conventional architecture to create a unique building that is the realisation of a dream. The Fondation Louis Vuitton aims to promote and support contemporary artistic creation for a wide international audience, and in particular the institution opens an exciting new cultural chapter for Paris. It offers the city a new space devoted to contemporary art, and a place for meaningful exchanges between artists and visitors by encouraging spontaneous dialogue and inspiring both emotion and contemplation. The collection, that is a combination of works owned by LVMH and Bernard Arnault, is unveiled to the public in three different temporary stages, each one focused on a specific topic.

Bernard Arnault

Bernard Arnault, born 1949, is a French luxury goods patron. He has been the chairman and CEO of LVMH since 1989, overseeing an empire of 60 brands, including Louis Vuitton, Dom Perignon, Bulgari, Fendi and Sephora. Bernard Arnault is the richest man in France and is the definition of a tycoon. Arnault grew up in northern France and after graduating from the École Polytechnique, France's esteemed engineering school, he worked as an engineer and ran his family's construction and property business firm. After some years working as a constructor in the USA, he began his rise to control of the world's largest luxury groups. Unique among the world's leading CEOs, Arnault has the ability to relate to both the creative and financial aspects of running a business, following a business model that balanced practice and creativity. He has frequently turned to artists for help with designing new products for his high-end brands: the most famous is the collaboration between Luis Vuitton and Takashi Murakami. Art patron and collector, he conceived and opened the Louis Vuitton Foundation Museum in Paris, which displays selections from LVMH's vast trove of contemporary art and his own personal art holdings, in addition to other exhibitions.

Garage Museum of Contemporary Art

The Garage Museum of Contemporary Art is a project of the IRIS Foundation, a philanthropic organisation dedicated to promoting the understanding and development of contemporary culture. Founded by Dasha Zhukova in 2008, the Garage Center for Contemporary Culture is an international project based in Moscow. Garage aims to bring important modern and contemporary art to Moscow, in order to raise the profile of Russian contemporary culture and to encourage new generations of artists. These aims are explored through a series of exhibitions, ranging from single artist retrospectives to group shows and surveys of important collections. The Garage Museum hosts a programme of special events including talks, film screenings, workshops, performances and creative activities for children, creating opportunities for public dialogue. The project was initially located in a glass pavilion designed by Japanese architect Shigeru Ban, one of the most progressive examples of hi-tech temporary architecture in the world. In June 2015, the Garage Museum moved to its first permanent home: a groundbreaking preservation project by Rem Koolhaas, that transformed the famous 1968 Vremena Goda Soviet Modernist restaurant in Gorky Park into a contemporary museum. The institution is the first archive in the country related to the development of Russian contemporary art from the 1950s to the present.

Roman Abramovich and Dasha Zhukova

Roman Abramovich, born in 1966, is a Russian multi-billionaire businessman and entrepreneur. Orphaned at the age of two, he was raised by an uncle in the north of Russia. While still a student, Abramovich set up a plastic toy production company, and its success enabled him to found an oil business in the Omsk region. He rapidly made a name for himself within the industry and joined the board of several companies. Nowadays, Abramovich is one of the richest men in the world, owner of Chelsea Football Club and of a private investment firm. Abramovich is among the richest art collectors and is believed to have bought several artworks at auctions over the years, including a Francis Bacon triptych. His third wife is the art collector and philanthropist Moscow-born Dasha Zhukova. After graduating with honours in Slavic Studies and Literature at University of California, in 2008 Dasha Zhukova founded the Garage Center for Contemporary Culture. This creative hub in Russia is part-funded by her husband. With her ambitious vision and campaign of launching the Garage Museum of Contemporary Art, Dasha Zhukova wants to connect Moscow with the international art world. The couple has recently bought the world's largest collection of works by Ilya Kabakov, the most expensive living Russian artist. Dasha Zhukova's collection is legendary and contains thousands of mostly contemporary artworks. Her husband seems to prefer modern and Impressionist art.

Fondazione Prada

For the last two decades, Fondazione Prada's activities have analyzed intentions and relevance through an evolution of projects, including solo and group international shows, contemporary philosophy conferences, architectural projects, cinematographic projects, shows presented abroad and publications. In 2011 Fondazione Prada opened the first exhibition space in Venice: Ca' Corner della Regina, a eighteenth century building overlooking the Grand Canal. In 2015, Fondazione Prada celebrated the opening of a new headquarters: a permanent complex in Milan that is a combination of an art gallery, a public museum and a private foundation. This spatial composition, a former distillery dating back to the 1910s, combines preexisting buildings with new structures and the courtyards provide a common public ground open to the city. This cultural hub represents a fresh opportunity for the funders, Miuccia Prada and Patrizio Bertelli, to enlarge their commitment to cultural community. Fondazione Prada embraces the idea that culture is deeply necessary for society, as well as being attractive and engaging, and art is considered the main instrument of learning. The Prada collection includes works mostly from the twentieth and twenty-first centuries and is partially displayed in Milan. The whole gathering of artworks is conceived as a resource from which to draw new perspectives: Fondazione Prada invites not only curators, artists and architects but also scientists, students and writers to provide new and unusual interpretations of the collection.

Miuccia Prada and Patrizio Bertelli

Miuccia Prada, born in 1949, is the Italian designer and entrepreneur behind the fashion house Prada. Having graduated with a PhD in political science from the University of Milan, she was involved in the women's rights movement during the 1970s. She took over the family-owned luxury goods manufacturer as head of the company in 1978 and around the same time met her future husband and business partner, Patrizio Bertelli. Since the 1980s, the company has reported a massive success and has acquired several other brands, transforming Prada into a multimillion-dollar fashion conglomerate. In 1993, she founded with Bertelli the PradaMilanoarte, later renamed Fondazione Prada, a non-profit organization dedicated to supporting various up-and-coming contemporary designers, architects and artists. The couple has a very meaningful idea of their position in the art system: they do not consider themselves collectors, and even less patrons. They want to be active part of shaping culture. Prada and Bertelli have always strived to keep their fashion business and their interest in art quite separate. In 2014, Miuccia was listed as the 75th most powerful woman in the world by Forbes and is an increasingly powerful figure in the art world.

Rachofsky House

Completed in 1996, the Rachofsky House is the private home of Cindy and Howard Rachofsky, located in Dallas and open to guided tours in order to display their private collection of contemporary art. On a rotating basis, the house is a laboratory in which architecture, landscape and the presentation of contemporary art integrate and overlap. Rachofsky House, designed by Richard Meier, revisits the importance of procession from exterior to interior, from formal to intimate, the role of natural light in defining living spaces, the relationship between handmade structure and its natural surroundings, and the correlation between the private and the communal. All of the spaces of the house act as landscapes in which artworks are displayed. The heart of the house is the second floor living room, where the secrets of the entire site are revealed through the double-height plane of windows that serves as a permeable membrane between nature and home. Whereas the front façade of the house is reserved and opaque, the back façade dissolves and allows constantly changing plays of light and silhouette to amaze people within and outside the house. The purpose of the Rachofsky House is to provide a place of residence and respite. The collection of roughly 800 works of contemporary art generally falls within two broad themes. The first of these, paralleling the architecture of the Rachofsky House, is the aesthetic of global minimalism, including but not limited to American minimalism and post-war European art with a specific focus on Italian art and post-war art in Japan. The second is an exploration of the post-war notion of identity, encompassing representational work from around the globe. Of particular significance to the collection are works by Alighiero Boetti, Alberto Burri, Lucio Fontana, Piero Manzoni, Donald Judd, Sigmar Polke, Richard Prince and Gerhard Richter.

Cindy and Howard Rachofsky

Howard Rachofsky (1947–2006) was a successful hedge fund and money manager and stock trader for more than 30 years. He was also one of Dallas' most engaged and generous arts patrons. For more than three decades, Rachofsky was deeply involved in a range of community based organizations including the Dallas Museum of Art, Dallas Symphony Association, Dallas Center for the Performing Arts, Dia foundation for the Arts in New York, East Dallas Community School, St. Phillips Academy, Booker T. Washington School for the Visual and Performing Arts, Dallas Theater Center, Dallas Architectural Foundation and the University of Texas School of Architecture. Nowadays his widow, Cindy Rachofsky, is a member of the board of trustees and sits on the executive committee of the Dallas Museum of Art. In 2010, she was awarded the TACA Neiman Marcus Silver Cup Award and with her husband received the Gertrude Vanderbilt Whitney Award for Outstanding Patronage of the Arts at Skowhegan in 2005. They both received the amfAR award for their longstanding support of the Foundation for AIDS research. As philanthropists, Cindy and Howard Rachofsky have focused on reinventing Dallas as a contemporary art capital and creating community and civic engagement through art collection.

Boros Collection

The Boros Collection is a private collection of contemporary art, housed in a converted bunker erected in 1942 situated in Berlin-Mitte, with 3,000 square metres of exhibition space spread over 80 rooms. Due to safety regulations, the bunker can only be visited in small groups accompanied by in-house guides. Entering the Boros residence is an experience unlike any home visit that might be expected. The structure exposes a not so distant history while simultaneously embracing the future. In the heart of this hermetic cube, different facets of the Boros Collection have been displayed since 2008. The first showing of the collection ran from 2008 to 2012 and attracted 120,000 visitors over 7,500 tours. The second exhibition of works from the Boros Collection, opened on September 2012, presents a total of 130 works. All media are represented in the current show: sculpture, installation, painting, drawing, video and photography. The exhibition juxtaposes artworks by 23 artists that range from the early 1990s up to the present day and include several new acquisitions, some purchased just a few weeks before the opening. Many of the installations work with sound so that visitors are confronted with various, overlapping sounds on each of the bunker's five floors. The artworks on display have been installed in the rooms by the artists themselves and fit with the spaces.

Christian and Karen Boros

Christian Boros, born in Poland in 1964 and settled in Berlin and New York, is the founder of an advertising agency and an art collector. During his studies in communication design at the Bergischen University Wuppertal in Germany, he was intensely engaged with the correlation between economics and culture. Besides economic enterprises and media brands, the customers of the Boros Group also include museums and cultural institutions. Additionally, he is an advisor to economic corporations and cultural institutions on communication and positioning. He often teaches on culture as an economic factor at the Bergischen University Wuppertal and is lecturer at the Witten-Herdecke private university and the Offenbach Academy of Art and Design. Since 1990, with his wife Karen, Christian Boros has built one of the largest collections of young contemporary art in Germany, gathering works by Olafur Eliasson, Wolfgang Tillmans, Sarah Lucas, and Damien Hirst. Unlike many other collectors, Christian and Karen Boros buy works in the year that they were created. The couple lives in one of the most unconventional homes in the world: an old bunker in Berlin which they partly converted into a private gallery, where since 2008 the Boros Foundation has presented highlights of the collection. Christian Boros is a member of the curatorship Circle of Friends of the National Gallery and of the Society of Friends of the Art Collection North Rhine-Westphalia.

Berardo Collection Museum

The Berardo Collection Museum is a museological space in Lisbon, where the visitor can enjoy the best of modern and contemporary art. The museum offers both the permanent presentation of the Berardo Collection and a vast array of temporary exhibitions. The Berardo Collection Museum presents the most significant artistic movements from the twentieth century to the present, establishing its position as the main museum for modern and contemporary art in Portugal. Names such as Pablo Picasso, Marcel Duchamp, Piet Mondrian, Joan Miró, Francis Bacon, Andy Warhol, Donald Judd, Bruce Nauman and Cindy Sherman, among many others, are presented within the framework of the artistic movements that their works helped to define, through a chronological sequence that allows a journey through time. The representation of more than 70 movements in a collection of more than 900 works demonstrates its strong museological and didactic nature. The Berardo Collection Museum also offers a broad programme of activities for all ages, such as paths through the exhibitions and family visit-workshops, which present the great names of art in an original and educational way. Temporary exhibitions held alongside the collection allow the museum to focus on specific artists, movements for art contexts that complement its broader panorama.

José Berardo

José Berardo, born in 1944, is a Portuguese businessman and one of the wealthiest people in Portugal. Born to a modest family, Berardo left school when he was 13 years old and got a low-ranked job in the Madeira wine industry. At the age of 18, he emigrated to South Africa where he worked in horticultural distribution and eventually set up large commercial ventures, becoming by the end of the twentieth century one of the most renowned and wealthiest Portuguese entrepreneurs. In South Africa, he focused on the gold and diamond mining industry. Berardo returned to Portugal in 1986 as a very wealthy and active stock trader and his businesses assets include hotels, tobacco companies, telecommunications, banking, and wine. José Berardo is one of the most successful contemporary art collectors in Portugal. His passion for collecting started as a schoolboy with stamps, postcards and matchboxes and graduated to modern and contemporary art in the 1980s. His various collections, which include art deco and Chinese porcelain, encompass more than 40,000 works. José Berardo devoted himself to art not only because culture is a pleasure to him, but also because he knew that financial resources are needed to allow culture and art to grow.

Sammlung Goetz

The Goetz Collection is an internationally renowned collection of contemporary art located in Munich, Germany. The building was designed by Herzog & de Meuron and completed in 1993. The development of the structured collection began from the mid-1980s and now encompass works of several hundred artists. The Goetz Collection includes art that critically examines the realities of society and their dubious social, political and aesthetic nature. The collection does not attempt to attain an encyclopaedic overview based on selected individual works, but rather to pursue, complete and expand on the production of individual artists over the years. The Goetz Collection promotes media diversity in today's artistic forms of representation. In addition to drawings, graphics, paintings, photographs and room-based installations, one of the collection's main focuses is time-based media such as video, film and multiple projections. In order to adequately show media artworks of the collection, the building's exhibition space was expanded in 2001 and nearly doubled by the addition of a multifunctional area. The Goetz Collection is fully aware of the significance of adequate conservation, carefully restoring and preserving artworks for future generations. Moreover, the Goetz Collection places high value on art-historical research into artists and artworks: the digital archive includes reports of artworks, correspondence with artists and galleries, and technical details for insurance. From the beginning, the collection has been accompanied by the development of a library that includes monographs and group catalogues for all artists.

Ingvild Goetz

The driving force behind the Goetz Collection and its wide range of activities is Ingvild Goetz, born in 1941, whose energy and passion launched the collection. Ingvild Goetz's commitment to art stems from the time she spent as a gallerist in Zurich and in Munich, hosting ground-breaking exhibitions by the leading artists of Arte Povera. In 1984, Ingvild Goetz decided to close down her gallery and concentrate on collecting. Works that she had acquired during her years as a gallery owner still form the cornerstone of her collection. Ingvild Goetz developed a strategy that she has continued to pursue to this day, based on two conceptual pillars: concentrating on emerging art and the new generation of artists on the one hand, and continuing to pursue and complement works already in the collection on the other. Today, she owns one of the largest private collections of contemporary art, video art and media works in the world, nearly half of which is composed of women artists. During her many years of experience as a collector, Ingvild Goetz has become an acknowledged authority in the field of contemporary and emerging art. Her resulting in-depth knowledge of contemporary art and her commitment and service to the city of Munich have won her high-profile recognition and accolades. In 1993 Ingvild Goez launched her private museum housing the collection in a building by Herzog & de Meuron.

Punta della Dogana

In 2006, the City of Venice launched a contest for the creation of a centre for contemporary art at Punta della Dogana. Palazzo Grassi, which since 2005 had hosted the *François Pinault Foundation*, won the contest and Punta della Dogana was entirely renovated by the architect Tadao Ando. In June 2009 the building opened to the public. The renovation required extensive work to safeguard the structure from humidity and high water, and the layout of the existing lofts was modified in order to create a space able to house the artworks. The triangular-shaped Punta della Dogana, an area of nearly 5,000 sq. ft., separates the Grand Canal from the Giudecca Canal in Venice. The facades of Punta della Dogana are pierced by 20 monumental gates. Its inner structure is divided into nine halls arranged transversely, each with an average width of 10 m and a beam height of 7 m. As a centre for contemporary art, the former customs house of the city presents a permanent display and temporary exhibitions of works from the François Pinault Collection. Some of the artists from the Pinault Collection displayed in Punta della Dogana are Mark Bradford, Marcel Broodthaers, Maurizio Cattelan, Jake & Dinos Chapman, Donald Judd, Jeff Koons, Takashi Murakami, Bruce Nauman, Thomas Schutte, Sigmar Polke, Richard Prince, Cindy Sherman, Elaine Sturtevant, Cy Twombly, and Chen Zhen. With its radical transformation from a commercial area into a bastion of contemporary art—and the ideal venue to share it with the world—Punta della Dogana has become a masterpiece of architecture and a symbolic building for Venice.

François Pinault

François Pinault, born in 1936, is a French businessman and art collector who created a retail empire, especially noted for its luxury goods. Pinault's earliest jobs were with his father's timber company, before he founded his first business in 1963: a timber and building materials firm. In 1988, the Pinault group went public on the French stock market. In 1990, Pinault decided to refocus the group's activities on specialized sales and retailing and to withdraw from the timber business. From then on the group began to acquire a wide range of firms and Pinault transformed the group into a luxury brand conglomerate. The group was renamed Kering (formerly Pinault-Printemps-Redoute) and became the third largest firm in the luxury goods sector worldwide after acquiring the Gucci Group. Pinault is an avid art collector, and by the early twenty-first century he had acquired some 3,000 works. In 1998 Pinault purchased nearly 30 % of the auction house Christie's, underlining his business interest in art. After his efforts to build a museum in France failed, in 2005 Pinault bought Palazzo Grassi in Venice, where he began displaying a small percentage of his collection in order to share his passion with the greatest number of people possible. From 2009, a large number of works from Pinault's collection have been hosted at Punta della Dogana. In 2006 and 2007, François Pinault was named the most influential person in the world of contemporary art by Art Review.

Crystal Bridges Museum

The Crystal Bridges Museum, founded by Alice Walton and designed by Moshe Safdie, officially opened in November 2011. Located in the heart of the country in Bentonville, Arkansas, Crystal Bridges explores the unfolding history of America by collecting and exhibiting works from its domestic artistic heritage, in order to enrich appreciation of traditional culture. With 120 acres of native Ozark forest, Crystal Bridges' grounds invite visitors to enjoy the natural environment as a continuation of their museum experience. The Museum's distinctive architecture immerses visitors in the landscape, while three miles of nature trails encourage exploration and reflection. Through the ever-expanding permanent collection of American art, temporary exhibitions, and a wide variety of entertaining and educational programmes, Crystal Bridges has become an invaluable resource for the local community, and a must-see attraction for tourists to Northwest Arkansas, offering the opportunity to view the glories of America's artistic heritage. In addition, a number of ground-breaking exhibition and education initiatives place Crystal Bridges at the forefront in scholarship and outreach innovation. The museum's permanent collection features American art from the Colonial era to the contemporary. All of the featured artists are United States citizens, though some spent most of their art careers in Europe. The collection includes art works by American giants from Benjamin West to Chuck Close, Georgia O'Keefe and Mark di Suvero, but also figures such as Jasper Johns, Jackson Pollock and Mark Rothko. Sculpture also figures prominently in the collection, displayed in interior galleries and along outdoor sculpture trails.

Alice Walton

Alice Walton, born in 1949, is the American heiress of the fortune of Wal-Mart Stores, daughter of Wal-Mart founder Sam Walton and Helen Walton. Her estimated net worth makes her one of the richest woman in the world. After graduating in Economics and Finance from Trinity University in San Antonio, Texas, she did not join her father's company right away: instead, she got her first job as an equity analyst at First Commerce Corporation. Her later business exploits include an investment bank. Despite her secrecy-shrouded persona, Walton's philanthropic efforts have not gone totally unrecognized. Her interest in art led the Walton Family Foundation to be involved in the developing of Crystal Bridges Museum of American Art in the heart of Bentonville, Arkansas. She is a passionate and visionary collector, and her amassing of such an impressive set of artwork in such a short period of time is almost unprecedented.

Rennie Collection

The Rennie Collection, one of the largest collections of contemporary art in Canada, is housed in Vancouver in the Wing Sang building, the oldest building in the city's Chinatown. The renovation of the structure, completed in 2009, was commissioned by Bob Rennie in order to display part of his collection in a sleek and modern showplace. The collection has evolved over a number of years to focus on works related to identity, social injustice, appropriation, painting and photography. The Rennie Collection is dedicated not only to the acquisition of established international artists, but also the work of emerging artists. Currently there are approximately 40 artists collected in depth with about 200 artists in total, including John Baldessari, Amy Bessone, Glenn Brown, Martin Creed, Gilbert & George, Dan Graham, and Mike Kelley. The collection, while based in Vancouver, is usually spread across the globe, on loan to institutions such as the Guggenheim New York, the Pompidou, the Smithsonian and the Tate, among many others.

Bob Rennie

Bob Rennie, born in 1956, is a Canadian real estate marketer based in Vancouver. Coming from humble origins, at the age of 19 he started selling first homes and then condos. In 1997 he established Rennie Marketing Systems, Vancouver's largest real estate marketing firm. At 18 he bought his first artwork, a print by Norman Rockwell, and in 2009 he opened his own museum that houses his collection of more than 1400 works. Bob Rennie, principal of Rennie Collection, is deeply involved in the art community in Vancouver and throughout North America. He is internationally active and is known for his commitment and his great intuition in finding artists way before they are on anyone else's radar. Moreover, by lending artworks of his collection to museums, Rennie has built a reputation as a generous custodian that has helped him gain access to the best works by artists he covets. Being included in prestigious exhibitions also boosts the works' value. He is Chair of the Tate North American Acquisitions Committee and a member of the Tate International Council. Locally, he sits on the Board of Governors of Emily Carr University of Art & Design in Vancouver as well as the University of British Columbia Provost's Committee on University Art.

Zabludowicz Collection

The Zabludowicz Collection is a philanthropic endeavour encompassing a dynamic and growing collection of art works with an associated programme of exhibitions and events in three venues (UK, USA and Finland). Founded in the 1990s by Poju and Anita Zabludowicz, the collection focuses on contemporary art from 1970 to the present day and includes works across all disciplines by artists from around the globe, with a major focus on artists from Europe and North America. The institution actively encourages the development of artists' practices beyond collecting by commissioning and supporting the production of new work as well as loaning works to other institutions. In 2007 the Zabludowicz Collection inaugurated a project space in London. A former Methodist chapel, built in Corinthian style between 1867 and 1871, was restored by Allford Hall Monaghan Morris with a minimum of interference to its natural fabric, providing a rich and challenging space for the presentation of contemporary art. The space presents a varied programme of self-initiated group and solo exhibitions, commissions and residencies, drawing on works from the collection or new works by artists linked to the collection. The programme features initiatives supporting emerging artists and curators without a commercial gallery representation in order to guarantee the opportunity to produce a solo exhibition. Moreover, the Zabludowicz Collection organizes an annual event to explore art and education with London's premier universities.

Anita and Poju Zabludowicz

Anita Zabludowicz, born in Newcastle in the early 1950s, studied Fine Art & History of Art at Newcastle's College of Arts & Technology. She subsequently spent 10 years working as a project manager in interior architecture before going back to study Modern Art & Auctioneering at Christie's. Her Finnish husband, Poju Zabludowicz, born in 1953 in Helsinki, graduated in Economics and Political Science from Tel Aviv University before joining Tamares, his family's holding company, which he has led since 1990. Anita and Poju Zabludowicz are deeply shaped by their commitment to engaging with local contexts and communities. Philanthropy is at the heart of all their activities: from donating major gifts to museums, to supporting community festivals, and from creating new opportunities for audiences, to engaging with emerging artists around the world. Poju and Anita

Zabludowicz founded the Zabludowicz Collection in 1994 to gather international emerging contemporary art and support their ongoing philanthropic endeavours. They are internationally active: they have opened an exhibition space in London; in New York City, a selection of works from the Zabludowicz Collection is temporarily on display at 1500 Broadway; and, since 2010, they have organized an international residency programme for artists on the Finnish island of Sarvisalo.

Yuz Museum

Located along the West Bund in Xuhui District in Shanghai, Yuz Museum is a non-profit organization under the umbrella of the Yuz Foundation, established in 2007 by the Chinese-Indonesian entrepreneur, philanthropist and collector Budi Tek. Yuz Museum in Shanghai is the second museum patronized by the eponymous foundation: in November 2008, as the first private official museum in Indonesia, opened Yuz Museum in Jakarta. The Yuz Museum in Shanghai is designed to provide exhibition opportunities to artists and enhance public appreciation of international contemporary art. The institution, opened in 2014, strives to promote the development of contemporary art and to enhance public understanding and appreciation. The space of the Yuz Museum in Shanghai used to be an airport hangar and by retaining a unique sense of grandeur, this enormous structure perfectly sets off the magnificence of the installations in the Yuz collection. The Yuz Museum's design approach is to maintain the historical style of the old hangar, redesigning the space of the building to create a large art exhibition space, and to use verdant trees and a bright open entry hall to prompt interplay between old and new architecture. While respecting the history of the facility, the structure has a flat-roofed glass hall that interacts with the clear formal characteristics of the old hangar. The Yuz Museum is focused on contemporary art: it promotes art movements, contributes to various art initiatives and takes an active role in the social and cultural welfare of the community. The Yuz Foundation will continue working to develop compelling and consistent ways of realizing the founder's desire to enhance appreciation for contemporary art and to promote contemporary artists. The new project, set to open in 2017, is a museum that blends art with landscape: Budidesa Art Park, created by US architects Aranda-Lasch, encompass a series of art gardens, exhibition spaces and a residence within the tropical environment of Bali.

Budi Tek

Budi Tek is a Chinese-Indonesian agricultural magnate, art philanthropist, and leading collector. He started his art collection at the beginning of the new millennium, when he discovered art's ability to take him to new and unknown worlds; he has been a serious collector ever since. He began with Chinese contemporary paintings, especially those created between the early 1980s and late 1990s. He has steadily expanded the scope of his interests beyond Asian art to include Western art as well. He is known for collecting mega works, art pieces larger than living rooms. Budi Tek considers himself not only a collector, but also an art patron. He has built up a considerable collection and is always willing to exhibit and lend his works to other accredited art institutions in order to raise the global profile and understanding of Chinese contemporary art. In 2007, with a strong desire to enhance public appreciation for contemporary art, he established the Yuz Foundation, a non-profit organization dedicated to the promotion of contemporary art and artists. Through his foundation, Budi Tek patronizes Asia Art Archive and in 2013 he sponsored the Indonesian Pavilion at the Venice Biennale. Budi Tek is part of the Tate's Asia-Pacific Acquisitions Committee, which aims to heighten international awareness of Asia-Pacific arts.

Long Museum

Founded by an art-collecting Chinese couple, Liu Yiqian and Wang Wei, the Long Museum owns two huge spaces for exhibition and related functions: Long Museum Pudong and Long Museum West Bund. Located respectively in Pudong New Area and Binjiang, Xuhui District, they constitute a unique ecosystem of art in Shanghai. As the largest private institution of collection in China, the Long Museum boasts the nation's richest collection. The collection is comprehensively large, covering traditional Chinese art, modern and contemporary Chinese art, and "red classics", as well as contemporary art of Asia and Europe. The Long Museum is devoted not only to professional art exhibitions, research, and collections but also to the promotion of public cultural education. It aims to take up the responsibility of propelling the continuous development and inheritance of art and focuses on the contrastive display and study of art—Western and Eastern, ancient and contemporary—while strengthening its local cultural roots. The couple has opened a third Long Museum in Chongqing, in the spring of 2016.

Liu Yiqian and Wang Wei

Liu Yiqian, born in 1963, is a Chinese businessman, investor in stock trading and real estate and chairman of a Shanghai-based chemical and pharmaceutical investment company. Liu Yiqian left school at 14 to help his mother with her handbag business. His stock trading big break came when he was 27 and today he is one of the wealthiest individuals in China. Liu Yiqian's passion for art is shared with his wife, Wang Wei, and they are among China's most successful art collectors and private museum owners. They both came from modest, working class families, but in recent years they have spent hundreds of millions in auctions building a collection that includes treasures such as ancient scrolls, Tibetan silk embroideries and imperial porcelain in addition to contemporary pieces. They built their own museum in Shanghai in order to display their complete collection, where Wang Wei is the general director and acts as curator of the museum.

Goss-Michael Foundation

The Goss-Michael Foundation is one of the leading contemporary British art collections in the United States. Founded in Dallas by George Michael and Kenny Goss in 2007, the collection is composed primarily of British contemporary art and includes approximately 500 works by more than 100 of the most prominent British artists working today, including Tracey Emin, Damien Hirst, Sarah Lucas, Marc Quinn and Michael Craig-Martin. Each work is personally chosen by the founders and therefore reflects their personal preferences, tastes and interests as well as those of the artists with whom they have formed friendships. George Michael and Kenny Goss have assembled a collection of innovative and provocative pieces that often relate to one another through shared themes: sexuality and its relationship to one's being; personal identity and societal roles; beauty, sensuality and death; as well as the social and political issues facing the current generation. The collection is augmented on a regular basis with very selective additions that are emblematic of a particular artist's work, serve as a catalyst for artistic discussion, or broaden the scope of the collection and enrich Dallas's artistic community. This ensures the inclusion of the most current and up to date pieces in the collection's catalogue of works. As part of the Goss-Michael Foundation's role in supporting and cultivating the arts within the community, the Foundation is committed to promoting a strong and focused educational program aimed at high school and university students. Moreover, in 2013 the Goss-Michael Foundation launched an Artist-in-Residence programme with the goal of supporting the development of artists of diverse ages, backgrounds and disciplines. A solo exhibition is held at the conclusion of the residency and become an important part of the Foundation's exhibition program. The Goss-Michael Foundation has become a significant player in international art circles and an invaluable addition to the local art scene.

George Michael and Kenny Goss

George Michael, born in 1963, is an English singer, songwriter, multi-instrumentalist and record producer. Kenny Goss, born in 1958, has been director of a cheerleading supply company for 20 years and a gallery owner and art collector based in Dallas. The collector and the pop star dated for 15 years, until their separation in 2009. The former couple began collecting contemporary British art in the early 2000s. They opened a commercial gallery in 2005 and their dialogue with important artists led the gallery activity to success. The gallery was moved to a much larger space, and commercial aspects were jettisoned in favor of setting up as a non-profit. In 2007, Kenny Goss and George Michael co-founded the Goss-Michael Foundation. The idea of the founders was to encourage young artists with scholarship money and inspire British galleries to participate in the Dallas Art Fair, of which the foundation is a founding sponsor. The institution based in Dallas is devoted to education, inspiring and engaging audiences and students. In addition to being the co-founder, Kenny Goss directly manages the foundation with Joyce Goss, his sister-in-law, as executive director.

Sifang Art Museum

The Sifang Art Museum is situated in the lush green landscape of the Pearl Spring near Nanjing, in the southeast of China. The museum's 21,500 sq. ft. exhibition space, designed by American architect Steven Holl, is an integral part of the Sifang Parkland, formerly known as the China International Practical Exhibition of Architecture. The project is the result of immense collaborative work, commissioning over 20 award-winning architects and artists over the course of 10 years to construct complex and functional spaces, as well as permanent and temporary art exhibition venues. The estate offers architects and artists unique circumstances and opportunities for developing and showcasing their works within this beautifully preserved forest area. Sifang Art Museum is a living, ever-evolving tribute to contemporary art and architecture. The institution is a combination of both natural and human beauty. Sifang is a response to China's rapid urbanization and the profit maximizing mentality. As the landscape of Chinese cities is quickly changed by the widespread construction of repetitive architecture at minimal cost, the Museum and the Park represent an architectural and artistic breath of fresh air. Based on a diverse collection of international and Chinese contemporary art, the Sifang Art Museum holds high quality, changing curatorial exhibitions throughout the year. It aims to introduce the newest forms of art and to contribute to the growth of public appreciation for contemporary art. The complex also includes a hotel, a conference centre and 20 residential villas designed by leading international architects.

Lu Jun and Lu Xun

Lu Jun, Chinese real estate developer and president of the Sifang Culture Group, was born in the mid-1950s. He and his son, Lu Xun, are two of China's most famous art collectors and owners of private art museums. The Sifang Art Museum houses Jun and Xun's respectable collection that includes artworks by some of the most prominent contemporary artists from all around the world. The director of the Sifang project is Lu Xun, who was studying engineering at the University of Cambridge in 2003 when his father, Lu Jun, bought a huge plot of land in the lush Pearl Spring forest. Lu and his father are taking a 'boutique' approach to the museum, commissioning new art to be shown inside as well as in the grounds of the park. In 2007 the younger Lu returned to China to devote himself full-time to the job of acquiring art to display in the museum. He and his father initially had a naïve approach to contemporary art, but the collection has grown rapidly and now includes between 200 and 300 works.

Hall Art Foundation

The Hall Art Foundation was founded in 2007 and displays postwar and contemporary art works from its own collection and that of Andrew and Christine Hall. The Hall Art Foundation operates an exhibition space on the site of an eighteenth-century farm in Vermont; shows are held seasonally, from May to November, and are open to the public by appointment, free-of-charge. In addition to operating the space in Vermont, the Hall Art Foundation collaborates with several public institutions around the world to organize exhibitions and facilitate loans from its own collection and that of the funders. The foundation has a strong exhibition partnership with the Massachusetts Museum of Contemporary Art (MASS MoCA), one of the largest centres for contemporary visual and performing arts in North America, and with the Ashmolean Museum of Art and Archaeology in Oxford, England, the world's first university museum. As part of its educational activities, the Hall Art Foundation has published, co-published and provided substantial financial support for catalogues and books relating to the exhibitions organized. Together, the collections of Andrew and Christine Hall and the Hall Art Foundation comprise some 5000 works by several hundred artists including Richard Artschwager, George Baselitz, Joseph Beuys, Olafur Eliasson, Eric Fischl, Jörg Immendorff, Anselm Kiefer, Julian Schnabel, Ed Ruscha and Andy Warhol.

Andrew and Christine Hall

Andrew Hall, born in Great Britain in the early 1950s, is CEO of the oil commodities trading firm Phibro, head of hedge fund Astenbeck Capital and an internationally renowned art collector. After studying for an MA in chemistry from Oxford University, Andrew Hall achieved an MBA from Instead where, in 1980, he won the Henry Ford prize for top graduate. Andrew Hall joined the petroleum sector where he served in a number of important positions on his route to the top. He gained notoriety for a highly criticized $100 million pay package during the financial crisis. Andrew Hall and his wife, Christine, are consistently counted among the world's top 200 art collectors by ARTnews magazine. He bought his first artwork in 1979, starting an eclectic collection. The collection is focused on contemporary German art, and particularly Anselm Kiefer, but includes a range of other works. Andrew and Christine Hall are attracted to great artists who, for whatever reason, remain slightly off the radar screen. Their initial response to an artwork is emotional and they are mainly interested in collecting works by artists with a solid record of museum shows over many years, rather than chasing the latest fad. They do not rely on advisers.

Kunsthalle Weishaupt

The Weishaupt Collection, one of the major private collections of contemporary art in Germany, consists of several hundred of important artworks and has taken more than 40 years to shape into its present form. The 16 m high glass facade facing Hans-und-Sophie-Scholl-Platz seems like a gigantic passepartout framing a highly visible piece of art. The Kunsthalle Weishaupt is sponsored and driven by the Weishaupt family: Siegfried Weishaupt is the founder and owner of the collection, whilst his daughter, art historian Kathrin Weishaupt-Theopold, is head of the *kunsthalle*'s board of directors. The Weishaupt collection does not merely show an extraordinary touch but also a vision and direction. It focuses on geometric art: Richard Paul Lohse, Friedrich Vordemberge-Gildewart, Max Bill and especially Josef Albers constitute the core of the collection. Over the years, colour has become the leitmotif of the collection, which comprises colour field paintings by artists such as Mark Rothko, Frank Stella and Ellsworth Kelly, along with European representatives such as Yves Klein. A selection of sculptures and installations completes the collection: artworks by Nam June Paik, Keith Haring, and Tony Cragg. A special place within the collection belongs to the US multimedia artist Robert Longo.

Siegfried Weishaupt

Siegfried Weishaupt, born in 1939, is an industrialist from Schwendi, a city near Ulm. He has an intuitive talent for discovering works of art and this passion has occupied him and his wife, Jutta Weishaupt, for more than four decades. Weishaupt's contact with the Ulm School of Design marks the beginning of his passion. In the early 1960s the collector's father, founder of the company, was successful in winning the prominent HfG product designers Hans Gugelot and Hans Sukopp for the company. Artworks by Josef Albers, who taught temporarily at the Ulm School of Design, formed Siegfried Weishaupt's conception of art. Over the following years, the collector and his wife have expanded their focus from geometric concrete art to other art movements: first to the Abstract Expressionism of US artists as Mark Rothko and the work of Robert Rauschenberg, then to Pop Art and contemporary art movements.

Museum of Old and New Art

The Museum of Old and New Art, MONA, officially opened in January 2011, after a $75 million renovation of its precursor, the Moorilla Museum of Antiquities. This art museum, founded by David Walsh, is located within the Moorilla winery in Hobart, Tasmania, and is the largest privately funded museum in Australia. The collection is guaranteed to impress: with over 400 art works, it includes controversial artists and pieces, such as a machine that turns food into excrement by Wim

Delvoye and Chris Ofili's famous *The Holy Virgin Mary*. At street level, the MONA building appears to be dominated by its surroundings, but in its interior a spiral staircase leads down to three larger levels of labyrinthine display spaces built into the side of the cliffs around Berriedale peninsula. With input from David Walsh, Greek-Australian architect Nonda Katsalidis decided to build MONA largely underground to preserve the previous heritage setting on the property. The building has no windows and the atmosphere is intentionally hostile. To see the art, the visitor must work back upwards towards the surface, a trajectory that has been contrasted with the descending spiral that many visitors follow in New York's Guggenheim Museum. Katsalidis's architecture for the museum has been appraised as not only fulfilling its function as a showcase for a collection, but also succeeding in extending the experience. Along with its frequently updated indoor collection, MONA also hosts the annual Festival of Music and Art, which showcases large-scale public art and live performances. The site also includes the Ether Building Function Centre, the Moorilla winery and vineyard, Cellar Door, the Wine Bar and Barrel Room, the Void Bar, the Moo Brew microbrewery, the Source restaurant, a cinema, the Mona Library and gallery and eight contemporary accommodation pavilions.

David Walsh

David Walsh, born in 1961, is an Australian professional gambler, winery owner and art collector. A high school graduate, David Walsh made his fortune by developing a gambling system used to bet on horse racing and other sports. He has a particular iconoclastic and autodidactic taste in art and an acute philosophical perspective. Walsh lacked in art expertise but he compensated with passion and curiosity. The collector favors a direct approach, buying straight from the studios of artists he appreciates and without a strategy, in a process dictated by interest and whim. In 2001 he founded the Moorilla Museum of Antiquities in Hobart, in order to display his idiosyncratic collection of antiquities, Australian modern art and international contemporary art. This closed in 2007 to undergo a massive renovation and was re-opened in January 2011 as the Museum of Old and New Art (MONA). MONA is the ultimate *wunderkammer* of the gambler, a cabinet of curiosities writ large.

The Broad

The Broad is the new contemporary art museum built by philanthropists Eli and Edythe Broad on Grand Avenue in downtown Los Angeles. The museum, which is designed by Diller Scofidio + Renfro, opened to the public on September 2015. The museum houses the nearly 2,000 works of art in the Broad Art Foundation and the Broads' personal collections, which are among the most prominent holdings of post-war and contemporary art. With a strong desire to advance public appreciation for contemporary art, Eli and Edythe Broad established the Broad Art Foundation in 1984. Dedicated to increasing access for audiences worldwide, the foundation has made more than 8,000 loans to over 500 museums and galleries around the world. The Broad Art Foundation keeps pace with the market, collecting with the agility and speed of a private collector, yet it does so with a public-minded objective: creating a unique repository of contemporary art with the sole purpose of display and study by public institutions. With its innovative "veil-and-vault" concept, the 120,000 sq. ft., $140 million building features two floors of gallery space to showcase The Broad's comprehensive collection and will be the headquarters of the Broad Art Foundation's worldwide lending library.

Eli and Edythe Broad

Eli Broad, born in 1933, is an American philanthropist and entrepreneur who built two Fortune 500 companies from the ground up over a five-decade career in business. Today, Eli Broad and his wife, Edythe, are devoted to philanthropy, through the Broad Foundations, which they established to advance entrepreneurship for the public good in education, science and the arts. The Broad Foundations include the Eli and Edythe Broad Foundation and the Broad Art Foundation. Over the past four decades, the Broads have built one of the most important private collections of post-war and contemporary art worldwide. Broad was the founding chairman and is a life trustee of The Museum of Contemporary Art in Los Angeles, a life trustee of the MoMA in New York and serves on the board of several other museums. He has been rewarded several times for his philanthropic commitment and in 2012 published his first book, *The Art of Being Unreasonable*: *Lessons in Unconventional Thinking*.

Museum Frieder Burda

The Museum Frieder Burda was inaugurated in the autumn of 2004 and is fully financed and run by the Foundation Frieder Burda, which was established in 1998. The museum was built by Richard Meier in Frieder Burda's home city of Baden-Baden in order to guarantee the public full access to the collection. The internationally-renowned Collection Frieder Burda concentrates on classical modernism and contemporary art and now encompasses around 1,000 paintings, sculptures, objects and works on paper. Originally, Frieder Burda's decision to buy a work of art was often motivated by spontaneous enthusiasm; he did not intend to establish a cohesive collection of works. The fascination of colour and the expressive emotional qualities of paintings were the centre of the collector's interest in art. This perspective has given rise to a collection with a personal style, bringing together pioneering painters of the twentieth century: Jackson Pollock, Mark Rothko, Clyfford Still, George Baselitz, Gerhard Richter, Sigmar Polke and Arnulf Rainer. A further interest of the collector was the tension between painting and sculpture, and indeed the collection includes important sculptures by artists renowned for their painting, such as Pablo Picasso and Willem de Kooning. Since the turn of the millennium, these concepts have determined the selection of works and the collection has grown in an organic and consistent manner, with a great deal of personal commitment from the collector. Over the past decade the Collection Frieder Burda has dedicated itself with increasing commitment to the current art of a younger generation. Works by Heribert C. Ottersbach, Karin Kneffel, Eberhard Havekost, Corinne Wasmuht and Anton Henning document the enduring fascination of the medium of painting and the search for new subject matter and themes. By presenting these contemporary positions, the Museum Frieder Burda is taking part in the current discourse on art.

Frieder Burda

Frieder Burda, born in 1936, is a German publisher and art collector. Born in Baden-Baden southwest Germany, the son of a renowned publisher and senator, Frieder Burda spent his childhood and youth in the town of his birth. After attending schools in Offenbach and Switzerland, Burda entered the publishing profession, first in his father's firm and later for long periods in France, England and the USA. He took over a printing house in Darmstadt and expanded this operation into one of the leading printing houses in Europe. In the early 1970s, with Lucio Fontana, he started to collect art, forming the foundation of his precious collection. In the mid-1980s he established a dialogue with contemporary artists, collecting artworks by German contemporaries including Gerhard Richter, Sigmar Polke, George Baselitz. The collection has now grown to include more than 1,000 works of art. Frieder Burda is highly regarded and has received awards for his philanthropic contribution to community. After creating a foundation with the purpose of promoting art, culture and science, in 2004 he inaugurated the Frieder Burda Museum, which is the spearhead of the territory's cultural community.

DESTE Foundation

The DESTE Foundation for Contemporary Art is a non-profit institution established in 1983 by collector Dakis Joannou. Through its exhibition space in Athens, Greece, DESTE engages in an extensive exhibition programme that promotes emerging as well as established artists and aims to broaden the audience for contemporary art, enhance opportunities for young artists, and explore the connections between contemporary art and culture. In its early years, the Foundation supported exhibitions that showcased the trends of art throughout the 1980s and 1990s in Greece and Cyprus, emphasizing the universality of contemporary art. In its first years the DESTE Foundation did not have a permanent exhibition space and shows were hosted in other institutions. In 1998 the DESTE Foundation moved to its first permanent space, a former paper factory in Neo Psychiko redesigned by

American architect Christian Hubert. In 2006, the DESTE Foundation moved to a newly renovated building in Nea Ionia that also houses a library, enriched by donations and exchanges, which serves as a research and educational resource on art and design. The Foundation's mission is to explore international contemporary art and to introduce iconic artworks to the Greek public for the first time. In an effort to act as a host for innovative thought and creativity, the DESTE Foundation's core exhibition schedule is complemented by a number of projects, such as the DESTE Prize, a bi-annual prize awarded to a young Greek artist, and the DESTE Fashion Collection, a project that aims to explore the connections between contemporary art and fashion. The DESTE Foundation collaborates with a number of internationally acclaimed curators and leading artists to showcase the most important artistic innovations and to organize curatorial projects and special events that reflect the global trends in contemporary art.

Dakis Joannou

Dakis Joannou, born in 1939, is a Greek Cypriot billionaire industrialist, art collector and founder of the DESTE Foundation of Contemporary Art in Athens. Having gained a BA and MA in Civil Engineering in the United States and a Doctorate in Architecture in Italy, Joannou entered the construction business in the late 1960s. He is chairman of several global scale companies. Over the last decades he has diversified his holdings through numerous areas of international industrial commerce, such as hospitality, shipping, aviation and real estate. He has been assembling a blue-chip collection of contemporary art since the mid-1980s and is considered to be one of the leading collectors of contemporary European and American art in the world. Although his enormous holdings cross genres, periods, and geographies, including Baroque figurines, Cypriot antiquities, couture, drawings, and modernist furniture, his more contemporary interests include the work of such artists as Andro Wekua, Seth Price, Tauba Auerbach, Haim Steinbach, William Kentridge and Pawel Althamer, among others. He also owns a yacht designed by Jeff Koons. Dakis Joannou is member of several boards of international institutions, such as the New Museum, the Museum of Modern Art, the Solomon R. Guggenheim Foundation, the Tate International Council and the Council of the Serpentine Gallery in London.

Colección Patricia Phelps de Cineros

Founded in the 70s by Patricia Phelps de Cisneros and Gustavo A. Cisneros, the Colección Patricia Phelps de Cisneros is based in New York City and Caracas. The collection is the primary art-related programme of the Fundación Cisneros, and has been a critical component of Patricia Phelps de Cisneros' efforts to enhance appreciation of the diversity, sophistication, and range of art from Latin America. The collection works to increase understanding and awareness of Latin America's contributions to the history of art and ideas, and to support innovation, creativity, and research in the field of Latin American art. The institution achieves these goals through the preservation, presentation, and study of the material culture of the Ibero-American world, ranging from the ethnographic to the contemporary. The Colección Patricia Phelps de Cisneros is focused on modernist geometric abstraction from Latin American artists and artworks of traveller-artists who explored Latin America and the Caribbean. The institution also gathers ethnographic objects and material cultural artefacts from the colonial era. A particular attention is given to contemporary art: the Colección Patricia Phelps de Cisneros actively works to support rising Latin American artists, through acquisitions of their artworks, support for residencies and artistic production, educational programmes, exhibitions, loans, and publications. Moreover, through grants, such as the CIMAM Travel Grant Program, and partnerships the institution supports the professional development of curators and scholars.

Patricia Phelps de Cisneros

Patricia Phelps de Cisneros is a Venezuela-born collector and art patron with a lifelong devotion to Latin American art and artefacts. Her husband is Gustavo Cisneros, born in 1945, a Venezuelan media mogul of Cuban descent and one of Latin America's most powerful figures. Together they are considered the most powerful Latin American couple both in business and the social scene. For more than four decades, Patricia Phelps de Cisneros has fervently supported education and the arts. In the 1970s, along with her husband, she founded the New York City and Caracas-based Fundación Cisneros. Its mission is to improve education throughout Latin America and to foster global awareness of the region's heritage and many contributions to world culture. Patricia Phelps de Cisneros supports a wide range of cultural institutions in the Americas and Europe. She is trustee and member of several institutions: MoMA, MoMA's Latin American and Caribbean Fund, Harvard University Art Museums, Tate London and Fundación Museo Reina Sofia, among others. In recognition of her effort and work to strengthen and promote education and arts in Latin America, Patricia Phelps de Cisneros has received numerous awards.

White Rabbit Gallery

The White Rabbit Gallery is a registered charitable institution in Sidney funded by the Neilson Foundation. The White Rabbit Gallery is one of the world's largest and most significant collections of contemporary Chinese art. Founded by Kerr and Judith Neilson, the gallery was opened in 2009 to showcase their private collection, dedicated to works made in the twenty-first century. Judith Neilson was inspired to establish the collection on a 2001 trip to Beijing, where she was thrilled by the creative energy and technical quality of the works she saw and wanted to share them

Appendix: Private Museums and Their Founders   157

with people outside China. She makes regular trips to China and Taiwan to augment the collection, which includes 1400 works by almost 400 artists, and new profiles are regularly added. Wang Zhiyuan was the first Chinese artist collected by the founders, and among the others, the collection includes artworks by Bai Yiluo, Bu Hua, Shen Liang, Sun Furong, Wang Zhiyuan, Zhou Xiaohu, Wu Junyong, Cang Xin, Chen Zhuo + Huang Keyi, Dong Yuan, Yan Baishen and Shi Jindian. The White Rabbit Gallery building, originally a Rolls-Royce service depot in the 1940s, was completely refitted as an exhibition space. Since the gallery can house only a fraction of the collection at any one time, there are two new exhibitions a year, each involving a full rehang of the entrance level and three upper floors of the building. The White Rabbit exhibitions provide an introduction for the audience to the several facets of contemporary art practice in China, showcasing works in very different media: painting, sculpture, animation, new media and installation. Through featured works it is possible to explore China's rapidly changing society, from Mao's oppressive Cultural Revolution to the excesses and exuberance of China's economic boom.

Kerr and Judith Neilson

Kerr Neilson, born in 1950, is an Australian investment manager. He started his financial management career in investments in London and, due to his ability to select high-performing stocks, moved to Australia as the head of retail funds management for Bankers Trust Australia. He and his wife, Judith Neilson, share a passion for art. The origins of their collection go back to the late 1990s, when Judith Neilson engaged Wang Zhiyuan, a Chinese artist living in Sydney, as her art tutor, introducing her to the astonishing explosion of creativity taking place in China. In 2009, Kerr and Judith Neilson opened the White Rabbit Gallery in Sydney to share with the public their extensive collection of contemporary Chinese art. Judith Neilson supports investments in research to investigate how art, architecture and design could be used as a powerful force for change. She serves as Member of Advisory Group at Asian Art Fairs Limited.

NEON Foundation

NEON is a non-profit organization based in Athens and opened in June 2013 by Dimitris Daskalopoulos. NEON, the Greek word for 'new', is committed to broadening the appreciation, understanding and creation of contemporary art in Greece in the firm belief that this is a key tool for growth and development. The founder has always been adamant that he would not build a temple to his collection, choosing instead to support contemporary art through an organization without walls. NEON operates within society and is also conceived to be part of a strong international network. Through many community projects NEON brings contemporary art programmes to Athenian neighbourhoods, stimulating the participation of local inhabitants, groups and artists. NEON constructively connects with several cultural institutions in Greece and supports their activities, implementing private-public partnerships and collaborations to enhance accessibility and interaction to public of contemporary art. NEON realizes its mission through free exhibitions, educational programmes, grants and scholarships, talks and events and a creation of a network of international partnerships.

Dimitris Daskalopoulos

Dimitris Daskalopoulos, born in 1957, is a Greek food and beverage entrepreneur. He is also well-known as a philanthropist, collector of contemporary art, owner of Daskalopoulos Collection and founder of the nonprofit organization NEON. He has been gathering art for over 20 years, amassing an impressive collection of more than 400 works by over 200 artists. He bought an edition of Marcel Duchamp's Fountain in 1999 and since then his collection has grown to include works from epically large-scale installations to smaller and more delicate pieces. His collection has been the subject of great exhibitions at the Guggenhein Bilbao and the Whitechapel Gallery in London. In 2014 he was honoured by Independent Curators International (ICI) with the Leo Award, which celebrates a "visionary" approach to collecting. Dimitris Daskalopoulos is active in many boards of international institutions and over the years he has contributed funds to facilitate exhibitions and acquisitions at major public art institutions worldwide. Daskalopoulos is a member of the board of trustees of the Solomon R. Guggenheim Foundation, the Tate International Council, the Director's Vision Council of the Museum of Contemporary Art Chicago, and the Leadership Council of New York's New Museum. He is also a founding partner of the Whitechapel Gallery's Future Fund.

Margulies Collection

The Margulies Collection at the Warehouse is a non-profit institution in Miami dedicated to the presentation of exhibitions and educational initiatives that explore contemporary art and culture. The Warehouse occupies a 45,000 sq. ft. facility located in the Miami Wynwood Arts District. Since its inaugural exhibition in 1999, the Warehouse has presented seasonal exhibitions of sculpture, photography, video and painting from 1940 to the present. The Warehouse is operated and funded by the Martin Margulies Foundation, that for 30 years has promoted the study and enjoyment of the visual arts. Recognized as one of the major collections of contemporary art in the world, it spans significant movements in art from Abstract Expressionism through Pop, Minimalism, and Conceptual Art, to monumental sculpture. In 1998, Martin Margulies along with his longtime curator and advisor began to consider creating a space suitable for displaying the growing vintage and contemporary photography, video and installation art segment of the extensive Margulies Contemporary Art Collection. In 1999, the first phase of the Margulies

Collection at the Warehouse opened to the public with an event to benefit the Lowe Museum at the University of Miami. Following a series of expansions, the last in 2004, admission to the Warehouse collection is now free. Lectures for students, guided tours, prominent guest speakers and national conferences are all factors designed by the Martin Margulies Foundation to improve public accessibility and interaction with contemporary art.

Martin Margulies

Martin Margulies is a Miami-based real-estate developer specialized in luxury housing complexes. He is also known as a philanthropist and one of South Florida's foremost collectors of contemporary art and photography. Martin Margulies' legendary collection is one of America's premier gatherings of modern and contemporary works in all media. Over the past two decades he has avidly collected photography that reflects his interest in the human condition. His art holdings, valued in hundreds of millions, are housed between his home and his non-profit institution. Along with other collecting families, including the de la Cruzes, he helped pioneer what became known as the "Miami model", in which private collectors opened their collections to the public and put the city on the art world's radar. Martin Margulies is very much appreciated in the Miami community due to his philanthropic activities. Among these, he is the benefactor of a homeless shelter for women and infants and of an orchestral academy, both based in Miami.

Museo Jumex

Museo Jumex is located within the Polanco area of Mexico City and was opened in November 2013. The museum is part of the Fundación Jumex Arte Contemporáneo, which distributes educational initiatives and art grants, and exhibits part of the Colección Jumex, an assemblage of over 2,700 artworks by contemporary artists, founded in 2001 by Eugenio López and his company Grupo Jumex. The five-floor museum, designed by David Chipperfield, is part of a wider urban redevelopment and has a distinctive roof that creates a geometric appearance. The building has been designed to accommodate gallery spaces that could offer the possibility for both in-house and guest curators to display artworks with new approaches. The institution presents both a programme of temporary exhibitions and a selection of the ever-expanding Colección Jumex. The museum features Mexican artists such as Gabriel Orozco, Carlos Amorales and Mario García Torres, as well as international artists such as Jeff Koons, Olafur Eliasson and Tacita Dean. Moreover, with an informal atmosphere, Museo Jumex provides a platform for discourse and educational activities. The lower floors of the building offer social and community spaces for lectures, talks, debates, conferences and film screenings for the enjoyment of both the local community and tourists.

Eugenio López Alonso

Eugenio López Alonso, born in the late 1960s, is the sole heir to the Jumex fruit juice fortune and is known as an arts patron whose foundation underwrites contemporary art exhibitions in Mexico. Eugenio López Alonso owns a huge collection that includes Mexican, American and European artists. Part of his gathering can be seen at the Colección Jumex, which opened to the public in 2001. Eugenio López Alonso has lived in Los Angeles for years, but he demonstrated loyalty to his homeland when in 2013 he established the Museo Jumex in the heart of Mexico City. It is the largest private museum in Latin America and houses selections from his personal collection. With his efforts he aims to share the passion of Latin American artists with North Americans and Europeans. Eugenio López Alonso is one of the most visionary collectors, a real art lover and supporter of the artists whose works he purchases. He began collecting 20 years ago, initially buying historical pieces of 1960s art, then concentrating on Mexican and international work of his own generation in the 1990s. López's 2,700-piece collection includes many works by American and European masters ranging from Cy Twombly and Robert Rauschenberg to Jeff Koons and Damien Hirst, along with Mexican artists such as Gabriel Orozco. He is a trustee and vice chair of MOCA in Los Angeles.

List of Contributors

Alessia Zorloni cultural economist and consultant specializing in the art markets and the museum field, is Adjunct Professor at IULM University and at Catholic University, Milan, Italy. Alessia Zorloni has developed her professional experience in international museums, in academia and in strategy consultancy. She worked as an Associate Researcher at The Boston Consulting Group in the Milan office, where she completes a research project funded by the European Community on economic management of museum and cultural institutions. She also advised art institutions across a wide range of strategic and organizational issues. Prior to joining BCG, Alessia worked at the Wien Kunsthalle, where she completed a 3-year research project on museum management funded by the Austrian Science Fund. Alessia has been a visiting scholar at the Tate Modern, Guggenheim Foundation and at the Smithsonian Institution, where she has been awarded the Smithsonian's Fellowship in Museum Practice. Alessia received a PhD in Communication Economics from IULM University of Milan and a Master's Degree in Arts Management from City University, London. She has published extensively in the fields of visual art management, covering topics such as art investments, museum management, art and design markets, creative industries, accountability and social reporting in cultural institutions, and art philanthropy. Her book, *The Economics of Contemporary Art. Markets, Strategies and Stardom*, published by Springer, has been translated in Italian and in Chinese.

Magnus Resch is a respected influencer in the art world, both as professor and entrepreneur. At the age of 20 he started an art gallery in Switzerland to finance his university career. Today he co-runs Larry's List and Magnus.net, the world's premier art platforms. He is author of *Management of Art Galleries*, and *The Art Collector Report*. Since 2014 he has taught art management at the University of St. Gallen, at Leuphana University, Germany and ZSEM, Croatia. His activities in the art market have been covered by more than 100 international newspapers. Magnus also has a track record as tech entrepreneur. At the age of 27, Magnus became Managing Director of Springstar, a Berlin based internet incubator (2,500 employees and $2 bn revenue). Here he started, failed and exited several internet start-ups, among them Gourmeo.com, Juvalia.com and Gymondo.de. Magnus studied business at Harvard, the London School of Economics, the University of St. Gallen and Hong Kong University. He holds a PhD in Economics, and was awarded scholarships by both the Konrad Adenauer Foundation and the Swiss National Foundation.

Antonella Ardizzone is Assistant Professor of Applied Economics at IULM University of Milan, Italy. She has been Visiting Research Assistant Professor and International Scholar at the Ithaca College, New York. She earned her PhD from the IULM University of Milan in Communication Economics and her MSc in Economics and Markets at the Erasmus University of Rotterdam. Dr. Ardizzone teaches graduate courses in Sector Analysis (Industrial Organization). Her research interests are in industrial economics, data analysis, cultural and creative industries, intellectual property, media and music markets, open source software, industrial districts and enterprises clusters, and experimental economics. She is co-author of a book on the Music Industry and of many papers published in academic journals and books.

Patrizia Sandretto Re Rebaudengo is an international art collector and President of Fondazione Sandretto. After graduating in business studies and economics, Patrizia Sandretto Re Rebaudengo first started collecting contemporary art in the early nineties. What started as a hobby, rapidly became a full time career when she founded the Fondazione Sandretto Re Rebaudengo in 1995, of which she is President. Patrizia Sandretto Re Rebaudengo is an extremely active patron of the arts. She is a Member of the International Council, Museum of Modern Art, New York (since 1996); Member of the Friends of Contemporary Drawing, Museum of Modern Art, New York (since 1996); Member of the International Council, Tate Gallery, London (since 1997); Member of the Leadership Council, New Museum, New York (since 2007); Member of the Advisory Committee for Modern and Contemporary Art, Philadelphia Museum of Art (since 2008).

Randall James Willette is the founder and Managing Director of Fine Art Wealth Management Ltd, a professional membership-based advisory firm based in London, that provides independent consulting, education, and proprietary research on integrating art into wealth management strategy. Prior to establishing the Company in 2003, Randall was Executive Director and Head of Art Banking for UBS Wealth Management in London responsible for helping to build its global Art Banking franchise in Europe and America. While there, he developed and implemented a global marketing strategy for UBS integrating art assets into the Bank's overall wealth management strategy for private clients. Before joining UBS Randall was a Managing Director in Corporate Finance with Citibank responsible for solving strategic problems facing corporate clients. His credentials include over 25 years combined experience in investment banking, structured finance, and private wealth management. Randall has lectured and published articles extensively on art wealth management and investment.

Sonia Pancheri is a PhD candidate in Communication and Market: Economics, Marketing and Creativity at IULM University, Milan, where she achieved an MA in Arts, Heritage and Markets. Her research is focused on the art market and in particular, on the impacts of art investments on collectors' well-being. She is involved in national publications on cultural management and, since 2015, she has been Regional Youth Ambassador of UNESCO.

The manufacturer's authorised representative in the EU is Springer Nature Customer Service Centre GmbH, Europaplatz 3, 69115 Heidelberg, Germany. If you have any concerns regarding our products, please contact ProductSafety@springernature.com

Printed and bound by CPI Group (UK) Ltd, Croydon, CR0 4YY

23/03/2026

02076360-0018